D1351195

# THE
# GARDEN IN FLOWER

*month-by-month*

# THE
# GARDEN IN FLOWER

*month-by-month*

## JOHN KELLY

*Photographs by John Kelly*

**David & Charles**

For my godson, Robin Cameron Aggleton, whose mother taught me this:

*June – too soon*
*July – they'll try*
*August – come they must*
*September – remember!*
*October – all over.*

Traditional Caribbean rhyme for predicting hurricanes . . .

. . . it is equally applicable to the flowering of hydrangeas.

## A DAVID & CHARLES BOOK

Copyright © John Kelly 1994
Photographs © John Kelly 1994

First published 1994

A catalogue record for this book is available from the British Library.

ISBN 0 7153 0076 8

Book design by Diana Knapp
Illustrations by Avis Murray
Typeset by ABM Typographics Ltd, Hull
and printed in Italy
by New Interlitho SpA
for David & Charles
Brunel House    Newton Abbot    Devon

# CONTENTS

# *INTRODUCTION*

 If you have the good fortune to live in a part of the world where the climate is cool-temperate and reasonably equable, gardening is a wide-open book of delights from which you can make an almost limitless choice of flowering plants. The permutations of plant associations and combinations are also virtually infinite – here is an unparalleled medium of self-expression.

Even if the chill fingers of a continental winter are apt to reach out and envelop your garden, or if the stalking figure of drought is wont to blight your summer, there is still a wealth of possibility in flower gardening. Gardeners are ingenious if nothing else, and it is always a pleasure to see a rock garden in the Arizona desert, Mexican dahlias in a Limerick rainscape, and Californian ceanothus like patches of fallen sky in Dorset or Cambridge.

Old habits die hard, however, and it is still commonplace to see gardens dedicated to only one month of the year and there may be a crocus or two here and there as a sop to the rest of the year. All too often the summer border and the spring garden rule – although it has to be admitted that they do so less now than a few decades ago – and the rest of the year merely serves as preparation for the two climaxes.

Paradoxically, this is precisely because the choice is so wide. Gardens are finite areas, and the space for flowering plants within them is often governed by factors other than the merely horticultural. Children must have somewhere safe and pleasant to play; adults need such things as fuel stores, washing lines, compost heaps, vegetable gardens, and somewhere comfortable to sit and enjoy an evening drink or a barbecue.

Given a minute patch of earth in which to plant flowering plants, and faced with a huge range of shrubs, perennials and bulbs, not to mention trees, from which to choose, it is not surprising that we tend to think 'summer' or 'spring' and go for broke. How can you possibly wade through all the garden literature and sort out a succession of flowering plants that will keep the garden reasonably colourful for nine, if not twelve of the months of the year? To do the necessary research means trawling for information about flowering times from a score of sources and then making some sort of chart, from which you then make your choice. The task would be a hard one for a full-time researcher, let alone someone who has to go to work, take the children to school, cook meals, clean houses, chair committees, entertain business contacts, bone up on tomorrow's history seminar, or whatever among the countless demands on one's time fall to your particular lot.

This book does not substitute for that work. What it does is collate enough information to set your feet upon the path of a balanced flowering garden, one in which there will be colour and interest every day of the year, and which will not have one or even two mighty explosions of flamboyance, but a steady output of harmony and grace.

No garden book, no matter how weighty and comprehensive a work it is or may claim to be, should ever set itself up as the answer to the seeking for perfection in which all good gardeners indulge. This one does not tell you all in one go how to have the garden to end all gardens. Its aim is to encourage experiment and the study of catalogues, and to enjoin you to approach your garden planning and planting with a wide-open and receptive eye. Its purpose is to nudge you towards

## SEASONS AND MONTHS

Under average conditions, the terms 'early', 'mid' and 'late' season are used throughout this book to correspond to the following months:

**SPRING**
Early: March
Mid: April
Late: May

**SUMMER**
Early: June
Mid: July
Late: August

**AUTUMN**
Early: September
Mid: October
Late: November

**WINTER**
Early: December
Mid: January
Late: February

*(opposite) At the height of summer, hydrangeas begin their long flowering season.
H. macrophylla 'Mme A. Riverain' among agapanthus*

gaining and using experience in a field in which a nudge is certainly essential.

It goes without saying that the attainment of a well-ordered garden of any sort is impossible without a grasp of the fundamentals of the practical side of gardening. If you do not understand how to prune without cutting away the season's flowers; suffer failure year in year out with sowing seeds of anything beyond the easiest annuals; cannot make a garden pond without its leaking, becoming choked with green slime and killing every living thing within it; and do not know how to make a piece of stem grow roots and evolve into a new plant, your gardening experience will be unsatisfactory, disappointing and probably boring.

Therefore, you will find here some guidance towards various practices, methods and techniques that will assist you in providing a home for an ever-increasing wealth of flowering plants. Stocking a garden is an expensive business. You have only to go to the garden centre and buy fifty assorted trees, shrubs and perennials to have spent the average weekly industrial wage. It is undoubtedly money well spent, and you will probably contemplate such levels of outlay for the framework of the plantings. But in order to have a really fine display of flowers throughout the year, you will find the need to propagate plants yourself almost overwhelming.

For this reason, I have devoted space to the techniques and equipment involved in propagating the widest possible range of flowering plants. You may think a mist propagation unit an extravagance, but just extrapolate from the figure I have given you above and you will realise that, far from being a luxury, it is something approaching a necessity.

Throughout the book I emphasise the concept of foresight, and extol it as the ultimate virtue in a gardener. At the FBI's Academy at Quantico, Virginia, they teach the six Ps (there are seven, but I have left one out for propriety) thus: Proper Prior Planning Prevents Poor Performance. It should be flown as a banner above every potting shed in the gardening world. Good gardening of any kind is impossible without good planning. When it comes to arranging for flowers to appear all year round without robbing summer's glory or demoting spring from its magical ascendancy, to fail to plan is to assure total failure.

Planning is one of the boring concepts like 'book-keeping' and 'doing the tax return', but it has been invested with its dullness by dull people. Planning a garden is quite the most enjoyable pastime I can think of, other than sitting in a Kenmare pub with a pint of black stout or watching the Cincinnati Reds win a World Series. It involves far more than sitting morosely over a piece of squared paper. It requires the investigative talents of Miss Marple, the cheek of a door-to-door salesman, and an appreciation of the fact that to steal ideas from one garden is plagiarism, but to steal them from several is research.

For planning means, among other things, going and looking at other gardens. Let me give you examples, drawn from my own garden-planning forays. I have studied the underplanting of roses at the home of the Royal National Rose Society, how to make the most of late winter bulbs at the Royal Horticultural Society's garden at Wisley, how to plant colourfully where the daffodils were flowering from my sister-in-law in Sussex, the best ways of deploying camellias from Leu Gardens in downtown Orlando, and how to make the most of water-lilies from a garden in Mombasa, Kenya. And that is a tiny fraction of the research I have done in garden planning. During the course of my career I have visited countless gardens, from the tiny to the grandiose, and learned something important from every single one.

To all the owners and operators of all those gardens I am exceedingly grateful, and you will be grateful to those whose gardens you may visit in the search for ideas for flowering plants to brighten the months that are usually on the dull side.

The more mundane aspect of planning involves looking constantly ahead. The times for choosing, planting and for flowers to appear rarely coincide. When they do it is usually during late spring or that part of the summer holidays that comes before the children's school uniforms have to be bought, which is one of the reasons for the burgeoning of gardens at those times. That bulb plantings are so often haphazard or thoroughly inappropriate is often because choosing and planting take place in autumn, while flowering happens in spring, fully six months or even more afterwards. To go and see bulbs in flower, notebook in hand, in a garden where they are labelled or where the owner knows their names, is an essential adjunct to good choice. Catalogue colours are often inaccurate and verbal descriptions (apart from mine, of course) not to be relied upon.

It is one thing to plant so as to achieve colour and interest throughout the year, quite another to ensure that your plantings will be harmonious. I am, in general, loath to give too many concrete examples or to draw too many planting plans, as I believe they can be restrictive. I would far rather succeed in inculcating the general principles of colour association than see any plan of mine rendered plant for plant. With the vast choice of plants that is available to us, the chances for self expression are legion, as long as such ideas as proper tonal order are adhered to. If you always try to combine a light tone of a light colour with a dark tone of a dark colour, rather than the other way round, it will be infinitely more worthwhile than executing a specific example.

Nevertheless, certain points are made more expressly by the use of examples, and where they serve a purpose I have given them. However, I would like to emphasise that they are only illustrations, and that your own plant associations and combinations stand a good chance of being better than mine.

There is an influential school that decrees that pastel colours are *de rigueur* in gardening and that strong, clear, even raw hues are in 'bad taste'. It is founded upon a fear and lack of understanding of colour, and has unfortunately acquired guru status. Its logical extension into retreat from colour is the white garden – a pity, as a drift of white flowers lightened by just one touch of another colour creates one of the most telling effects of all.

The pastel garden is a garden that misses the point. It denies the joyousness of nature and relegates to 'bad taste' the works of the Almighty. Of course, colour is easily deployed in ways that shock or offend those with sensitive aesthetic perceptions – and sometimes they do not have to be so sensitive. But to be so offensive as

to dismiss as bad taste the love and attention that have gone into a garden is unforgiveable. By all means be as bold as you like, use fierce orange and satanic red; let vivid purple add a royal touch to your plantings, enjoy near-black hellebores if you like them and do not eschew green flowers if you find them fascinating. Garden for you and yours, and not for the censorious passer-by.

The love of flowers is deep in the heredity of all of us. The world we came into as primitive beings many thousands of years ago knew colour only through nature, and the most colourful things in nature were the flowers. This book will, I hope, help you to surround yourself with flowers for as much of the year as your climate allows. If the result is a deepening of your gardening perceptions and pleasure, it will not have been written in vain.

## USING THE BOOK

This book is divided into months so that practical information is quickly accessible to the gardener at any time of the year. If, for example, you want to check that you have done all the necessary routine jobs in the garden in a particular month, simply turn to the appropriate maintenance section. Plant Profiles for each month list a selection of the most attractive plants in flower for that month; the Plants in Flower section provides a more comprehensive list with, necessarily, less information about individual plants – the aim is to give the reader an idea of the wealth of choice available. Other sections in each month tell you how to propagate, how to plan and plant so that you have an attractive garden all year round. Finally there are suggestions for practical projects to improve your garden, or your gardening.

For ease of use the book is divided into twelve months, or sections. However, flowering periods vary greatly depending on weather conditions so more general terms, for example mid-spring and late autumn, are used, allowing the gardener, who is more used to his or her own area, to judge when projects and planting are best undertaken. The table on page 7 is a guide to the average conditions.

### LISTS AND TABLES OF PLANTS IN FLOWER

The lists of plants for each month are meant to be a guide and are neither comprehensive nor precise. Comprehensiveness is prohibited by reasons of space; precision by the ways of nature.

The flowering times of plants are highly variable, especially in winter and spring. The factors governing flowering time are the prevailing climate (continental, maritime, etc), the local climate, microclimates, altitude, soil (heavy soils are late, light ones are early), the strength of the light (governed in turn by climate and latitude) and often the age of the plant.

The length of the flowering season of a given plant varies also, but it is often cultural conditions that determine for how long a plant will bloom.

In addition to these factors, there are others that are imperfectly understood, either by your author or by science. An example of the variability of flowering is that of *Pieris* 'Taiwanensis', which is usually cited as flowering in the British Isles in April. In fact, it can start flowering at the end of January in the south-west of Ireland, to finish in mid-March, or it can begin in May in the northern parts of Scotland, where its season is shorter and it is likely to finish in the same month. In the United States of America, the same shrub will flower at radically different times in the mild, maritime climate of much of Washington and Oregon, and the colder, continentally-dominated climate of upper New York State (where it would be likely to need winter protection).

Many plants flower in more than one month. To have included every plant flowering in every month would have made demands on space that I could not have met, and I have omitted plants from those months during which, although they may be very nearly in full flower, they are not at their peak – given the provisos above.

Thus, from the lists early summer appears to be as good a time for shrub flowering as midsummer, which is not the case. Many shrubs that are at their best in early summer also flower in midsummer, and space does not allow their being mentioned there.

*The best way to use the lists and tables for any given month is to read them in conjunction with those for the months before and after. This will give a broader picture upon which you can with some realism base your gardening plans.*

*Bright and bold* Dianthus 'Sweet Beauty' *and* Lychnis chalcedonica *combine with* Nepeta 'Six Hills Giant' *apparently flouting conventional colour-matching*

# JANUARY

The English winter – ending in July,
To recommence in August
BYRON

*Well, he would say that, wouldn't he, a man who was never happy unless by the shores of the warm Aegean. If he had stayed around long enough he would have realised that the English winter seems long only because it is so mild. Autumn, winter and spring are merely variations on a theme when compared with the difference between August and January in New York or Boston. The colder months have subtle differences between them, to discern which my Lord Byron appears to have lacked the patience. This month is colder than last, but the days are gradually lengthening, not much, but enough to trigger certain plants – the earliest irises, the very first spring crocuses, winter aconites and snowdrops – into bloom. Its milder spells will, with increasing certainty, tempt hamamelis, winter-flowering cherry, wintersweet and Christmas box into flower, and release the fragrances of viburnums.*

*Now is the beginning of the end of winter – the first Act of the year's drama truly begins. This month it is not yet curtain up, but time for the overture. It starts quietly, with a tentative theme that passes through its variations with increasing confidence until, by the month's end, there is a hint, if not of merriment, then of relief that the worst is over. Next month can see a return to the bleakness, but never the blackness of the depths of winter.*

*It is at this time of year that a gardener's spirit proves its worth. In his or her mind's eye there is no longer the gloom of winter, there is a soaring picture of perfect borders to be achieved, blossoms generously falling to paths below, luscious scents and birdsong. Oh, cynical Byron! If only you had listened to Wordsworth!*

# tasks

## FOR THE

## *month*

## 1

**PREPARE FOR HARDY ANNUALS**
*In a dry spell, prepare the ground for early-spring sowings of hardy annuals. Dig the sites over, removing any perennial weed seeds, and incorporate organic matter such as peat or garden compost.*

**MANURE VERSUS BONEMEAL**
*Now is the time to top dress roses with either well-rotted manure or bonemeal, but not both at the same time. They react together, driving off the nitrates in the manure as ammonia gas.*

**WOODY WASTE**
*Any bits of twig, prunings you failed to pick up, or any woody debris at all, can all too readily set up infections of coral spot fungus. In no time, it can destroy your favourite tree. Burn them.*

## CHECKLIST

- As bulbs emerge, rake gently among them with a hand fork to break up and aerate capped soil
- Check your hardwood cuttings. If they have been disturbed by frost, firm them back
- Continue to plant trees and shrubs in open weather
- Continue pruning deciduous shrubs and trees and pay special care to removing all dead wood. Return to Japanese maples later, at leaf-break, and head back branchlets whose tips have died back
- You can still plant roses if necessary
- Protect crocus flowers from mud splash by mulching the area with a fine grade of composted forest bark
- You can plant winter-flowering heathers now if you like, to give some instant colour, but aim to plan better in future. Foresight is characteristic of the better gardener
- Make plans for planning a mixed border

## PLANTING

### PLANTING DISTANCES

Read the plant-buyer's guide on page 19 to save you a great deal of work in winters to come. Then follow these planting guidelines. No matter how small the specimen you fondly carry home, plant according to the best information you have.

When it comes to width, or crown spread, in trees and shrubs, take care that you do not make the extremely common mistake of planting so that the centres of the plants are separated by the amounts of their spreads only. For example, if you buy two shrubs whose spreads after ten years will be 2m (7ft) each, do not plant them 2m (7ft) apart (ie at 2m (7ft) centres). If you do and they grow the slightest bit more than that – as they will, one supposes – in year eleven – they will grow into one another and become misshapen.

Always allow for more than the ten-year spread. If I am planting shrubs whose spreads are likely to be 2m (7ft), I allow half that distance as the ten-year gap between them. When planting shrubs of differing spreads, I allow half the spread of the larger shrub as the gap.

The way you will save winter work is in not having to move shrubs that have become overcrowded. This is the most usual and the most easily avoided reason for transplanting semi-mature shrubs and trees.

## PLANNING

### THE MIXED BORDER

The above shows that it is not a good ambition to have a shrub border in the strict sense. When the young shrubs are planted there will be large distances between them, and there should still be significant gaps after a decade. These areas should be rendered unrecognisable as mere gaps between shrubs by your planting perennials, which can easily be reduced in number as the shrubs grow, whereas the shrubs cannot be reduced in size without ruining them. Close to the roots of the shrubs you should grow annuals such as nicotianas, which can be sown in situ and removed without disturbance. Bulbs, too can be planted among the shrubs.

What you will have created, in short, is a mixed border, and it is this towards which your ambitions should be directed. If it is, you will find yourself planning it as a whole, so that the colours and shapes of the flowers of the shrubs harmonise with those of the perennials, annuals and bulbs, and everything is in balance and there is none of the distortion, darkness and disease so common among shrub plantings.

## PROPAGATION

### ROOT CUTTINGS

Many perennial plants and just a few shrubs are better propagated from root cuttings than by any other method. There are many reasons tor this. With border phloxes, particularly varieties of *Phlox paniculata*, it

## PLANTING DISTANCES

Incorrect – after 10 years

Correct – after 10 years

Correct spacing for shrubs of different spreads

is the only certain way of producing plants free of eelworm. *Geranium* 'Ballerina', a highly popular rock-garden plant, is one of a group of geraniums that make little stem-cuttings material and cannot be divided. From root cuttings a good increase can be obtained.

This is the best month for taking root cuttings, as the plants are dormant and will not suffer from loss of a proportion of their root systems. Of course, if a large number of cuttings are taken from a plant, it will die, so you take either a few and keep the parent going, or many and do away with it.

■ Lift the plant with the root system as intact as you can and wash the soil away from part of it. You will find that the plants mentioned above will have long, thick roots with a consistency somewhere between woody and fleshy. Look for one the thickness of a pencil – from diary pencil to regular desk model. Cut it off, making a horizontal cut, and unravel it from the rest of the system.

■ Now cut it into sections 3-5cm (1¼–2in) long, each time cutting with a horizontal cut. Immediately you have severed a cutting, re-cut the bottom with a slanting cut. In this way you will always know which way is up.

■ There are two ways of setting the cuttings. With slender, malleable ones, such as are obtained from phloxes, lay them lengthwise on the surface of a 50/50 mixture by volume of sharp sand and moss peat in a pot, and cover them only 1cm (½in) deep, firming the compost down onto them.

Other, stouter cuttings may be inserted vertically into the compost so that their tops are just covered. It is for these that the difference between top and bottom is vital: an upside-down root cutting will never root.

■ Whichever method you use, put the pot in a cold greenhouse or frame, water it well, and keep it moist but not wet. In spring, you will see little green buttons on the surface, and these rapidly grow into new shoots.

■ Where most people fail with root cuttings is in disturbing them too early. The shoots develop before the new roots and live for a while on the food reserves in the cuttings. Moving them at this stage will inhibit root development. Allow the shoots to grow on well and then tap out the contents of the pot. Gently separate the newly rooted plants and, with great care, pot them up.

Root hairs, the organs that do the actual job of absorbing water and inorganic salts from the soil, are one cell thick and invisible. One single cubic inch of soil may contain as much as six thousand miles of root hairs. If you damage many of those newly formed on a root cutting you lessen its chances of establishment, but by not being too hasty you increase them many hundredfold.

## PLANTS FOR ROOT CUTTINGS

*Acanthus*
*Aesculus parviflora*
*Ailanthus*
*Anchusa*
*Arnebia*
*Brunnera*
*Campsis*
*Carduncellus*
*Centaurea* (some)
*Clerodendrum*
*Convolvulus*
*Crambe*
*Dicentra*
*Echinacea*
*Echinops*
*Erodium*
*Gaillardia*
*Halesia*
*Japanese anemone*
*Limonium*
*Morisia*
*Papaver orientale* (oriental poppy)
*Primula denticulata*
*Rhus*
*Romneya*
*Verbascum*

# plants
## OF THE
## *month*

### IRIS
#### *Iris unguicularis (*syn. *Iris stylosa)*

The Algerian iris is one of the most surprising of plants. It is bone hardy, which is strange for a plant from North Africa, its flowers are unusually large for one that blooms in winter, its winter flowering itself is a surprise, and it lives practically on nothing. Its beauty is little short of astonishing.

| | |
|---|---|
| type | Evergreen perennial |
| flowers | Typical of a beardless iris. Lilac-lavender and pinkish-lavender forms are the earliest flowering. Darker, purple forms such as 'Mary Barnard', rarely flower before spring. Lightly fragrant. Midwinter to early spring |
| foliage | Grassy |
| height | The plant's height is in its leaves. Ideally it should be not much more than 30cm (1ft), but when fed rather too well it can be twice that and liable to hide the flowers |
| spread | 60cm (2ft) |
| hardiness | Hardy |
| planting | Plant from a pot at any time, otherwise in late summer to early autumn |
| position | Hot and dry, preferably at the foot of a sunny wall |
| soil | Poor, preferably limy and rubbly. Do not feed. Richer conditions encourage leaves at the expense of flowers |
| propagation | By division of established clumps in late summer or early autumn if dry conditions persist |
| varieties | 'Walter Butt' is early and free flowering, but the flower shape is not very good. There is a white form. *Iris lazica* is a similar species with broader leaves flowering later in the winter. Its flowers are a good violet-blue |

### WINTER ACONITE
#### *Eranthis hyemalis*

The common winter aconite flowers towards the end of the month in warmer parts, a little later where it is cooler. It naturalises freely in leafy places beneath trees, and is highly valued for its yellow flowers at a time of year when most at ground level are in the lilac to lavender range.

| | |
|---|---|
| type | Tuberous perennial |
| flowers | Buttercup-like, rich yellow |
| foliage | Basal, much divided. The 'leaves' below the flowers are bracts |
| height | 8cm (3in) |
| spread | Colonises |
| hardiness | Hardy |
| planting | Plant when available |
| position | Full or part shade. It should be left alone to naturalise |
| soil | Leafy |
| propagation | By lifting self-sown tubers |
| alternatives | *E. × tubergenii* is a larger plant but it does not self-seed. *E. × t.* 'Guinea Gold' has deep yellow flowers with bronze tints and is a little later |

### WITCH HAZEL
#### *Hamamelis mollis* 'Pallida'

This is possibly the most popular of the witch hazels. It flowers very freely, with its naked branches wreathed in clusters of curious, spidery flowers. Their scent is not heavy and sickly, as in some others, but is a strong and yet delicate fragrance. It may flower at any time between early winter and early spring, but is usually at its best towards the end of this month. Its leaves turn rich, butter-yellow in autumn.

*IRIS UNGUICULARIS*

*CROCUS TOMASINIANUS*

| type | Deciduous shrub |
|---|---|
| flowers | Lemon yellow |
| foliage | Wide, hazel-like |
| height | 2m (7ft) after 10 years |
| spread | 1.8m (6ft) |
| hardiness | Hardy |
| position | Sun or part shade |
| soil | Any good garden soil |
| pruning | None |
| propagation | By layering in midsummer or spliced side-veneer grafting (see p.154) onto *Hamamelis virginiana* seedlings in spring. Seeds of the other species are decidedly reluctant to germinate, even when sown as soon as ripe. I have had little success with cuttings of any kind, even under mist |
| alternatives | *H.m.* 'Brevipetala' has orange-yellow, short-petalled flowers with a heavy scent. 'Coombe Wood' has darker yellow flowers and a fine scent |

## CROCUS

*Crocus tomasinianus* hybrid

There are several forms of the 'Tommy' crocus. Some are very free-seeding and crop up all over the place, others just quietly get on with establishing themselves in rapidly increasing clumps. An occasional flower may suffer the attentions of an inquisitive creature looking for nectar, but among so many it makes hardly a difference. The true species is now considered unobtainable and all corms offered are really hybrids. *Crocus tomasinianus* is quite the most cheekily cheerful of plants and a great companion on a fresh, sunny day later in the month.

| type | Corm |
|---|---|
| flowers | Vary from purple-lilac and reddish purple to mauvish blue, occasionally white |
| foliage | Grassy, flowers and foliage borne together |
| height | 8cm (3in) |
| spread | Spreads by seeding |
| hardiness | Hardy |
| planting | Plant in autumn |
| position | Almost anywhere |
| soil | Almost any |
| propagation | By lifting naturalised corms when dormant |
| varieties | Crocuses under the name of the species and given names such as 'Albus', 'Rose', 'Ruby Giant' and 'Whitewell Purple' are excellent propositions. The latter two are ideal for naturalising |

# plants

IN

# *flower*

| SHRUBS | colour | flower type |
|---|---|---|
| *Camellia sasanqua* 'Narumi-gata' | White | Small, single, fragrant |
| 'Crimson King' | Red | Small, single |
| Chimonanthus praecox (Wintersweet) | Pale yellow | Very fragrant |
| *Garrya elliptica | Greenish | Tassels |
| *Sarcococca spp (Christmas box) | White | Small, highly scented |

Also: **Erica carnea, Erica × darleyensis, Hamamelis** (many vars), **Jasminum nudiflorum, Lonicera fragrantissimum, L. × purpusii, L. standishii, Viburnum × bodnantense, V. farreri, V. tinus.**

| PERENNIALS | colour | height |
|---|---|---|
| *Iris unguicularis | Lilac-lavender | 30cm (12in) |

| CLIMBERS | | |
|---|---|---|
| *Clematis cirrhosa balearica (Fern-leaved clematis) | Pale yellow, red spots | |

| BULBS | | |
|---|---|---|
| Crocus ancyrensis | Orange-yellow | 5cm (2in) |
| imperati | Violet inside, buff outside | 10cm (4in) |
| tomasinianus | Lavender or pink | 10cm (4in) |
| Eranthis hyemalis | Yellow | 8cm (3in) |
| Galanthus graecus | White, green markings | 10cm (4in) |
| Iris danfordiae | Lemon yellow | 12cm (5in) |
| histrioides major | Royal blue, white and gold markings | 10cm (4in) |
| 'Katherine Hodgkin' | Cream, overlaid with pale yellow and blue | 10cm (4in) |

Also: **Cyclamen coum** aggregate.

## TREES for ornamental twigs and bark

| | | |
|---|---|---|
| Acer davidii | Red 'snake-bark', marked snakeskin fashion with white | |
| griseum | Mahogany orange, peeling bark | |
| grosseri var. hersii | Snake-bark marbling | |
| pensylvanicum | Snake-bark maple in green and white | |
| Betula albo-sinensis var. septentrionalis | Peeling bark in soft, fawnish pink | |
| utilis var. jacquemontii | White | |
| papyrifera | White, peeling | |
| pendula | Silver birch | |

---

**KEY**

\* = evergreen    spp = species
vars = varieties

**ROCK GARDEN**

The main flowers on the rock garden will be among the bulbs listed right

**ORNAMENTAL BARK AND TWIGS**

When there are few flowers in the garden, it is not just berries and autumn foliage that can provide the missing colour. Deciduous trees and shrubs with beautiful bark are invaluable this month and next, when most berries have gone and deciduous trees and shrubs are leafless. The list on the right is a selection only; it is not comprehensive.

| | |
|---|---|
| ***Eucalyptus* spp** | *Many different kinds: flaking, peeling, in blue, blue-grey, green-grey, cream and combinations of these* |
| ***Prunus serrula*** | *Bright mahogany, glossy* |
| ***Salix daphnoides*** | *Violet with a white 'bloom'* |
| *irrorata* | *'Purple with a white 'bloom'. Sometimes a shrub* |
| *alba* 'Britzensis' | *Brilliant orange-scarlet branches. Prune hard every other year* |

### SHRUBS for ornamental twigs and bark

| | |
|---|---|
| ***Acer palmatum* 'Senkaki'** | *Brilliant coral red twigs and branches* |
| ***\*Arbutus andrachne*** | *Cinnamon brown* |
| ***Cornus*** (European) – several kinds | *Bright red or yellow. Stool every other spring* |
| ***Leycesteria formosa*** | *Green stems* |
| ***\*Myrtus luma*** | *Cinnamon orange, peeling* |
| ***Parrotia persica*** | *Flaking stems like old iron. Sometimes a tree* |
| ***\*Rhododendron thomsonii*** | *Deep, glowing crimson main stems* |
| ***Rubus cockburnianus*** | *Arching stems appear as if whitewashed* |

## THINK OF AUTUMN

Plant *Rosa moyesii,* which has long, erect-arching, clean branches, near to *Acer griseum.* The brilliant red flowers are beautiful in their own right, but the large, long-lasting hips, like upside-down, sealing-wax-red amphorae, are unbelievably gorgeous in combination firstly with the tree's daring, coal-fire-at-bedtime autumn colour, and then with the peeling, mahogany bark, whose flakes are bright orange with the sun behind them.

## A PLANT-BUYER'S GUIDE

*The days of the altruistic nurseryman are gone. No longer can you expect universally to hear the truth when you ask questions about plants. Many people in the trade, though perhaps well-trained in horticulture, work for enterprises that are, like so many today, ruled by accountants. If they wish to keep their jobs, they must sell. This is not universally so, but enough that you should wear a sceptical garment when buying trees, shrubs and perennials.*

*Here are the rules for the well-informed plant buyer:*

■ *Never ask how tall a tree or shrub grows. You will be told 'Not very big', or 'Oh, it takes ages to get to any size'. If, on the other hand, the salesman spots that you really do want a large tree, his tune will change. Always ask, 'How tall will this shrub/tree become ten years from now?' If he does not know, or does not find out, go elsewhere.*

■ *Adopt the same approach concerning the spread of the tree or shrub, but be specific: 'How wide will the crown or head of branches become in ten years from now?' Spread, when applied to herbaceous plants, means the span of the plant when in leaf: take care that you are not told the width of its crown, which is at ground level and much narrower.*

■ *Never ask in what conditions a plant will grow: always ask in what conditions it will not grow. The question, 'Will it grow in my conditions' expects the answer 'Yes', and will probably get it. 'Tell me what soils and situations it does not like' forces the salesman to tell the truth.*

■ *Never dismiss a salesman who admits to lack of knowledge. However, if he makes not the slightest move towards finding out the answers to your questions, go elsewhere.*

■ *Never ask, 'Is this plant hardy?' Again, it expects the answer 'Yes'. If the nursery or garden centre is local, ask instead, 'Will this plant stand the worst winters round here?' If you are far from home ask if it will stand the worst winters in exposed conditions in the south/east/north or wherever you live.*

■ *Never buy a 'dwarf' or 'slow-growing' conifer without either looking it up in a good book or asking a nurseryman whom you trust how large it will become after ten years. In the less scrupulous areas of the trade 'slow-growing' conifers become forest trees with remarkable speed and 'dwarf' ones are merely slow growing.*

■ *Gardening is not a trade into which dim children are sent as a last resort. People buying plants can be extraordinarily rude and patronising, usually, one hopes, without meaning to be. Get the sales person on your side and you will come away with better information.*

# F E B R U A R Y

Here comes February, a little girl with her
first valentine, a red bow in her wind-blown
hair, a kiss waiting on her lips, a tantrum
just back of her laughter.

HAL BORLAND
*(1964)*

*This month can charm you with sunshine as strong as that of
autumn, it can freeze the falling rain into terrible ice, it is
perfectly capable of gales of hurricane force, and it can bury all
thoughts of gardening beneath a duvet of snow.*

*Generally, in those parts of the world where gardening is usually
possible now, it is not as wet as in late autumn and early winter.
Yet, like the little girl with a curl in the middle of her forehead,
this month, when very bad, can be horrid. It can rain, in an off
year, as if the future of the world depended on it. Then it becomes
'February fill-dyke' (Thomas Tusser c.1564), and you should
resolutely stay off the soil and keep to the paths – or the armchair
– until the fit passes.*

*The flowers that brave all this are equipped with hardiness of
quite astonishing proportions. Crocuses will stand under water
for days at a time and then open as if nothing had happened. The
reticulata irises, brave enough in any case at this time of year,
surpass themselves in courage and beauty when thrusting their
indomitable flowers through snow. And snowdrops take
everything that comes, nod sagely, and carry on as if to aver that
a few million years of evolution have taught them that this is
nothing, really.*

*Overhead, some shrubs and a few trees keep up the continuo to the
overture to spring. They bear the flowers of winter and have done
so for some time now, off and on. Soon, however, their final
chord will die away, the opening fanfare of true spring will
sound, and Act I of the gardening year will commence once again.
As Marcus Aurelius said, all things from eternity . . . come round
in a circle.*

# tasks

## FOR THE

## *month*

## 1

- Sow seeds of trees and shrubs under glass
- Sow seeds of alpines in a garden frame
- This is the last month during which you can safely plant out bare-rooted roses
- Lilies may be transplanted towards the end of this month in milder districts. Be careful to keep as much soil round them as possible
- Go round coloured-leaved shrubs such as *Spiraea* 'Gold Flame', removing any green, reverted shoots
- Plant clematis
- Prune late-flowering, large-flowered clematis and hydrangeas
- Remove suckers from roses
- Order summer-flowering bulbs, such as galtonias, gladioli and crinums
- *Buddleia davidii* varieties may be pruned hard back now, but in colder areas leave until next month

## MAINTENANCE

### PRUNING CLEMATIS

There is more confusion over this one small facet of gardening than almost any other.

Clematis are natural climbers of trees and large shrubs. With the exception of alpine species, it is of no advantage to them to produce leaves and flowers all along their stems, as it is only at the ends that they will be in sun; the greater part of the stems are hidden among the leaves of the host tree.

Gardeners, however, require flowers from near ground level upwards. To achieve that, they have to ensure a framework of the sorts of stems that do flower. These are either (A) produced on short growths from the wood of the previous year, or (B) on the growth of the current year.

Group A clematis should have previously flowered, dead growths removed; this should really have been done last autumn but can be done now. Growths made last year may be cut back to a strong pair of buds, thus diverting energy into all the leaf axils from which flower stems will be made. This pruning is *not* essential, just advisable. Old, tangled plants may be pruned to within 30cm (1ft) of the ground, but you will lose the flowers for that particular year.

Group B clematis should have the entire head of branches made last year removed, as you are only interested in the new growth that will flower this year. Prune all growths back to within 30cm (1ft) of the ground. This pruning *is* essential.

You can tell Group A from Group B thus:

■ Group A clematis flower in late spring to early summer, and then again in early to mid-autumn.

■ Group B clematis do not start flowering before midsummer.

■ Group C consists of species clematis that produce their flowers before the end of spring, including *C. montana, alpina* and *C. macropetala.* The only pruning required is the removal of weak or dead stems.

### NOTE

■ *Please note that it is an excellent idea to grow large-flowered clematis into trees and over large shrubs. The logic of the above paragraphs demonstrates that they should not be pruned at all* ■

Hearty growers among the species, such as *C. orientalis,* may be thinned as needed. The winter-flowering *C. cirrhosa balearica* need not be pruned if it is allowed to do its job of covering dead trees or old walls.

### PRUNING HYDRANGEAS

Hydrangeas may be pruned later this month and into next.

*H. macrophylla* varieties, which include all the 'mopheads' and 'lacecaps' – in other words the best-known hydrangeas – are easily pruned incorrectly. This is the correct way:

■ Firstly, go over each bush and remove the dead flowerheads, cutting each stem back to the first strong pair of buds below the head. You should not have done this earlier, as the old flowerheads afford an important measure of frost protection.

■ Now go down to the very bottom of the bush and remove as close to ground level as possible all growths that are old, gnarled, weak, badly crossing or diseased. With a bush that has not been pruned for years, you may need to do this in two or even three annual 'bites'. This will encourage the production from the base of straight, strong, rapid shoots that will flower the same summer.

■ Even well-grown hydrangeas should have some of the older growths removed each year once they have become established, otherwise flowering will gradually decline.

### PLANNING

### SCENT

Scented plants are often planted with little thought to how the scent is best to be appreciated. It is little use, for example, going to the trouble of seeking out shrubs with scented flowers and then planting them on the eastern boundary of the garden when the prevailing wind is westerly.

Equally, it makes poor sense to plant shrubs with winter scent anywhere but near a path. The last thing you want to do is to have to plunge through mud, snow and dripping branches to take a sniff of a pleasant perfume; you are more than likely not to bother.

Although a few plants have scents that do not waft on the air and demand that you approach them closely, the majority are better appreciated when they take you by surprise. A garden is by definition a contrived place, and its surprises are therefore planned, but that does not reduce the surprise value of scents. It is physiologically impossible consciously to remember a scent. We think we remember them, but in fact recall only that they were pleasant or unpleasant. Each time a scent is encountered, it has about it a degree of novelty, even though it may recall with great vividness a partly forgotten episode in one's life.

You can, therefore, deliberately plan to surprise yourself, and this use of scent is one of the more subtle aspects of gardening. To do so, you should arrange for the scented plants to 'arrive' at or approaching head height, or near to where you are likely to linger. To this end you might grow the smaller daphnes in raised beds, scented climbing roses on a pergola, *Viburnum carlesii* 'Aurora' near the garden frame, and nicotianas, mignonette and night-scented stocks around the part of the garden where you sit out on summer evenings.

It is a good idea to plant the general run of scented plants (all other aspects of your design being equal) towards the centre of the garden, rather than at the boundaries. You will then be able to enjoy them no matter in which direction the wind happens to be blowing.

*IRIS PROTECTION*
*If heavy rain or snow threatens while Iris reticulata is in flower, have a pane of glass ready with which to protect the blooms. They are very tough, but can look tatty after a battering.*

*LILIES IN POTS*
*If you receive lily bulbs now, plant them in pots, plunge them in a cold frame, and plant out the entire pot contents in two months' time, cushioning the bottoms of the planting holes with 3cm (1¼in) of sand.*

# plants
## OF THE
## *month*

### HELLEBORE
#### *Helleborus orientalis*

Depending on your botanical viewpoint, the Lenten rose is either a very variable species or one of about five. As gardeners rarely involve themselves in botany if they have any sense, they may take it that we are talking about those beautiful hellebores that flower in late winter and early spring and have nodding flowers in shades of purple and plum, usually beautifully spotted inside, and occasionally almost white, with some of the darkest approaching black.

| | |
|---|---|
| type | Evergreen perennial |
| flowers | Wide open, nodding, saucer shaped |
| foliage | Dark green. The leaves lie flat, allowing the flowering stems to rise unobstructed |
| height | 45cm (18in) |
| spread | 60cm (2ft) |
| hardiness | Hardy |
| planting | Preferably in spring, but autumn planting is satisfactory for pot-grown plants |
| position | Part shade |
| soil | A good, organic, moisture-retentive soil |
| propagation | By division of established clumps only, immediately after flowering. Seeds should be sown as soon as ripe |
| varieties | There are many and they should be chosen if possible when in flower. The species you may find them under are *H. guttatus, olympicus* and *abschasicus* |

### CAMELLIA
#### *Camellia × williamsii* 'St Ewe'

Camellias as a whole have a long season that varies greatly according to the climate. In the south-eastern states of the USA, for example, flowering is well under way in autumn and is over by the end of this month. In the British Isles the first williamsii camellias are out this month in the south, and start a season that finishes with the last japonicas towards the end of spring. The further north you go, the later the camellia seasons get, but they are also more compressed, so that camellias flowers are rarely seen after mid-spring.

| | |
|---|---|
| type | Evergreen shrub (*C. japonica* × C. *saluenensis*) |
| flowers | Funnel shaped, single, deep phlox-pink |
| foliage | Semi-glossy, pointed |
| height | 1.5m (5ft) after 10 years |
| spread | 1.2m (4ft) after 10 years |
| hardiness | One of the hardier camellias, but requiring shelter from freezing winds, particularly when young |
| position | Part shade. Camellias should never face the morning sun as frozen buds are killed if they thaw too quickly. In cooler areas, camellias should face south but have a little shade from the hottest sun at midday. Here, the williamsii camellias flower very much better than the varieties of *C. japonica* |
| soil | Lime-free, leafy, moisture-retentive but well-drained soil |
| pruning | None |
| propagation | By semi-ripe cuttings taken after midsummer and rooted under mist |
| alternatives | Many. Among the most celebrated williamsii camellias are 'Donation', large, semi-double, pink; 'Anticipation', medium, deep rose, peony-form double; 'Brigadoon', medium to large, semi-double, wavy, pink; and 'Debbie', neon-pink, large, ruffled peony-form double |

*CAMELLIA × WILLIAMSII 'ST EWE'*

*GARRYA ELLIPTICA*

## PRUNUS
### *Prunus mume* 'Beni-Chidore'

This form of the Japanese apricot demonstrates the flexibility of trees and shrubs that flower as winter gives way to spring. It will, in a mild or even reasonable year, cover itself with blossom even in midwinter, while in harder years it may wait until well into spring. It is sensational when flowering with *hamamelis*, particularly those with clear yellow flowers, and it is worth planting for the association even though their flowering may not always coincide.

| | |
|---|---|
| type | Small deciduous tree |
| flowers | Rich, dark phlox-pink, single (not double as sometimes stated) almond-scented, up to 9mm (¼in) wide |
| foliage | Leaves up to 10cm (4in) long; long-pointed |
| height | 3m (10ft) after 10 years |
| spread | 3m (10ft) after 10 years |
| hardiness | Hardy |
| position | Sun or part shade, sheltered |
| soil | Any good garden soil |
| pruning | None |
| propagation | Hardwood cuttings taken in autumn may root |
| special comment | Although the name given above is the one I believe to be correct, you may find it as 'Ben-shidon', 'Beni-shidare', or 'Beni-shidori' |

## GARRYA
### *Garrya elliptica*

In places where the winters are mild, this unusual and strangely beautiful evergreen shrub thrives and produces its large crops of silvery-grey catkins at some time during mid-to late winter. If sheltered from winds it will tolerate quite severe cold, but it is not safe in the colder regions.

| | |
|---|---|
| type | Evergreen shrub |
| flowers | Catkins like silky tassels. They are longer in male forms, which are the ones usually sold. Their average length is 15cm (6in) in colder areas, 25–30cm (10–12in) in warm ones |
| foliage | Leaves tough, leathery, roundish, dark glossy green above and woolly-grey beneath |
| height | Dependent on climate; 1.8–3.5m (6–12ft) after 10 years |
| spread | Dependent on climate; 1–2m (3–7ft) after 10 years |
| hardiness | See above |
| position | Part shade, shelter |
| soil | Any reasonable garden soil |
| pruning | None |
| propagation | By semi-ripe cuttings taken in summer and rooted under mist. In early autumn they may be tried in a garden frame |
| varieties | *G.e.* 'James Roof', if the true plant can be obtained, has catkins well over 30cm (1ft) long |

# tasks

## FOR THE

## *month*

## 2

*If you want to have as colourful a year-round garden as possible, growing trees, shrubs and perennials from seed will save you a great deal of money and provide you with excitement and a much deeper knowledge of plants than you might otherwise gain.*

*WATERING SEED TRAYS*
*When watering pots or trays of seed, use a fine rose and water in a series of passes over the surface of the compost, pausing between them. This allows the water to drain down and soak the lower levels of the compost, but prevents ponding on the surface. Ponding washes the seeds together and ruins your best efforts to sow thinly.*

## PROPAGATION

### SOWING SEED

This is the best time for sowing seed of trees and shrubs. I also sow many perennials now, under the same conditions, as I prefer to give them the longest growing season possible in their first year.

Early sowing is best done with some artificial heat. I use a frame on the greenhouse bench, which is fitted with under-soil heating cables, but for small quantities of seed heated propagators are perfectly adequate. Soilless compost seems to give far higher germination rates than a soil-based, John Innes type of compost.

Seed sowing can become far too complicated. The majority of these sorts of plants can be given identical treatment as far as compost, watering and the germination environment go. If you have no artificial heat, simply sow everything in pots in a cold frame. Different seeds will come up in different environments. With artificial heat, plants from warmer countries will germinate readily; in a cold frame, it will be cold-country plants that emerge in the main.

Far more important than technical details is an understanding of what makes seeds germinate, and what can inhibit them.

### Factors in germination

The germination of seeds is governed by moisture, temperature and light. They act like alarms, waking the seed from its sleep. All three have to act in the right way, otherwise the seed will not awaken and start the chemical processes that lead to germination. Moisture must enter the seed and

must be constant or nearly so in the environment of the seed. The temperature must be at the right level and constant within certain limits. The amount of light falling on the seed must be within certain limits.

> ### WARNING
>
> ■ *Inconsistency is death to most seeds. Fluctuating moisture, a failure of the temperature to 'inform' the seed that it is safe to germinate, and too much or too little light will severely inhibit germination* ■

You should water the seeds regularly but not heavily. You should keep the temperature within a fairly constant range, and you should provide about 50 per cent of the ambient light by shading the frame or propagator, but not too heavily. Light is also governed by the depth of soil over the seed. Cover the seeds with a depth of compost no deeper than the breadth of the seed. The smallest seeds – primulas, meconopsis, hydrangeas and so on, as well as certain other specific seeds, such as birches – should not be covered at all.

### Seed dormancy

A fairly constant temperature of about 18°C (64°F) will 'convince' most seeds that spring has arrived and that it is safe to germinate. Other seeds, however, are more sceptical and need more evidence than that. They have to go through a notion of winter first, otherwise their inhibition mechanisms will not be broken down. Still others, less sophisticated, have time-delay mechanisms in the

shape of hard, impenetrable seed coats.

To deal with the former kinds, two methods are open. One is to sow all seeds from cold countries in a frame in autumn and let the fluctuating temperatures of winter do their job. However, not all such seeds are available to you in autumn. You can still sow them in a frame if they arrive in the early part of the year. Some will receive enough information, while those that do not will wait another year or even two. Thus, a gardener with no more than an unheated frame and some patience will obtain good results, but in the longer term.

The second method is to break the dormancy by 'kidding' the seed that winter has been and gone and that spring has arrived. Many cold-country seeds, including a large number of alpines, appreciate being mixed with a mixture of damp sand and peat in plastic bags and placed in the refrigerator for thirty days or so. They can then be removed for a few hours to warm up and then given another ten days, after which the entire mixture can be sown in heat. Or, you can sow the seed, wrap each pot in clingfilm, and put it in the fridge. It is a mistake to think of seed as being frozen; 'chilled' describes it much better.

The second kind of dormancy, that engendered by tough seed coats or those with built-in chemical inhibitors, has to be broken down mechanically. The pea family is notorious for this. Sowing in autumn in a frame allows hard coats to be rotted away naturally and chemical inhibitors to be leached out. Spring or late-winter seed may be soaked in water that starts hand hot and is then allowed to stand for 24 hours, after which the seeds are sown normally.

| TREES | colour | flower type |
|---|---|---|
| **Prunus mume** vars | Red, pink or white | Various |
| ***Rhododendron arboreum** forms and hybrids | Red, pink or white | Trusses |

### SHRUBS

| | colour | flower type |
|---|---|---|
| **Abeliophyllum distichum** | White, tinged pink | Small, fragrant |
| ***Camellia × williamsii** vars (a few) | Various | Various |
| **Cornus mas** vars | Yellow | Small, on bare twigs |
| **Daphne mezereum** | Pink | On bare branches, fragrant |
| odora *'Aureomarginata' | Purplish | Fragrant |
| ***Mahonia japonica** | Yellow | Drooping racemes, fragrant |
| ***Rhododendron dauricum** | Rose-purple | Funnel shaped |
| *'Praecox' group | Rose-purple | Funnel shaped |

Also: **Camellia sasanqua** vars, **Chimonanthus praecox, Erica carnea** vars, **E.** × **darleyensis** vars, **Garrya elliptica, Hamamelis, Jasminum nudiflorum, Lonicera fragrantissima, L.** × **purpusii, L. standishii, Sarcococca, Viburnum** × **bodnantense** vars, **V. farreri.**

### CLIMBERS

| | colour |
|---|---|
| ***Clematis cirrhosa balearica** (Fern-leaved clematis) | Pale yellow, red spots |

| PERENNIALS | colour | height |
|---|---|---|
| ***Bergenia** vars | White, pink or red | 30cm (12in) |
| **Helleborus orientalis** vars | Plum, purple or white | 60cm (24in) |
| ***Iris unguicularis** and vars | | |

| BULBS | colour | height |
|---|---|---|
| **Crocus chrysanthus** vars | Yellow, blue, purple, white | 8cm (3in) |
| **angustifolius** | Yellow and bronze | 8cm (3in) |
| **biflorus** and vars | White or grey-white | 9cm (3½in) |
| **sieberi** vars | White, blue or violet | 8cm (3in) |
| **Galanthus** (Snowdrop) many | White, green markings | 10cm (4in) average |
| **Iris reticulata** vars | Blue, reddish purple | 15cm (6in) |
| **Narcissus asturiensis** | Golden yellow | 20cm (8in) |
| **bulbocodium** vars | Yellow, hooped petticoats | 15cm (6in) |
| 'February Gold' | Yellow | 30cm (12in) |
| 'February Silver' | White, lemon cup | 30cm (12in) |
| 'Peeping Tom' | Yellow, reflexed | 40cm (16in) |

Also: A few other narcissus vars, **Eranthis hyemalis, Iris histriodes major, Cyclamen coum** aggregate

# plants
IN
# *flower*

**NOTES**

**Rhododendrons** prefer lime-free soil as do **camellias**.

**ROCK GARDEN**

**Hepatica** spp
***Polygala chamaebuxus**
**Primula marginata**
***Saxifraga** (**kabschia** and **engleria** spp and vars)
**Also the smaller bulbs**

# MARCH

In our hearts those of us who know anything worth
knowing know that in March a new year begins . . .

JOSEPH WOOD KRUTCH
*The Twelve Seasons (1949)*

*Spring comes in several different ways for the gardener. There is
the official season, of course, the one that starts with the equinox;
but for most of us who watch plants grow, spring has been under
way for some time by then.*

*Did it start when the snowdrops hopefully declared the hostilities
of winter to be over? Some people, invariably optimistic by
nature, would say that the true spring began even earlier, with the
first lengthening of the days, when* Iris danfordiae *joined the most
precocious crocuses in braving the ferocity of those last winter
days. In fact the coming of spring varies by several weeks from one
area to another. If we are to be scientific about it, and I suppose
we should, the best criterion is based on the average soil
temperature above which plant growth can take place –
5°C (41°F).*

*What gardeners everywhere have in common is a capacity for
simply feeling the arrival of spring. It is not an occasion that is
marked off on the calendar like an annual holiday, nor is the
secret of its magic to be found in the bulb of a thermometer. It is a
stirring in the soul, a bubbling up of the spirit. Spring renders you
impatient of wintry pastimes and draws you gently but inexorably
outside. It is at this moment that the gardening year really begins.
The long largo of the overture ends as the allegro vivace of spring
moves into brisk, happy brilliance. For the great majority of us,
it is happening now.*

# tasks

## FOR THE

## *month*

## *1*

*SETTLE BACK*
*Look for newly planted perennials and any alpines that have been lifted by frost and settle them back in the soil, firming finally with the foot where possible.*

## CHECKLIST

- Carry out path cleaning and maintenance
- Treat bearded irises against fungi
- Start dealing with slugs
- Prune roses, hydrangeas and buddleias
- Get your main planting season under way

## MAINTENANCE

### PATHS

Algae are highly dangerous on paths so it is worth a little labour to get rid of them. By the early spring every path laid with 'pavers', slabs, stone, or any material without a really rough finish will have developed by the early spring a coating of invisible algae as frictionless as a skating rink.

Obtain some potassium permanganate, also known as permanganate of potash, from your pharmacist. It comes as purple crystals and a few grams cost very little. Dissolve some in your watering can until the solution is about the colour of Beaujolais nouveau. If you don't know what it is like, imagine the colour of the phoniest wine you can think of, and that will be it. Water the path and leave it for 24 hours. Then take your yard brush, sluice the path down with clean water and scrub,

wetting whenever you need to. The original colour of the path, dulled by algae and general dirt, will be restored, and, when it dries, the path will hold a wet wellington boot in full flight.

Apply a residual contact and pre-emergent weed-killer to gravel drives and paths. Applied this month it will give a year's protection against weeds; if you wait until later it may be too late, as it does not work well once the soil warms up.

### WARNING

- *Go carefully over any paving you have. Frost can lift this, and in an increasingly litigious society it might cost you a lot of money if a tradesman or visitor should trip* ▪

### IRIS RENOVATION

Bearded irises are all the better for being treated to a little surgery. Lift them – it is easy because their rhizomes are on the surface – and cut away any parts of rhizome that are diseased, squashy or extremely elderly. Cut with a very sharp, extremely clean knife, and dust the cuts with flowers of sulphur. Remove all dead leaves from the rhizomes and surrounding soil and put down bait for slugs.

When replanting them, scatter a few generous handfuls of bonemeal over their patch. It will feed the irises slowly and will also help to keep the soil on the alkaline side, which they like. If your soil is acid, it does no harm to add a handful of hydrated lime, too. However, you must not add lime if you are also giving the irises any animal manure. The lime reacts with the nitrates in the manure to give off ammonia, and all the goodness is lost.

## IRIS RENOVATION

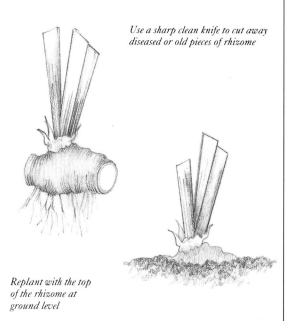

*Use a sharp clean knife to cut away diseased or old pieces of rhizome*

*Replant with the top of the rhizome at ground level*

## SLUG BAITING

Slugs mainly take bait at night. The bait is harmful to birds, which may come across doped, dehydrated, but still living slugs in the morning. If they eat them, they probably eat undigested bait as well. However, you have to fight slugs if you want a good garden, so rise early and pick the offending objects up. Gardens with plenty of birds have few slug problems, so think twice before accepting a kitten. It will grow up to be a highly efficient bird-scarer.

### NOTE

■ *Go over the garden with a critical eye for dead leaves, heaps of blown twigs and general litter. Woodlice, slugs, snails, vine weevils and other animal pests love to hide and breed among such rubbish, and disease fungi thrive* ■

## PRUNING HYDRANGEAS

Now is the best time for pruning hydrangeas and removing any dead heads left on to protect the buds underneath from frost. Cut back strong shoots to the first pair of fat buds (they are opposite one another). Next, go down to ground level and remove old, weak and crossing branches at the bottoms of the bushes. This will induce thick, hearty new shoots to arise from near the ground.

Annual pruning of *Hydrangea paniculata*, by cutting back each of last year's flowering stems to within a few centimetres of the old wood, is not recommended. The result looks like a horticultural cripple. Pruning like this is essential once in a while, otherwise flowering falls off, but every three years is quite enough.

## PRUNING BUDDLEIA

Varieties of common buddleia should be pruned now, too. It is astonishing how drastic you can be with them. Nothing looks worse than a spindly buddleia, and the way to produce a vigorous, well-furnished shrub is to cut it down to within 45cm (18in) of the ground – every year. Buddleias seem to live on thin air, and I have carried out this treatment on specimens growing in nothing but old rubble for years and years. Every summer, without fail, there are the butterflies having a whale of a time on the massed flowerheads of the healthiest buddleias for miles around.

Yellow buddleias are different. *B. globosa* should be pruned seldom if at all, and its hybrid, *B.* x *weyerana*, of which there are some lovely forms without any mauve in the yellow, will need hardish pruning about once every six or seven years.

## PRUNING ROSES

Prune the roses. Would that it were that simple! However, it does not have to be the solemn ritual that many would have you believe. Hybrid Teas and floribundas need quite hard pruning. This is because they produce their flowers on new wood and you want to induce a lot of it. The harder you prune at this time of year, the greater the response. Light pruning creates a twiggy mass of shoots and many flowers, but these will be on the small side; prune hard and you induce fewer but longer and stouter shoots, and fewer but larger flowers because the shoot buds left on the old wood will be fewer. Also aim

## PRUNING ROSES

■ With both hybrid teas and floribundas, cut out dead and diseased wood, pruning back any damaged shoots to good wood. Remove weak or crossing shoots then cut everything to between 15 and 22cm (6–9in) from the ground ■

to remove crossing branches and encourage an open, chalice-shaped bush. This is where the 'prune to an outward-facing bud' advice comes in. Although not cast in tablets of stone, it is common sense.

## PLANTS FROM POTS

Planting of shrubs, trees and perennials from pots can start as soon as the weather feels spring-like and the soil less like a cold, wet sponge.

## BARE-ROOTED PLANTS

Anything arriving bare-rooted should be put in as soon as ever it is possible, as this is about its last chance. Plant them to the depth mark left from when they were in nursery containers.

*FEEDING ALPINES*
*Top dress alpines with hoof and horn for slow-release nitrogen, and top up the surface layer of pebbles to about 2.5cm (1in) deep.*

# plants
## OF THE
## *month*

*PLANTING TIMES*
*Please note that, as almost all trees and shrubs are sold in containers, they can be planted at any time of the year unless the ground is waterlogged or frozen. In this book, planting times are only given for perennials, which may be supplied bare-rooted, and for bulbs.*

### FORSYTHIA
*Forsythia* – 'Beatrix Ferrand'

Forsythias are among the most colourful of the shrubs that flower in early spring, with bright yellow blooms on the naked branches. They are hardy, reliable and, especially when a good variety is chosen, very free flowering. The flowers of *F.* 'Beatrix Ferrand' are particularly large.

| | |
|---|---|
| **type** | Deciduous shrub |
| **flowers** | Rich canary yellow |
| **foliage** | Leaves 10cm (4in) long, slender, and fresh green |
| **height** | 2m (7ft) after 10 years |
| **spread** | 1m (40in) after 10 years |
| **hardiness** | Hardy |
| **position** | Full sun or part shade |
| **soil** | Any good garden soil |
| **pruning** | Immediately after flowering, cut back old flowering shoots to within 5cm (2in) of the old wood and remove crowded or crossing branches. Forsythia hedges should be trimmed hard after flowering |
| **propagation** | By semi-ripe cuttings, early to mid-summer. Root in a propagator at 15.5°C (60°F). Hardwood cuttings taken in late autumn will root in a cold frame |
| **alternatives** | 'Karl Sax' is similar in colour and has leaves that turn purple in autumn. *F. viridissima* 'Bronxensis' is a dwarf form for small gardens and is later flowering |

### HELLEBORE
*Helleborus corsicus*

In an unconventional way, this is one of the most beautiful of all garden plants, let alone those that flower in winter and early spring. It usually flowers now although it may be earlier. It is easy to grow.

| | |
|---|---|
| **type** | Evergreen perennial |
| **flowers** | Drooping, pale green cups |
| **foliage** | Leaves have three prickly-edged, grey-green leaflets |
| **height** | 60cm (2ft) |
| **spread** | 90cm (3ft) |
| **hardiness** | Hardy, but should be protected from freezing winds |
| **planting** | Usually container-grown; plant any time in open weather |
| **position** | Sun or part shade, sheltered from cold winds |

*MAGNOLIA CAMPBELLII VAR. MOLLICOMATA*

| | |
|---|---|
| **soil** | Any good garden soil |
| **propagation** | Divide the plants immediately after flowering and plant straight away. Sow seeds in late spring in an outdoor seed bed |

## MAGNOLIA

*Magnolia campbellii* var. *mollicomata*

This is hardier than the larger *M. campbellii*. It flowers later in the season and is not as likely to lose its flowers to frosts. This variety also flowers at about twelve years old instead of thirty or more.

| | |
|---|---|
| **type** | Tree |
| **flowers** | Very large, like pink waterlilies, before the leaves |
| **foliage** | Large and paddle shaped |
| **height** | 3m (10ft) after 10 years |
| **spread** | 2.5m (8ft) after 10 years |
| **hardiness** | The tree itself is reasonably hardy. Flowers are spoiled by hard frosts, but shelter helps to protect them |
| **position** | Part shade, protected from frosty winds |
| **soil** | Peaty or leafy, lime-free soil. Add well-rotted organic matter generously when planting |
| **pruning** | None |
| **propagation** | From seed, sown as soon as ripe |

## SCILLA

*Scilla sibirica*

There are several species and varieties of scilla. These are underrated plants, ideal for the rock garden and places such as occur round the boles of mature trees or among the trunks of smaller ones. They are most attractive when grown among patches of early daffodils.

| | |
|---|---|
| **types** | Bulbs |
| **flowers** | Star shaped, shades of blue and violet-blue |
| **height** | 5-10cm (2-4in) |
| **spread** | Clump-forming |
| **hardiness** | Hardy |
| **planting** | Plant 8cm (3in) apart and 8cm (3in) deep in early autumn |
| **position** | Partial shade and in company with other small bulbs |
| **soil** | Any good garden soil |
| **propagation** | Divide the clumps, which increase freely, in summer when dormant, or in leaf immediately after flowering |

*FORSYTHIA 'BEATRIX FERRAND'*

| | |
|---|---|
| **alternatives** | Try to obtain the variety 'Spring Beauty', which is deeper blue. *S. tubergeniana* is earlier-flowering as is *S. bifolia*, which has a longer flowering period. All have blue flowers |

# tasks
## FOR THE
## *month*
## 2

**NOTE**

Hemerocallis prefer not to be disturbed more than once in every five or six years. They should be left alone until flowering declines perceptibly

## CHECKLIST

☐ Divide perennials of all kinds
☐ Plan bulb planting carefully

### PROPAGATION

#### DIVIDING PERENNIALS

This is quite the best time for dividing perennials of all kinds. The soil is – well, we hope it is – warming up, and the plants are at a stage when they are bursting with urgency, positively longing to put out new roots and get on with growing.

### Primulas

Primulas enjoy being divided, and it is a satisfying task. Lift a good clump and soak off the soil in a bucket of water. Ease the soil right away and the plant begins to fall apart into individual crowns. A little gentle teasing and tugging soon leaves plenty of young plants – and some for your neighbour, too.

### Gentians

If you have the good fortune to grow Asiatic gentians – the kind that flower from late summer onwards on lime-free, peaty soils – divide them now.

At the moment, the growing plants show as buttons of green, just extending into individual stems. These are at the heads of stout, white, thong-like roots. Often there will be more than one crown per button, and they tease apart with the greatest of ease if you are deft. Plant them immediately, allowing about a hand's-span between them, and autumn should bring a dazzling show of sumptuous blue.

### Achilleas and larger herbaceous perennials

Larger herbaceous perennials can be lifted and attacked with unplantsmanlike ferocity. The roots of an old clump of achillea are like so much fine wire and about as penetrable. Take two garden forks and thrust them back to back into the clump. Done properly, this leaves the handles at an outward angle to one another. Press the handles together and immediately wrench them apart. The achillea should split into two with a crack.

Of course you may find yourself indulging in a wrestling match with your plant. Little harm will be done, and you can go on subdividing until you have several small, wholesome divisions, each furnished with a few strong young crowns and a plentiful share of roots. Make sure the roots are actually attached to the crowns. Throw away the tired centre of the old plant.

### PLANNING

#### BULBS

Lack of planning is one of the main reasons why bulbs are often not used as well as they could be in private gardens. Trained gardeners and bulb experts can do the most wonderful things with bulbs, chiefly because they plan ahead, but most people lead busy lives doing other things, and planning is easier said than done.

Unlike other plants, bulbs are not easily bought on impulse, unless you are taken in by the pictures that usually accompany the bins of bulbs on sale in autumn. A particular daffodil seen in flower in spring cannot be

**DIVIDING PRIMULAS**

bought straight away; you have to wait for six months, by which time it is highly likely that you will have forgotten all about it.

Use the spring to gather information. There is no substitute for seeing bulbs in growth, and visits to gardens that are open to the public can be supplemented by keeping your eyes and mind open to them in other people's private gardens as you pass by.

Public gardens have the advantage of labels, and it is a mistake to visit one without a notebook. Write down the name of the bulb and a short description of it. If, subsequently, that variety is not available, this description will be helpful in choosing something else close enough to give much the same effect. I once made a note to, 'Remember *Narcissus* 'Ice Wings'; new white cyclamineus hybrid, approx 10in'. It was growing in the famous Keukenhof garden in Holland and had pure white flowers and neatly swept-back petals. That autumn, I could not find 'Ice Wings' on sale anywhere, so bought a few bulbs of 'Dove Wings' instead. 'Wings' in the name of each variety refers to the characteristically backswept petals of this group of hybrids. 'Dove Wings' differs from 'Ice Wings' in that it has a pale yellow trumpet with its white petals and is a couple of inches taller. The main thing was that it was quite easily obtainable and would fit my planting scheme almost as well.

## NOTE

- *After flowering allow the leaves of bulbs to die down, thus replenishing the bulb for next year's display* ▪

### KEY

1 *Narcissus* 'Suzy'
2 *N.* 'Scarlet Gem'
3 *N.* 'Actaea'
4 *N.* 'Tête à Tête'
5 *Tulipa* 'Juan'
6 *T.* 'Candela'
7 *T.* 'Berlioz'

*MAPPING OUT YOUR DISPLAY*
Draw a 'map' of your border (see below) – or wherever you will be planting bulbs in the autumn – and designate areas for where you would like bulbs. Then look at those in flower and choose the bulbs that, ideally, you would like. If a particular niche cannot be filled, write 'red, short-stemmed tulip' or whatever, and see what is on offer when the time comes. How it should turn out is shown left.

# plant
## *selections*

### PERENNIALS

The great majority of perennials are easy to divide. However, a few are best propagated by other methods and you should not try to divide them:

*Althaea*
*Anemone* (some)
*Aquilegia*
*Codonopsis*
*Cynoglossum*
*Dianthus*
*Erodium*
*Euphorbia myrsinites*
*Gentiana* (except autumn-flowering gentians)
*Gypsophila*
*Helleborus*
*Incarvillea*
*Linum*
*Lysichitum*
*Malva*
*Ostrowskia*
*Phlox* (border)
*Phyteuma*
*Platycodon*
*Primula denticulata*
*Salvia* (some)
*Verbascum*

### PERENNIALS

**Pulmonarias** are among the most valuable groundcover plants you can grow. Choose a selection of species for flowers throughout spring. Their foliage, evergreen with the exception of *P. angustifolia*, is always present, lending an intriguing note in its often silvery-spotted dress. Pulmonarias are happy to spread gently in light shade, and the bright pink flowers of *P. officinalis* have a tone that is strong enough to cope with early spring light. This species was grown in gardens for medicinal use. It was known as Lungwort, since the Doctrine of Signatures decreed that because a diseased lung lobe was blotched and spotted, the leaves, also spotted and much the same shape, must contain the cure. We shouldn't scoff: many gardening practices are based on even flimsier premises.

### BULBS

Spring and **daffodils** are inseparable, and they are now well into their stride. The choice is extremely wide and often daunting, with the catalogues bright with pictures of tall, gracious 'daffs' and long-stemmed, elegant 'narcissi'. There are few sights as magical as a daffodil-strewn wood or glade; if you have the room, plant as many of these cool beauties as you possibly can.

The great majority of gardens, however, are quite small, and large flowers on stems of 45cm (18in) or more seem out of scale and tend to be planted in blobby clumps because drifts of them become overpowering. This is where the dwarf and shorter-stemmed daffodils are so valuable; not just because they are in scale, but also because the owner of an average garden can enjoy so many more varieties.

*PULMONARIA OFFICINALIS*

*Narcissus* 'Tête à Tête' is only 15cm (6in) high but holds its twin heads up in the teeth of the most bellicose gales. Almost every stem has two flowers, perfect miniature daffodils in bright golden yellow. The Lent lily, *Narcissus pseudonarcissus*, one form of which is the Tenby daffodil, differs from the wild daffodils to be seen elsewhere in Britain in that its petals are the same deep yellow as the trumpet; those that Wordsworth saw had light yellow, contrasting petals. It only grows 15–30cm (6–12in) high so if you have room, naturalise it in grass, but if not, it is still small enough to provide a host of daffodils even more golden than those that so entranced him. *Narcissus cyclamineus* 'Jumblie' has the swept-back petals of the species combined with the simple grace of the true daffodil. 'Little Witch', obviously a kissing cousin of 'Jumblie' and well under 30cm (1ft) high, carries on flowering into later spring.

**Chionodoxas** are close relatives of the starry-flowered, blue scillas. The most widely grown is *Chionodoxa luciliae*, often known as 'glory of the snow', although it is said that the name refers to its flowering as the snows melt in the mountains of Turkey. It is only 13cm (5in) in height and makes a charming clump of starry flowers of an eye-catching, vivid blue. *C. sardensis*, which is about the same height, is as brilliant a gentian blue as you could wish to see twinkling at you on a bare day.

The big, fat 'Dutch' **crocuses** flower this month, and they are preferred by many gardeners for their size. They lack the natural air that seems so essential in flowers if they are to carry off such an early appearance, and they can appear coarse. Nevertheless, they have their place and are ebulliently cheerful.

### SHRUBS

***Rhododendron*** 'Praecox', is among the earliest of all shrubs. Generally speaking, early-flowering rhododendrons cause as many heartbreaks as a bevy of debutantes. A whiff of frost – no rare occurrence this month – and the flowers are gone for another year, crumpled brown mush at the branch ends. 'Praecox' is made of sterner stuff and, as long as it is in shelter, will survive to continue its display of rosy purple.

***Stachyurus praecox*** is a shrub whose 10cm (4in) flower-tassels are formed in autumn to open unerringly in spring. They hang stiffly down, not a leaf in sight, with up to twenty-four small golden cups ranged along them. It belongs in more spacious gardens not because it is very large, but because its appeal is limited

*MAHONIA AQUIFOLIUM*

to its budding and flowering. For more prolonged interest, there is 'Magpie', a variety of *S. chinensis*, which flowers two weeks later. Its leaves have white margins with a pink blush – most effective in a shady spot.

**Mahonias** bear long tassels of gold too. These may be upright or lax or – as in *Mahonia aquifolium* – what the botanists call 'terminal clusters'. This species is, according to our chronology, the earliest, as its more distinguished congeners flower mainly in winter, which for us is late, not early. It is a plant that combines humility with determination, and its holly-like, evergreen foliage is to be treasured, rather than scorned. Solicitude pays off – if it is allowed decent light it gives a bright show of bold, golden flowers set off against the occasional scarlet tint among its foliage.

No two components of a floral arrangement go better than fresh spring daffodils and **willow** catkins when they are at their velvety best.

Pussy-willows appear on the naked branches and have a way of catching the low, seasonal light that induces moments of magic of the kind that are the stuff of nostalgia. You may hanker for sub-tropical warmth as you listen to the lashing rain, but if you were eventually to move to warmer climes would you not occasionally pine for that pale sunlight, picking out the tinsel on the lowly willow flowers?

# plants

IN

*flower*

**KEY**

\* = evergreen    spp = species
vars = varieties

**NOTES**

Many **Prunus** have other points of interest, such as:

**P. sargentii** coloured bark
**P. cerasifera 'Pissardii'** purple leaves
**P. 'Moerheimii'** is a weeping form
**P. 'Pandora'** has rich autumn colour.

**HEATHER**

Varieties of Erica carnea and E. × darleyensis are lime-tolerant.

| TREES | colour | flower type |
|---|---|---|
| **Magnolia campbellii mollicomata** | Purplish pink | V. large, open saucer-shaped |
| **dawsoniana** | Pale rose | Large, flat |
| **denudata** | White | Cup-shaped, fragrant |
| **Prunus cerasifera 'Pissardii'** | White from pink buds | Small, but profusely borne |
| **dulcis** (Almond) | White or pink | Single or double |
| **incisa** (Fuji cherry) | White, from pink buds | Small, freely borne |
| **'Kursar'** | Deep pink | Small, freely borne |
| **'Moerheimii'** | White, pink in bud | Small, freely borne |
| **mume** (Japanese apricot) | Pink to almost red | Single to semi-double |
| **'Okame'** | Carmine | Small freely borne |
| **'Pandora'** | Pale pink | |
| **sargentii** | Pink | Single |
| **subhirtella** | Pink | Small |
| **× yedoensis** | White, blushed | Single, almond scented |
| **\*Rhododendron arboreum** and hybrids (mild areas only) | White, pink or red | Trusses |
| **Salix aegyptica** | Yellow | Catkins |
| SHRUBS | | |
| **Camellia japonica** vars | Various | Various |
| **Chaenomeles speciosa** vars | White to crimson | Small saucers |
| **Corylopsis pauciflora** | Yellow | Short racemes, scented |
| **Daphne mezereum** | Reddish purple | Scented |
| **\*Erica carnea** vars | Various | |
| **× darleyensis** vars | Various | |
| **Forsythia** | Yellow | |
| **Magnolia stellata** | White | Star-shaped |
| **\*Mahonia aquifolium** | Yellow | Close clusters |
| **Rhododendron** several, including **dauricum, leucaspis, oreodoxa** var. **fargesii, pemakoense, 'Praecox', racemosum, strigillosum, 'Seta'** | | |
| **Salix apoda** | Catkins are silvery-furry, then become covered with yellow anthers | |
| **caprea** (Pussy willow) | Female form has silver catkins | |
| **gracilistyla** | Catkins are silvery grey at first, becoming red as pollen appears | |
| **'Melanostachys'** | Catkins almost black, becoming red, then yellow | |

**TULIPS IN TUBS**

Devote one or two containers to Kaufmanniana tulips. Set off their strongest colours, like the red of 'Show Winner' or the orange and salmon of 'Shakespeare', against the foliage of an evergreen shrub. *Pieris* 'Forest Flame' is a good companion for them, as it will turn red itself next month when its new foliage unfurls, and then carry on a spectacular foliage display into the beginnings of summer.

| | colour | height |
|---|---|---|
| *Stachyurus praecox* | Yellow | Cup-shaped racemes of up to 24 |
| *chinensis* | Yellow | Up to 35 flowers in a raceme |
| *Viburnum tinus* vars | White | Flattish heads |

### PERENNIALS

| | colour | height |
|---|---|---|
| *Helleborus corsicus* | Green | 60cm (2ft) |
| *Primula farinosa* | Lilac | 15cm (6in) |
| *rosea* | Rose | 15cm (6in) |
| *denticulata* | Various, red forms are most desirable | 30cm (1ft) |
| *Pulmonaria rubra* | Coral red | 30cm (1ft) |
| *saccharata* | Blue, from pink buds | 30cm (1ft) |
| *Saxifraga* – cushion forms | Various | A few inches |

### BULBS

| | colour | height |
|---|---|---|
| *Anemone blanda* | Various | 10cm (4in) |
| *Chionodoxa luciliae* | Blue | 13cm (5in) |
| **'Pink Giant'** | Pink | 13cm (5in) |
| *sardensis* | Gentian blue | 13cm (5in) |
| *Crocus* Dutch hybrids. Many others overlap from last month | | |
| *Muscari armenaicum* | Cobalt blue | 18cm (7in) |

*Narcissus* – daffodil types and early 'narcissi' dwarfs, **'Apricot'**, **'Beryl'**, *cyclamineus*, **'Jumblie'**, **'Little Witch'**, **'Tête â tète'** and many more

| | colour | height |
|---|---|---|
| *Scilla bifolia* | Blue | 4cm (10in) |
| *sibirica* **'Spring Beauty'** | Deep blue | 20cm (8in) |
| *Tulipa kaufmanniana* hybrids | Various | 13–20cm (5–8in) |

### ROCK GARDEN

| | colour | height |
|---|---|---|
| *Alyssum saxatile* **vars** | Yellow | 20–30cm (8–12in) |
| *Aubrieta* **vars** | Mauve, blue, purple | 8–10cm (3–4in) |
| *Draba* **sps** | Yellow | 5–10cm (2–4in) |
| *Omphalodes verna* | Bright blue | 15cm (6in) |
| *Primula denticulata* | Pale lilac to deep red | 30cm (1ft) |
| × **pubescens** | White, crimson, violet, brick red | 7–12cm (2¾–8in) |
| *Saxifraga oppositifolia* | Red, purple, white | 2cm (1in) |

## CONTAINER CONTRASTS

If you like gardening in tubs, urns, and other ornamental containers – or if your gardening is done in a city yard where you have no choice but to use them – you may find yourself with little colour in March. It is easy to brighten up your containers with small bulbs. Chionodoxas and scillas look lovely with very small daffodils, but be careful about tonal order. Choose a light-toned narcissus, such as the cyclamineus hybrid 'Ibis', which has reflexed, white petals and lemon-yellow trumpets on 20cm (8in) stems, and plant it with *Scilla sibirica* 'Spring Beauty', whose blue is deep and rich. Tonal order is the key to making grape hyacinth (*Muscari*) look right. They so often appear out of place because their blue, which is quite deep, often appears near yolk-yellow daffodils.

## SILVER AND GREEN

In the open garden, you can set up a subtle, year-round foliage contrast by growing pulmonarias as ground cover beneath camellias. The slightly whiskery, matt, silver-dotted pulmonaria leaves highlight the glossy, deep green of the camellias, and they make a quietly splendid picture when flowering together.

## HEATHER COMPANIONS

*Erica carnea* is a species that grows in limestone mountains – it is not a moorland heather. In nature, you find it associated with all sorts of other plants, many of them shrubby. Varieties of the species and of *E.* × *darleyensis* should be planted with suitable companions to give structure and purpose. Try small willows, which are perfect when placed among them. They can provide early colour where deciduous azaleas will bloom later, and the cool white of *E.* × *darleyensis* 'Silberschmelze' deceives nicely, hinting little at the hot oranges, reds and yellows that are to come.

# APRIL

April, April,
Laugh thy girlish laughter;
Then, the moment after,
Weep thy girlish tears!

SIR WILLIAM WATSON
Collected Poems *(1905)*

*This month is the early adolescence of the year; up one moment,
down the next – never knowing when to smile or cry. Dawning
poise and serenity are interrupted by stormy episodes when
childhood seems to break through, but the promise is always there.
Adulthood is just around the corner.*

*The weather is showery and cool, but the sun can be every bit as
strong as it is in high summer. The soil is warming up quickly,
absorbing heat faster than it is prepared to release it to warm the
air. Plants whose natural home is the dappled shade of trees
scamper into growth in the full light, in order to flower and set
seed before the leaf canopy closes over.*

*This is pure spring; there is nothing transitional about it. This
month rushes, bustles, agonises, has moments of forgetfulness,
bursts into tears, and leaps with joyful life. It is a time when the
patience of gardeners is sometimes sorely tried and when their
ability to take the long view can be put to the test. Frosts are not
as devastating as they can be a few weeks later, but it is a rare
year when some flowers are not lost. On a well-drained slope this
month is full of flower; in a frost pocket it is a lottery in which
some years are almost completely barren of bloom.*

*There is still a wide difference between climatic zones. The full
bubble and bounce of spring may not arrive for another month in
colder, northern areas, and it is sometimes early summer before
the seasons briefly coincide. Spring can be somewhat telescoped at
higher latitudes and altitudes, but it is more a state of nature than
a thirty-day period and always arrives – some time.*

# tasks
## FOR THE
## *month*
## 1

## CHECKLIST

- Feed the lawn as necessary and begin regular mowing
- Mulch beds and borders
- Give roses a top dressing of fertiliser
- Stake herbaceous perennials
- Plant out any perennials raised from seed last summer
- Plant gladioli and dahlias
- Order alpines from specialist nurseries and plant out
- Prune *Kerria japonica*, forsythias and flowering currants when they have flowered

## BEDS AND BORDERS

Make certain that all perennial weeds are absent and then, as the soil warms up, mulch with a weed-free material such as forest bark. This should preferably be 'composted' bark; if it is not, add 30g (1oz) of sulphate of ammonia per square metre (yard). This prevents the bark from taking nitrogen from the soil as it breaks down.

The mulch should be at least 4cm (1½in) deep to be effective. It will not only suppress weeds, but will also conserve moisture and make watering in summer much less of a necessity.

## MAINTENANCE

### THE LAWN

A flower garden with an unkempt lawn always looks shabby. Mowing is essential, but is also one of the most repetitive chores in gardening. There are, however, ways of reducing the frequency of the labour to give you more time for your plants.

The main one is to realise that almost everyone overfeeds their lawn. This is not only unnecessary but also produces soft, sappy, quick-growing grass that has to be mown often. Feed the lawn about one-third as often as most other people and you will have a good, hard-wearing lawn. Your mower will last much longer, and furthermore you will avoid adding to the excess of fertiliser that is leaching down to the water supplies and creating a major environmental problem. I feed my lawn once every *three years*.

Mark out a section of your lawn into square metres (yards) using bamboo canes. Apply the required amount of fertiliser and then move the canes on, until the complete lawn has been fed.

Mowing begins when the soil starts to lose its sogginess and the hardest frosts are over, which is usually this month. Unless you want to play bowls or practise your putting, there is no point in mowing with the blades set lower than 3cm (1¼in) – it only accelerates wear.

## ROSES

Feed established roses with a rose fertiliser. Scatter 35g (1oz) over the root area of each rose and hoe in gently, taking care not to damage any main roots as this can stimulate suckering.

## PERENNIALS

I prefer to support tall or floppy herbaceous perennials with twigs, much as one would peas. If you live in the town you may find them hard to obtain, and you will have to resort to bamboo and string or proprietary plant stakes.

Whichever supports you choose, have them ready at hand from now on and put them into place when the perennials break ground – if you leave it until early summer it will be too late.

If you cut twigs of willow, poplar or hazel, make sure to do so a couple of weeks before you need to use them or when they are put into the soil they will take root.

## PLANTING

### Dahlias

If you live away from the mild areas where dahlias can be grown in the ground all year, plant them out later in the month. Any new dahlia shoots could be frosted, so earth them up like potatoes.

### Summer-flowering bulbs

Plant gladioli 10cm (4in) deep and ensure that the base of each corm is on soil and not over an air pocket. Well-rotted manure or garden compost can be dug in beforehand to provide good growing conditions. Peat is excellent on heavy soils, but only as a conditioner. Do not plant all your corms at once, but make successional plantings over a number of weeks in order to have a season of flowers, rather than one burst of bloom.

Early this month is your last chance for planting bulbs such as galtonias and especially lilies.

### Alpines

In many areas this is the ideal month for planting alpines. It is also the time of year when alpine plant nurseries are getting into full swing with sending out their mail orders. The range of alpines that is sold in most garden centres is small, with often only the sketchiest descriptions to be found on the labels – and sometimes none at all. If you are a keen alpine grower it is better to order most of your plants by mail.

## PRUNING

As soon as *Kerria japonica*, forsythias and flowering currants have finished flowering, prune them back to encourage them to produce flowering wood for next year. The best method is to remove some of the older stems at ground level and then clip back any others that are unwieldy or unbalancing the shrub.

*BARE-ROOTED PLANTS*
*Beware of nurseries offering cheap, bare-rooted plants this month. You may think they are no end of a bargain, but they will fail. The time for open-ground plants is now well past.*

*WEED-FREE PLANTING*
*Whenever you plant a pot-grown specimen, always scoop away the top 0.5cm (¼in) or so of compost. This is where the weed seeds are, especially those of that awful pennycress which fires its seeds all over the place for months on end, germinates in what seems to be five minutes flat, and flowers again five minutes after that.*

## LABELS

*Never plant anything without a label. You may think you can remember the names of the plants, but Murphy's Law decrees that you will forget just the one you thought you knew best.*

*Labels should be permanent, which is to say they should be legible after twenty years. By far the best are strips of anodised aluminium, on which ordinary pencil remains decipherable for more than two decades. Plastic of whatever kind looks ugly and succumbs to ultra-violet light in no time. So-called 'permanent' marking inks and many of the pens sold in garden centres for 'permanent, waterproof labelling' last about a year before they have you holding the labels up to the light as you vainly try to work out what on earth they used to say.*

*Form a 'stake' from 12 gauge wire as illustrated. Then bend an anodised aluminium label around the loop in the wire to make a permanent label.*

# plants
## OF THE
## *month*

### RHODODENDRON
*Rhododendron* Loderi

This name covers a group of hybrids between *R. fortunei* and *R. griffithianum*. They are considered to be the best hybrid rhododendrons ever raised and have very large, lily-like flowers in loose, many-flowered trusses. Their hardiness, free and regular flowering and delicious scent are inherited from *R. fortunei*.

| | |
|---|---|
| type | Evergreen shrub |
| flowers | Vary, but usually some shade of pink, shading and fading more or less to cream or white |
| foliage | Leaves quite large and mid-green |
| height | 2m (7ft) after 10 years |
| spread | 2m (7ft) after 10 years |
| hardiness | These hybrids require shelter from wind. In shelter, they are hardy away from the coldest areas |
| position | Grow in the dappled shade of trees, preferably where you can enjoy their scent without getting wet and muddy. The larger the leaf of a rhododendron, the less sun it can take |
| soil | Must be lime free and as leafy as possible |
| pruning | None |

| | |
|---|---|
| propagation | Propagation of rhododendrons of this type is not easy and is best left to the nursery trade |
| varieties | All stand on their own merits |
| alternatives | *R. fortunei* bears bell-shaped, lilac-pink flowers next month; the sub-species *discolor*, which is strongly scented, bears its pale pink blooms in early to midsummer. There is no real alternative to *R.* Loderi in spring |

### AZALEA
Japanese Azaleas

The evergreen 'Japanese' azaleas are considerably shorter and more compact, and flower earlier, than the deciduous azaleas. These extremely well-known plants belong, in fact, to a special section of the genus *Rhododendron* and require the same conditions. However, they are also ideal for culture in raised beds or tubs, where a rhododendron-type soil can be used even in a limy garden.

| | |
|---|---|
| type | Small, evergreen shrubs |
| flowers | A wide range of colours from white through various pinks and lilacs to red, including some doubles. In flower during second half of this month and first few days of next |

*RHODODENDRON LODERI*

| | |
|---|---|
| foliage | Leaves small and densely packed, making for neat, rounded bushes that are always decorative |
| height | 0.5–1m (1½–3ft) after 10 years |
| spread | 0.75–1.25m (2½–4ft) after 10 years |
| hardiness | Hardy, apart from a few of the older varieties, which are hardy only in milder areas |
| position | Plant in sun as long as the soil is moisture retentive, but try to allow for a little shade during the hottest part of the day |
| soil | Peaty, leafy and lime free |
| pruning | None |
| propagation | Take semi-ripe cuttings in summer and place in a heated propagator or mist unit. On no account attempt to pot up the rooted cuttings until they begin to grow again the following spring |
| varieties | All stand on their own merits |

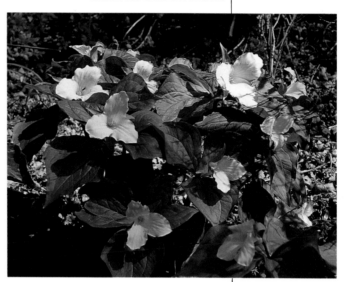

*TRILLIUM GRANDIFLORUM*

## MAGNOLIA

*Magnolia × soulangeana*

This is the most familiar of all the magnolias, bearing its enormous chalices on bare branches in the best forms. There are several varieties, with flowers ranging from pure white to deep purple.

| | |
|---|---|
| type | Tree or large shrub |
| flowers | White in 'Alba Superba' and 'Amabilis', variously shaded purple from the base, until fully red-purple in 'Rustica Rubra' |
| foliage | Large and paddle shaped |
| height | 2m (7ft) after 10 years; 10m (35ft) after 30 years |
| spread | 1.5m (5ft) after 10 years; 7m (24ft) after 30 years |
| hardiness | Hardy |
| position | Full sun or part shade |
| soil | The soil must be lime free. Add plenty of well-rotted organic matter to the soil. Magnolias dislike sticky clay. Dry, sandy soils should be thoroughly mixed with copious amounts of organic matter, but not fresh manure |
| pruning | None |
| propagation | By air layering in mid-spring or early summer. Simple layering is sometimes possible |
| alternatives | There are now many different kinds of this general type of magnolia. The following are excellent: 'Jane', 'Betty', 'Heaven Scent', *liliiflora* 'Nigra', 'Sayonara' |

## TRILLIUM

*Trillium grandiflorum*

Trilliums are among the aristocrats of spring flowers. They are often thought of as difficult, but if you follow the notes below you should find them no problem. All parts of the plant except the stems and roots are in threes – the leaves are in whorls of three, and the flowers have three petals.

| | |
|---|---|
| type | Herbaceous perennial |
| flowers | White; there are single and double forms |
| foliage | Whorls of leaves at the tops of the stems, just below the flowers |
| height | 30cm (1ft) |
| spread | 30cm (1ft) |
| hardiness | Hardy |
| planting | Container-grown plants may be planted at any time in open weather. Plant open-ground specimens between mid-autumn and early spring |
| position | Part or complete shade, but not dry shade |
| soil | The peatier and leafier the soil the better. Trilliums abhor dryness, but must nevertheless have good drainage |
| propagation | By careful division in early autumn or early spring. Each division must have at least one growing point |
| alternatives | *T. sessile* and *T. chloropetalum* have flowers that vary from pink to deep maroon |

# tasks

## FOR THE

# *month*

# 2

## CHECKLIST

- Check seed trays every day for signs of germination
- Prick out seedlings when large enough to handle
- Continue to sow hardy annuals in the positions in which they are to grow. Thin those that have germinated
- Continue dividing perennials
- Divide bulbs
- Pot up rooted cuttings
- Decide on container-grown or open-ground perennials

## PROPAGATION

### SEED

Examine pots and trays of seed every day. The purpose of this is so that you can take trays from the shade of a frame as soon as possible after germination and put the seedlings into full light so that they will remain short-stemmed and sturdy, and not become weak and drawn out.

Seeds that have been germinated over bottom heat, which includes most trees and shrubs, should be taken from their heated, humid environment and placed on the greenhouse bench in full light, but the temperature should not drop below 0°C (32°F).

Water freshly germinated seedlings with Cheshunt Compound in order to forestall damping-off disease. This should not be necessary, however, if you treated the trays at sowing time.

You should finish direct sowing of sweet peas now. Those you sowed in pots last month should be thoroughly hardened off and then planted out now.

If you sowed any hardy annuals last month, keep an eye on them. As soon as you can tell weed seedlings from plants, tweak them out while they are still small. Thin the plant seedlings at the same time, so as to produce short, bushy specimens. With a good, fertile soil you should not need to apply any fertiliser to them.

## PRICKING OUT SEEDLINGS

*Seedlings of trees, shrubs and perennials should be pricked out as soon as they can be handled. The conventional wisdom states that you should wait until there is a pair of true leaves in addition to the seed leaves (cotyledons). That is all very well, but many seedlings are far too small at that stage. The best advice is simply that you should prick seedlings out when they are large enough to handle – but of course when they have some true leaves.*

*The cotyledons of many seedlings make useful handles with which to hold them as* *they are lifted from the compost. On no account hold the stem of a seedling – it will be far too delicate to stand the lightest grip without becoming damaged. Lightly hold a cotyledon or leaf, and support the root ball underneath as you move the plant from the seed tray to its individual pot.*

*There are all sorts of gadgets for lifting seedlings. Most are designed to make twee little Christmas presents for gardening relatives. They are, by and large, useless and compare badly with the sensitivity and delicacy of which human fingers are capable.*

## PERENNIALS

Continue dividing perennials, but only those that flower late in summer. If you have not got round to those that flower earlier, such as oriental poppies, hemerocallis and iris, you should leave them until early autumn or early next spring, as they are now growing strongly and would be set back badly by being disturbed.

## BULBS

It is not generally appreciated that many bulbs can be lifted and divided while still green. Just after flowering is the best time for daffodils and narcissi. I reserve this procedure for bulbs that are in the wrong place or that I have hitherto forgotten. Do not try to break down the clumps very far, look after the roots, and replant immediately. Remove the old flower stems so that the plant's energies do not go into making seed.

Bulbs are storage organs. They hold a reserve of food so that the plant is capable of a long resting period. The food is manufactured in the leaves so if they are removed or have knots tied in them this may result in the bulb not being formed properly and failing to flower in subsequent years.

The leaves should be left in place until they have turned quite yellow. Next month, as the danger of frosts recedes, you will be able to disguise them with plantings of annuals. Meanwhile leave them to get on with their job.

## CUTTINGS

Many gardeners make the basic mistake of potting up all their cuttings soon after they have rooted. Many will tolerate it, and in fact it is the best thing to do with the majority, but there are some that bitterly resent it and they will die.

If you root your cuttings in pure sand you really have to pot them on quickly, but few of us do, and then usually only with soft cuttings (especially of alpines); the standard mixture – 50/50 by volume of moss peat and sand – will hold enough moisture to keep the plants going during the winter.

What kills the young plants is disturbance. No matter how careful you are you will still damage the root hairs, which are only one cell thick, and the plants are unable to renew them in the later part of the year. In spring, however, the plants are not attempting to go dormant but are growing fast, and the root hairs are quickly re-grown.

The plants most seriously affected are listed, although several more will succumb

to some degree. Potting of cuttings late in the year is a major cause of failure with magnolias and is also the reason for the extreme scarcity of the beautiful Chinese shrub *Dipelta floribunda,* which roots easily under a mist system but does not survive potting until the following spring.

## PLANNING

### PERENNIALS

If you decide to carry out a planting project involving more than just a few perennials, it is a good idea to consider ordering open-ground plants for autumn delivery. They are larger and more robust than pot-grown plants and will give you a good display in their first year, whereas pot-grown perennials take two years to be effective. In the open ground, too, root growth is unrestricted, whereas perennials in pots rapidly become rootbound and very difficult to establish properly.

The decision whether to buy potted perennials or plants from the open ground should be taken now. If you decide to buy them in pots from the garden centre, make up your mind to visit about once every two weeks from next month onwards; otherwise, by the time you come to plant in autumn the best will have gone and you will be left with the rubbish. If, on the other hand, you choose bare-rooted, open-ground perennials, start your research now and determine to visit as many gardens open to the public as possible. The ideas for plants and plant associations that you pick up on these visits will make all the difference in the world to your ultimate design.

**PERENNIALS TO DIVIDE**

**Aster**
**Helenium**
**Helianthus**
**Kniphofia**
**Monarda**
**Phlox**
**Rudbeckia**

**CUTTINGS TO POT UP
IN SPRING**

**All these are prone to failure if potted up in autumn.**

**Azalea**
**Camellia**
**Conifers**
**Crinodendron**
**Cytisus** (broom)
**Eucryphia**
**Ilex** (holly)
**Rhododendron** (many)

# plant
# *selections*

*Kaufmanniana
tulip 'Glück'*

## BULBS

The difference between **'daffodils'** and **'narcissi'** is, of course, an artificial one. There are official groupings within the genus *Narcissus* that differentiate between 'Trumpet daffodils or narcissi of garden origin', and 'Large-cupped' and 'Small-cupped' narcissi of garden origin.

As far as I am concerned, a daffodil is what looks like a daffodil, and a narcissus is one of the sophisticated sorts of flowers that generally has a shorter cup, which is more openly flared and less trumpet-like. What matters is the fact that the flowers of 'narcissi' look more appropriate this month than earlier in the year.

Many modern narcissi are long-lasting in flower, and these are the ones that everyone with a garden that is on the small side should seek out. Plant just a few in fair-sized groups and you will obtain a much better effect than by trying to buy all the toys in the shop.

With the striking contrasts in modern narcissi between the colours of the petals and the cups, you can make for much stronger statements than were made by the innocent daffodils of last month. 'Professor Einstein', for example, which flowers early this month, has brilliant orange-red cups against pure white petals. 'Romance', which is later, is on the same plan but with smaller, lighter-coloured cups and is very long lasting. 'Actaea', which blooms late in the month, is beautifully scented. Its flowers have small cups, which are yellow with red rims, and broad, white petals.

Collectively, **tulips** have a far longer season than most gardeners realise. It starts in early spring, or sometimes even in late winter, when the dwarf Kaufmanniana hybrids trustingly open their wide, star-shaped flowers to the fickle weather, but begins in earnest this month, with the Fosteriana tulips.

These are to all intents and purposes short, early Darwin types. Fosterianas flower early in the month zestfully coloured in a full range of hues and tones from vivid vermilion (the dreadfully named 'Rockery Beauty') to rich orange ('Orange Emperor') and the almost edible lemon-yellow fading to cream of 'Sweetheart'.

The Early Single tulips are better known for forcing than for growing in the garden, but the tougher varieties are perfectly at home in the open. 'Couleur Cardinal', which is 35cm (14in) tall, is renowned for its vigour and ability to stand up to the weather. It is cardinal red, as you might expect, but deepens to plummy crimson at the bases of the petals. 'Keizerskroon', bicolored in scarlet and yellow, is superb, but needs a bed to itself unless offset by the pure white of 'Diana' or something like 'Apricot Beauty'.

## TREES AND SHRUBS

Just occasionally you come across a shrub, or group of shrubs, whose foliage for a short time plays the part of flowers. I do not mean the fickle display of colour that autumn leaves may or may not put on in any particular year, but the reliable show that is an intrinsic part of the development of the leaves of some shrubs.

**Pieris** are a perfect example. For a period in spring, which varies according to how the season is going, the new leaves on these evergreen shrubs make as dramatic a display of red or pink as any that may be in flower. If they are planted in association with camellias, which is logical, as both genera like the same, leafy, lime-free soils, a richness will be achieved to which camellias on their own could never aspire. Admittedly, the effect may be spoiled by frost, but you take that risk at this time – it is part of gardening.

It is inescapable that those who garden on lime-free soils have by a very long way the best of this month as far as trees and shrubs go. The great spring shrub genera – *Magnolia*, *Camellia* and *Rhododendron* (which, of course, includes the azaleas that come at the end of the month) – are only available to gardeners on limy soils if they resort to raised beds and containers. Spring for them means concentrating on bulbs, **cherries**, **crab apples**, **berberis**, **daphnes**, **osmanthus** and **viburnums** – all of which will grow on lime-free soil as well. Many are caught out of pocket when they buy the snowy mespilus, **Amelanchier lamarckii.** It is one of the very finest of small trees, bearing its massed white flowers this month, but it must have a lime-free soil.

**Japanese cherries** (*Prunus* vars), on the other hand, are never entirely happy on moisture-retentive, acid soils. They will grow, flower and attain maturity, but they will also be subject to canker, martyrs to fungus disease, and liable suddenly and dramatically – sometimes when in full flower – to collapse and die. On alkaline, calcareous soils, and especially on chalk, they are much better.

Their peak season is from middle to the end of this month, although some flower earlier and some spill over into next. There are many of them, some of which are too large for the average garden, while a few others are afflictions rather than assets. Among the latter is the egregious 'Kanzan', whose costume is more fitting to a red-light district than to the myriad of suburban streets in which it has been planted at the expense of the unsuspecting public. The great majority, though, offer a feast of delights from which it is not always easy to choose.

Your choices will be between double or single flowers, white or some shade of pink, and rounded or spreading crowns to the trees. Some research will be needed, but here I can only tell you of those that figure highest in my own personal favour. 'Mount Fuji' wins in the double white, spreading class. Its branches are horizontal, eventually bowing towards the ground, and laden with very large, semi-double, pure white blossoms. 'Tai Haku' comes top of the single whites, although it needs a larger than average garden. It is known as the 'Great White Cherry' and has very large, single, white flowers and coppery young foliage. 'Shogetsu', also known as 'Shimidsu Sakura' (Sakura means cherry), is the best spreading tree for small gardens, with a flat crown of branches, all along which hang large, pure white, frilled flowers that open from pink buds. Of the double, pink, 'typical' Japanese Cherries, 'Ichiyo' is almost in a class of its own for delicacy of colouring and general elegance. 'Ama-no-gawa', upright like a little Lombardy poplar and the most widely planted Japanese Cherry of all, has become a cliché and a fairly tiresome one at that.

**Camellias** are misunderstood beauties, as capable of growing in cold as in mild climates. If you want to see them flower in chilly areas, however, you should choose varieties of *Camellia × williamsii*. In colder climates, such as the north-east of North America, and places with low light levels, such as Scotland, *C. × williamsii* varieties flower freely whereas *C. japonica* varieties tend to fail.

Where the sun is strong camellias should be planted in at least part shade. If you plant any camellia facing the morning sun you will see few flowers, as frosted buds will be killed. Don't plant the bushes where cold winds can reach them, for the simple reason that the plants will die. They are essentially hardy, especially after passing their third year or so, but only in relatively still air.

If your soil is alkaline, you need not exclude all **magnolias**. *Magnolia kobus*, a small tree, will grow on chalk, but rarely flowers until it is between twelve and fifteen years old. Much better are the forms of its hybrid with *M. stellata*, which go under the name *M. × loebneri*. The best known of these is the extremely floriferous 'Leonard Messel', which has flowers like those of *M. stellata*, but lilac-pink. 'Merrill' is becoming more widely known; it is more tree-like and less bushy than 'Leonard Messell', but still small enough as magnolias go. Its flowers, abundantly borne, are pure white. These are two of the best of the smaller magnolias of spring.

*MAGNOLIA STELLATA*

CAMELLIAS IN THE UNITED KINGDOM
*Plant facing south in the north, west in the middle, and north in the south – that is to oversimplify it, but it is not a bad guide.*

*Camellia × williamsii 'Golden Spangles'*

# plants
## IN
## *flower*

**KEY**

\* = evergreen  spp = species
vars = varieties

**NOTES**

*Arctostaphylos uva-ursi* and *Pieris* need lime-free soil.
*Magnolia kobus* is good on chalk but does not flower until 15 years old.

## TWICE FLOWERING

The ornamental crab apples are excellent trees for small gardens and give good value, especially if you obtain varieties that flower freely in spring and then bear conspicuous fruits in autumn. *Malus* 'Eleyi' is very popular, with crimson-rose flowers and very fine, deep red fruits. *M.* 'Golden Hornet' has white flowers of good size and its yellow fruits stay on the tree for many weeks.

You can make a crab apple tree 'bloom' twice by growing a clematis into its crown. If you select varieties that do not flower late, you will avoid detracting from the impact of the fruit. Try the crimson 'Mme Edouard André', the light blue 'Perle d'Azur' or the soft pink 'Comtesse de Bouchaud', which flower throughout summer.

Once you realise the benefits of growing clematis into trees you will soon find many other combinations. One of the great advantages is that you can forget about how to prune the clematis – there is no need.

| TREES | colour | flower type |
|---|---|---|
| *Amelanchier lamarckii* | White | Racemes along branches |
| *Magnolia kobus* | White | Small chalice, scented |
| *liliiflora* | Purple outside, cream inside | Slender, erect |
| *liliiflora* 'Nigra' | Rich purple | Slender, erect |
| × *loebneri* 'Merrill' | White | Star shaped, scented |
| 'Leonard Messel' | Lilac pink | Star shaped |
| × *soulangeana* vars | Various | Large chalice |
| *stellata* | White or pink | Star shaped |
| *Malus* vars (Ornamental crab apple) | Various | Like apple blossom |
| *Prunus* many (Japanese cherries) | Various | |
| *Pyrus salicifolia* 'Pendula' | White | Like pear blossom |
| **SHRUBS** | | |
| \**Arbutus andrachne* | White | Urn shaped |
| \**Arctostaphylos uva-ursi* | White, tinged pink | Urn shaped |
| \**Berberis darwinii* | Orange | Drooping clusters |
| \* × *lologensis* | Orange | Clusters |
| \**Camellia japonica* many vars | Various | Various |
| \* × *williamsii* most vars | Various | Various |
| *Chaenomeles speciosa* and *C.* × *superba* vars | White, pink, red or orange-red | Saucer shaped |
| *Corylopsis pauciflora, C. spicata, C. sinensis* (syn. *C. willmottiae*) | Yellow | Hanging clusters |
| *Cytisus praecox* 'Warminster' | Rich cream | Massed, pea shaped |
| \**Daphne blagayana* | White | Clusters, scented |
| \* × *napolitana* | Rose pink | Clusters, scented |
| \**Erica carnea* – later vars | Various | |
| 'Myretoun Ruby' | Ruby red | Bell shaped, racemes |
| 'Vivellii' | Deep carmine, bronze foliage | Bell shaped, long racemes |
| \**Erica* × *darleyensis* 'A.T. Johnson' | Magenta | Bell shaped, racemes |
| *Forsythia* | Yellow | Star shaped |
| *Kerria japonica* | Yellow | Single and double forms |
| \**Mahonia aquifolium* | Yellow | Terminal clusters |
| \**Osmanthus* × *burkwoodii* | White | Small |
| \* *delavayi* | White | Small |

| | colour | flower type |
|---|---|---|
| ***Pieris*** – many vars | White | Urn shaped |
| ***Rhododendron*** – many spp and vars | Various | |
| ***Ribes*** (Flowering currant) | Pink | Hanging clusters |
| ***Skimmia japonica* 'Foremannii'** | White | Small, scented |
| ***Viburnum* × *burkwoodii*** vars | White | Large, clusters, scented |
| *carlesii* | White or pink | Large clusters, scented |

## PERENNIALS

| | colour | height |
|---|---|---|
| ***Bergenia*** | White, red or pink | 30–40cm (12–16in) |
| ***Caltha palustris* 'Plena'** (Double marsh mallow) | Yellow | 30cm (12in) |
| ***Doronicum* 'Miss Mason'** | Yellow | 45cm (18in) |
| ***Epimedium perralderianum*** | Bronze yellow | 25cm (10in) |
| ***Euphorbia polychroma*** | Sulphur yellow | 45cm (18in) |
| ***Helleborus foetidus*** | Citron, maroon edge | 45cm (18in) |
| *orientalis* | Various from white to purple | 40cm (16in) |
| ***Lamium maculatum*** vars | White spikes | 15cm (6in) |
| ***Omphalodes cappadocica*** | Blue | 15cm (6in) |
| ***Peltiphyllum peltatum*** | Pink, before large leaves | 1m (40in) |
| ***Primula* 'Wanda'** | Wine purple | 10cm (4in) |
| ***Saxifraga umbrosa*** | Pink | 15cm (6in) |

## BULBS

| | | |
|---|---|---|
| **Anemone nemorosa** | White | 10cm (4in) |
| **Corydalis solida** | Purple-pink | 15cm (6in) |
| **Tulips** – *fosteriana* and **greigii** types | Various | Various |
| **Erythroniums** | Yellow, white or lilac | 12–30cm (5–12in) |
| **Fritillaria meleagris** | Various | 22cm (9in) |
| **Daffodils** and **narcissi** many | Yellows, white | Various |
| **Muscari** spp | Blue or white | 12–30cm (5–12in) |

## ROCK GARDEN BULBS

| | | |
|---|---|---|
| **Narcissus** 'Hawera' | Lemon-yellow | 15cm (6in) |
| 'Lintie' | Yellow, orange-cupped | 15cm (6in) |
| 'Pipit' | Light lemon and white | 25cm (10in) |

## SCENTS OF SPRING

The scented shrubs of spring are more noticeable than the ones that came into flower during the winter months, but only because you are there to catch their perfumes instead of inside by the fire. Nevertheless, they are among the most deliciously fragrant of all and are not to be missed.

When planting, remember that this is a showery month and put the shrubs where you can enjoy them fully. It is most frustrating to catch a waft of perfume and not be able to get nearer because of not wanting to tread on sodden ground. If you do not already grow *Osmanthus* × *burkwoodii*, *O. delavayi*, *Viburnum* × *burkwoodii* or one of the varieties of *V. carlesii* such as 'Aurora', make a note now to do so – and to find just the right position.

## A CARPET OF BULBS

One of the most effective ways of growing spring bulbs is round the bases of trees. Close to the trunks, the roots are deep and are acting as anchors rather than actively feeding. You can quite safely plant bulbs in the pockets of soil between the main roots, and it is perfectly in order to add organic matter to the soil to give the bulbs a good start. All spring bulbs, including erythroniums – the gorgeous trout lilies and avalanche lilies from America and the dog's tooth violet from Europe – can be grown in this way.

If you have trees as lawn specimens and keep a circle of clean soil round the base of each one, make use of the space by planting it with bulbs such as *Fritillaria meleagris*, the snakes head fritillary. It grows to about 20cm (8in) and bears nodding flowers like cloche hats. They always have a reticulate pattern of veining, and are prettily and modestly coloured in shades of purple-red, purple-pink and white.

## ROCK GARDEN

*Adonis vernalis*
*Alyssum saxatile* **'Compactum'**
*Aubrieta*
*Haberlea*
*Primula auricula* **vars**
*Primula marginata* **vars**
*Pulsatilla vulgaris*
*Ramonda myconii*

# M A Y

Whan that the month of May
Is comen, and that I here the foules singe,
And that the floures ginnen for to springe,
Farwel my book and my devocioun!

CHAUCER

*This is the month of freshness and perfection. Everything in the
garden looks forward fearlessly to the future and there is none of
the hedging of horticultural bets that goes on later, when the rush
to discard flowers and concentrate on setting seed sets in. Flowers
have a boisterous glow and only the insensitive fail to detect the
burgeoning celebration of the return of warm weather.*

*Early in the month, however, it is still possible to find that a
sharp reminder of winter has browned a magnolia or reduced
rhododendron flowerheads to a pulpy mass. On the whole,
though, this is the time when you can relax and think about
planting out tender subjects that you could not risk before.*

*Now is the height of the shrub season. It is all too easy to fall for
the beauty of the late spring garden, to the extent that you fill it
with the bounty of spring and leave no room for the other seasons,
but restraint must prevail. The nature of your garden will to some
extent make your choice for you. If you garden on a soil with lime
in it, the world of rhododendrons, deciduous azaleas and their
allies is closed to you, but for an occasional favourite in a tub.
Never mind, you only have to visit some of the largest gardens to
see how drab in later months an over-emphasis on one group can
be, and the richness of the late spring allows you full rein
without them.*

*This is the gardening month. Enthusiasm swings to great heights,
but we must beware of summer ennui. Month by month our
gardens flower; let us enjoy the late spring festival, but let us also
remember that it is but one twelfth of the year. There is much more
to come.*

# tasks

## FOR THE

# *month*

# 1

## CHECKLIST

- [ ] Watch out for late frosts
- [ ] Harden off all plants raised under glass before planting them out
- [ ] Plant out early chrysanthemums towards the end of the month
- [ ] Prune camellias if necessary
- [ ] Check all tree ties
- [ ] Check rhododendrons for signs of disease
- [ ] Look out for the first signs of greenfly on roses and start regular spraying. Remove any suckers
- [ ] Keep a strict eye out for slugs, especially around developing hostas and delphiniums
- [ ] Plant magnolias and water-lilies

## MAINTENANCE

### LATE FROSTS

Although this is indeed the time for beginning to put out tender plants, hanging baskets and so on, it pays never to be too complacent – frosts can strike surprisingly late. On the other hand, gardeners cannot afford to be too pessimistic, either, otherwise they would find themselves never getting anything done. Keep a sharp eye on the weather forecasts – tune in to the forecasts for farmers – and have contingency plans ready (a clear space in the shed for baskets, for example.

### WARNING

■ *A damaging frost can set you back an entire year, destroying 'geraniums' (pelargoniums), fuchsias and the half-hardy annuals you have gone to the trouble of raising* ■

### CAMELLIAS

If you are growing camellias in containers – tubs, barrels and so on – as you may well be if your garden soil is limy, survey them for top-heaviness and for odd branches that grow out of balance. In the open ground the plant would set itself to rights over the next couple of years, but container growing demands more immediate discipline. If you cut back now, while new growth is still active, some restoration of balance will take place. Leave it much longer and extension growth will stop (this happens usually towards the middle of next month).

### TREE TIES

Try to find time this month to check all your tree ties. The wilder winds of the year should be over, and this is the period when you should remove ties from trees and taller shrubs that have become firmly anchored. Those that need to remain

for a further year should be examined and tightened if they have worn loose, or loosened if they have become too tight because of the growth in diameter of the stems.

It is not only false economy but folly to attempt to economise on tree ties by using string, nylon stockings, strips of rubber inner tube, or any of the gimcrack efforts seen in the gardens of otherwise intelligent people. Nylon string cuts into the stems as they expand, creating a groove which is such a source of weakness that it is an absolute certainty that the stem will eventually snap. Stockings or panty-hose do exactly the same, and have the added disadvantage of combining untidiness with a distinct air of the ridiculous. Gadgets made with rubber strips merely give with the motion of the tree stems and cause abrasions.

It is hard to understand how gardeners can invest ten per cent of the average weekly industrial wage on a tree and then abjure the few pennies it costs to ensure its proper development.

### RHODODENDRON DISEASES

Rhododendrons of several kinds, but most particularly the Cinnabarina subsection of the genus, which includes the 'Lady Roseberry' and 'Lady Chamberlain' groups, must be regarded as vulnerable to rhododendron powdery mildew. Bi-weekly spraying with a systemic fungicide, starting in early spring and continuing until late autumn, should prevent its appearance. Branches showing the symptoms should be removed and burnt. If this disease is left unchecked, the entire shrub becomes leafless and dies.

It is not a good idea to exclude any particular group of rhododendrons from your garden. As time goes by it will be found that a large number of species and hybrids will become infected. As the disease spreads to encompass hitherto unaffected areas of the country, preventive treatment will increasingly become the rule, rather than the exception.

Rhododendron bud blast is another disease that is gradually widening its geographical range. This manifests itself in blackening of the flowerbuds, which then grow what appear to be black whiskers and are in fact the fruiting bodies of the infecting fungus. You can pick off all such buds early in the year, taking care to touch none that are free of the disease, and burn them. My experience is that you will be putting off the inevitable and it is probably better to dig up affected plants and consign them to the bonfire, as one or two blackened buds, missed in the picking off, can infect several more bushes through their windborne spores. It is not easy, however, to bring yourself to destroy a mature shrub with just a few infected buds.

### ROSES

Examine all your roses, especially those that have been planted for about three years, for suckers.
Left alone they will take over and destroy the rose. The purpose of doing this job now is to remove the suckers while they are still young, tender and manageable; leave them until later and they will have become tough, rendering the roses liable to damage when you attack the suckers.

> ### NOTE
>
> ■ *It is not difficult to identify rose suckers. They emerge from below the burr (where the rose was budded) and usually have seven or more leaflets rather than five* ■

## PLANTING

### MAGNOLIAS

This is an excellent month in which to plant magnolias. They have tender, fleshy roots that are easily damaged, and if this happens in autumn or earlier in the spring they do not regenerate and the plant is liable to start on a slow decline. Far too many gardeners find themselves bewildered by the 'going backwards' exhibited by their magnolias and think they cannot grow them, whereas it is merely a matter of understanding their needs.

Cultivate an area 1m (1yd) square to a depth of one spit (spade's depth) and a half.

■ Dig it over thoroughly and incorporate generous quantities of moss peat as a conditioner. Magnolias love soft but firm going in their early years and can penetrate heavier soils only when they are older.

■ Use one of the short-stake methods of support (see page 151). It will allow the magnolia to be held firmly against rocking but will not involve disturbance of the root ball.

### WATER-LILIES

This is also the best month for planting water-lilies.

## PLANTING MAGNOLIAS

←70cm→
(2ft)

clay

solid

**WRONG**

**RIGHT**

Your supplier will give you advice about which sorts of lily pots or crates to use (they depend on the variety of water-lily), about compost, and concerning the proper depth for each plant, but the most important point is that they must not be planted to their full depth straight away.

Water-lily leaf stalks grow to the precise depth of the water they are in, but can only do so relatively slowly. Put the new plants in too deeply and the leaves will die. The way to overcome this is to put the pot fairly near to the edge of the pond and over a period of several days gradually move it further into deep water.
Alternatively, you can set the pot on stones or bricks and remove one at a time until the plant is at its optimum depth.

### RECOMMENDED WATER-LILIES

**This is not an exhaustive list.**

**WHITE**
'Carolinia Nivea' *(small, fragrant)*
'Marliacea Albida' *(medium, fragrant)*

**PINK**
'Marliacea Rosea' *(medium, deep pink)*
odorata 'W.B. Shaw' *(medium, fragrant)*

**RED**
'Attraction' *(free-flowering, medium, garnet red)*
'Escarboucle' *(free-flowering, medium, vermilion)*
'Laydekeri Purpurata' *(small, wine red)*

**YELLOW**
'Marliacea Chromatella' *(free-flowering, medium*
pygmaea 'Helvola' *(free-flowering, small)*

# plants
## OF THE
## *month*
## *1*

## AZALEA
### Deciduous Azaleas

These are quite different from the Japanese azaleas. They are much taller and lose their leaves in winter, almost always with a dazzling display of autumn foliage colour. Their branch structure is more open and their flowers are a good deal larger, typically open-trumpet shaped, and their colour range is wider and more flamboyant, including brilliant orange and many shades of yellow. Some varieties, however, are more restrained.

| | |
|---|---|
| type | Deciduous shrubs |
| flowers | A wide range of colours |
| foliage | Leaves 10–12cm (4–5in) long, not broad. Light green |
| height | 1.5m (5ft) after 10 years |
| spread | 1m (3ft) after 10 years |
| hardiness | Hardy |
| position | Full sun or part shade |
| soil | Lime-free, peaty or leafy, moisture-retentive soil |
| pruning | None |
| propagation | By cuttings. Heat and artificial light are essential; not a subject for home gardeners to try |

## PRIMULA
### *Primula* 'Guinevere'

A primula with a character all of its own. It is also known as *P*. 'Garryarde Guinevere' and was one of a series of 'Garryarde' hybrids, of which it is now virtually the sole survivor. It is easily grown and increases well. Its great virtues are the freedom with which it produces its flowers, their unique shade of soft, carmine pink, and the beautiful bronze foliage – as desirable a ground-cover feature as one could wish.

| | |
|---|---|
| type | Herbaceous perennial |
| flowers | Almost stemless, carmine-pink with yellow 'eye' |
| foliage | Rugose (wrinkled), varied shades of deep green-bronze |
| height | 10cm (4in) |
| spread | To 30cm (1ft) |
| hardiness | Hardy |
| planting | Avoid planting primulas in summer – otherwise any time in suitable weather |
| position | Part shade |
| soil | Any good garden soil. Soils over chalk should not be too shallow |
| propagation | By division after flowering. Plant the larger divisions immediately and pot up the small ones to grow on in a frame |
| alternatives | There are many primulas, but none like 'Guinevere' |

## VIBURNUM
### *Viburnum plicatum* 'Mariesii'

The 'wedding cake' virburnum is aptly nicknamed. The horizontal branches, wreathed in heads of flowers all along their length, have a tiered effect that is unmistakable. It is an easy plant to grow but has an air of quality that suggests an aristocratic ancestry. Its attractiveness is by no means confined to flowering time.

| | |
|---|---|
| type | Deciduous shrub |
| flowers | White, in heads somewhat similar to those of a 'lacecap' hydrangea |
| fruits | Black, not often borne |
| foliage | Softly green, pleated (hence *plicatum*). Quite good autumn colour in some years |
| height | 2m (7ft) after 10 years |
| spread | 2m (7ft) after 10 years |
| hardiness | Hardy |
| position | Part shade |
| soil | Any good garden soil |

*DECIDUOUS AZALEA SEEDLING*

*PRIMULA 'GUINEVERE'*

| | |
|---|---|
| **pruning** | None |
| **propagation** | Semi-ripe cuttings taken in summer require heat at 21°C (70°F). Hardwood cuttings taken in late autumn may be rooted in a garden frame |
| **alternatives** | *V.p.* 'Lanarth' is stronger growing. 'Pink Beauty' has flowers that become blushed with pink as they age. 'Rowallane' bears its fruits freely |

## CLEMATIS
### *Clematis* 'Nelly Moser'

'Nelly Moser' has become the classic clematis, but it is only one of many that have a first flush of flowers in late spring to early summer, followed by another in late summer to early autumn. It is not realised often enough that 'Nelly Moser' fades badly in sun and is the ideal clematis for growing on a shady wall.

| | |
|---|---|
| **type** | Deciduous climber, requiring support |
| **flowers** | Large, lilac-pink with carmine-pink bar: two flushes each year |
| **foliage** | Mid-green |
| **height** | 2.5m (9ft) |

| | |
|---|---|
| **spread** | Varies with training |
| **hardiness** | Hardy |
| **position** | Full or part shade – out of strong sun |
| **soil** | Any good garden soil. Make a 30cm (1ft) cube planting hole and fill the bottom with well-rotted manure and the rest with rich, friable soil |
| **pruning** | This variety has its first flush of flowers on wood made the previous year and should therefore not be pruned heavily in spring. After flowering, cut back the old flowering wood, taking care not to damage the wood that will flower the next year |
| **propagation** | By internodal cuttings in summer. Difficult |
| **alternatives** | Several. Choice becomes a matter of colour as between varieties enjoying similar conditions |
| **special comment** | Great care should be taken not to allow the stems of clematis to buckle, particularly during planting and pruning. Buckling causes damage that allows the ingress of the clematis wilt fungus |

*M A Y*

# tasks
## FOR THE
## *month*
## 2

*Even though the rock garden may be at its best for flowering, it may well be approaching its peak as a source of softwood cuttings*

## PROPAGATION

### SOFTWOOD CUTTINGS OF ALPINES

A very large number of alpine plants can be propagated from cuttings of soft wood at this time of year. Whereas the majority of garden shrubs are best increased by semi-ripe cuttings from mid- to late summer, this is the preferred method for alpines.

The cuttings are taken when they are just large enough to handle. They may be anything from 2.5cm (1in) long or more in shrubby penstemons and many dianthus, to as little as 1.5mm (¹/₁₆in) in cushion plants such as dionysias.

Softwood cuttings do not require artificial heat. They root extremely rapidly if you take them just at the right stage and give them the right conditions. The idea is to allow them sufficient natural heat, while at the same time shading them from sun scorch.

### Taking softwood cuttings

*Phlox douglasii* 'Boothman's Variety' is a good example of a typical subject. You should look for cuttings material not just immediately flowering is over, but while the last few flowers are still out. The plant makes a neat, slightly domed mat of mid-green foliage with a greyish tint. Peeping between the stems you will see fresh, bright green ones, and if you part the plant you will find that they are about 1.8cm (¾in) long.

Take an extremely sharp knife or razor blade – I use a surgical scalpel – and make a neat horizontal cut to remove the cutting just below its lowest leaf joint. Put the cutting into a plastic bag and close the neck. I usually put the neck of the bag under my foot. Then move on across the plant, until you have all the cuttings you want.

### Preparing the cuttings
Take your blade and, cutting down onto a block of wood, cut away the lowest pair of leaves flush with, but not so as to damage, the stem. Longer cuttings may need to have the next pair up removed as well. Preparing soft cuttings by pulling off the leaves tears the tender bark of the stems; cutting with a razor-sharp blade while the cutting is held in the hand is just plain stupid.

### Inserting cuttings in the rooting medium
Use clay pots. Plastic ones distort when lifted and can disturb the fine, new roots. Place an inverted crock over

the drainage hole. This is to prevent the compost running out and, as you are going to use pure sand, it is most important.

Fill the pot with silver sand or any other sharp sand, but not fine builder's sand. Immerse the lower part of the pot in water and wait until the surface of the pot darkens.

Now, using a dibber the size of a matchstick, insert the cuttings in the sand so that no two touch one another and no single cutting fails to have its base in contact with the sand. Place the pot in a frame.

### Frames for softwood cuttings
An ordinary garden frame, facing the sun but shaded with netting to about 50 per cent, will provide heat and enough light to root the cuttings quickly. They will need to be lightly and carefully watered with a fine rose at least twice a day. If you are away from home all day, place the frame in a less sunny position.

### Potting up the cuttings
Test the cuttings by tugging very gently indeed. When most appear to have rooted, lift them out with care, one at a time, and plant them in 8cm (3¼in) pots in a soil-based potting compost. Sand has no food value, so pot up the cuttings as soon after rooting as possible.

### Difficult cuttings
Alpine gardeners who want to try their hand at difficult subjects like dionysias should take the new rosettes as they emerge from between the leaves of the old ones and remove them with a keen blade. Handling must be so gentle as to cause no bruising. Place the cuttings, which may be extremely tiny, in sand which has previously been watered and is in a propagating tray. The

lid of the tray should have ventilators in it. Replace the lid with the ventilators open and put the whole propagator at the foot of a shady wall. Cover the ventilators with small, flat stones or pieces of slate so that air can get in but not rain. The sand must never be watered again and should stay damp for six weeks or more, by which time the cuttings will have rooted or rotted. Potting on is tricky and you can expect 50 per cent losses.

### Rooting times
Such a long rooting time is exceptional. Most softwood alpine cuttings will root within two weeks or a little longer. I have on occasion rooted alpine phloxes in as little as four days, but that is also exceptional.

## PLANNING

### PLANNING BORDERS

Many gardeners make the mistake of neglecting to plan ahead at this time of year. There is so much to do, so many good things to enjoy, and it does not feel like a planning time at all.

Nevertheless, you should not take your eye off the ball. No sooner has this period passed than you will find yourself embroiled in school or family holidays or both, followed by the scramble to recover from them, and suddenly autumn is upon you.

This is why you see so many badly planned herbaceous borders. Start thinking about a new one (or even refurbishing the existing one) now, and you will have the whole summer to go round looking at other people's borders and appropriating the best ideas for plants and colour associations.

*CUTTING FROM ALPINES*
*With most of the alpines that can be propagated from cuttings, the cuttings are best taken at the softwood stage. Some, however, should be taken later, when they are half ripe (see p90); among these are aubrieta, most dwarf shrubs and dwarf conifers*

*CLEAN CONTAINERS*
*No matter what technique you are using or what the pots or trays are made of, always take time to wash containers for cuttings or seed in advance. A dilute solution of a mild antiseptic will help to promote hygiene. Make sure the pots are dry before you fill them with compost, otherwise you will find the job becomes messy.*

*GAPS IN THE BORDER*
*If gaps appear where herbaceous plants have failed to come up after their winter rest, mark the centre of the space with a slender cane to which you have attached a label. Then plant the space with annuals. Nicotiana 'Lime Green' is a good one of which to have a stock, as its colour goes with everything and it is tall and robust enough to compete with the perennials.*

M A Y

# plants
## OF THE
## *month*
## 2

### RHODODENDRON
*Rhododendron* 'Lady Rosebery'

This is in fact a group of rhododendrons, all of which have similarly shaped flowers in rich shades of pink. The 'Lady Chamberlain' group have the same type of flowers but with more or less orange in their red. The many-flowered clusters are unmistakable because of the long, narrowly bell-shaped blooms and their waxy texture.

| | |
|---|---|
| type | Evergreen shrub |
| flowers | Clusters of six or more, pink to carmine, waxy |
| foliage | Distinctive: long-oval, sea-green |
| height | 2m (7ft) after 10 years |
| spread | 1.25m (4ft) after 10 years |
| hardiness | Hardy |
| position | Part shade |
| soil | Must be lime free, leafy or peaty, and moisture retentive |
| pruning | None |
| propagation | Semi-ripe summer cuttings will root in a mist unit |
| alternatives | The 'Lady Chamberlain' group |
| special comment | These groups of rhododendrons are susceptible to rhododendron powdery mildew. This disease has only occurred in recent years, but is spreading and potentially lethal. The symptoms are irregular, greyish-purple patches, not to be confused with frost damage. Spraying with a systemic fungicide as a preventive is the best course of action |

### LILAC
*Syringa* × *josiflexa* 'Bellicent'

*Syringa* is the lilac genus. The well-known, large-clustered varieties can be seen perhaps too much during late spring and lose something of the grace of the species. 'Bellicent' is sufficiently close to nature to show the daintiness and charm of species lilacs while putting on a sumptuous show

| | |
|---|---|
| type | Deciduous large shrub or small tree |
| flowers | Large panicles of rose-pink; fragrant |
| foliage | Fine, deep green leaves |
| height | 2.5m (9ft) after 10 years |
| spread | 1.5–2m (5–7ft) after 10 years |
| hardiness | Hardy (raised in Ottawa) |
| position | Sun or part shade |
| soil | All good, well-drained soils, especially happy on chalk |
| pruning | Remove the old flowering wood after flowering. This, however, is not as essential as it is with the usual garden hybrids, and suckering is not a problem |
| propagation | Best by semi-ripe cuttings taken in summer with a heel of old wood and rooted in a heated propagator 18°C (65°F) |
| alternatives | *Syringa* x *persica* (Persian lilac); similar, but with smaller panicles |
| special comment | *Syringa* is the correct generic name for lilacs. Philadelphus, though often called 'syringas', are entirely different (see p.81) |

### WEIGELA
*Weigela* Hybrids

The most rewarding weigelas (pronounced wi'jeel'ias) are the selected hybrids, of which there are about thirty. They vary in flower colour but are reliable, free-flowering shrubs for late spring and early summer. They are of easy culture, although attention should be paid to pruning if flowering is to remain free and the shrubs are not to grow too large.

*RHODODENDRON 'LADY ROSEBERY'*

| | |
|---|---|
| type | Deciduous shrub |
| flowers | Red, white, or shades of pink |
| foliage | Ovate-oblong, smallish leaves with tapered points |
| height | 1.5m (5ft) after 10 years |
| spread | 1.3m (4½ft) after 10 years |
| hardiness | Hardy |
| position | Full sun or a little shade |
| soil | Any good garden soil |
| pruning | Immediately flowering is over, shorten or remove the old flowering shoots and shorten any over-long branches that may unbalance the shrub |
| propagation | Semi-ripe cuttings taken in late summer will root in heat at 21°C (70°F), or softwood cuttings taken in early summer will root in a garden frame |
| varieties | 'Abel Carrière' – carmine, 'Eva Rathke' – crimson, 'Looymansii Aurea' – pink, gold foliage, *W. florida* 'Variegata' – pink with cream-edged foliage |

## CEANOTHUS
### *Ceanothus × veitchianus*

Ceanothus are known as Californian Lilacs. That they come from California may alert those of us in colder climates to a suspicion of tenderness, but the 'lilac' sobriquet is misleading; ceanothus and lilacs are not related. They can be evergreen or deciduous, there is a small-leaved group and one with considerably larger leaves, the flowers can be blue, pink or white, although the majority are in shades of blue. This hybrid is the hardiest, and the most prolific with its flowers.

| | |
|---|---|
| type | Evergreen shrub |
| flowers | Clusters of rich blue |
| foliage | Small, slightly wrinkled, wedge-shaped leaves |
| height | 1.25m (4ft) after 10 years |
| spread | 1.5m (5ft) after 10 years |
| hardiness | Hardy in all but the coldest places |
| position | Full sun or a little shade |
| soil | Ceanothus are lime-tolerant but do not do well on shallow, chalky soils. Good drainage is essential |
| pruning | None |
| propagation | Semi-ripe cuttings taken in summer require heat at 21°C (70°F) or a mist unit |
| alternatives | 'Blue Mound' (deciduous, light blue); 'Cascade' (evergreen, bright blue); *impressus* (evergreen, dense habit, dark blue, hardy in shelter); 'Puget Blue' (evergreen, very long-flowering, deep blue). All flower late spring to early summer |

*CEANOTHUS × VEITCHIANUS*

# *practical* project

### CREATING A
### GARDEN POND

*DON'T RUSH*
*A garden pond should be regarded as a living, balanced, co-operating entity. Do not be in too much of a rush to see it achieve stability.*

*FINDING THE LEVEL*
*Water finds its own level. If you do not get the rim of the pond perfectly level, the liner will be exposed in the shallow areas and will eventually split through the action of ultra-violet light. Knock in pegs round the pond's edge and use a spirit level to make sure all is well. If it is not, build up the low places and lower the high ones.*

Water-lilies are among the most spectacular flowers we can grow in temperate climates, and they are among the glories of the summer garden. You must have water for them to grow in and, unless you are going to restrict yourself to the very small ones, you will have to consider making a pond for them and some other water and marginal plants – including oxygenating plants, which are essential.

There are several ways in which you can make a pond, but let us assume you would like it to look as natural as possible and have decided to excavate it, rather than build it up from ground level. As the great majority of garden ponds are made with liners these days, especially now that butyl materials have become so tough and reliable, there is little point in going to the trouble, expense and back-breaking labour of attempting to line your pond with concrete.

This is the perfect month for the job, as it is the ideal time for planting water plants and the soil will be much drier and lighter than it was earlier. Furthermore, it should not yet be too hot for a good bout of manual labour.

## DESIGNING THE POND

Make sure that the site you have chosen is the right one, and then look again to make sure – it is rather late to change your mind after you have moved several cubic metres of earth. The pond should not be on any sort of rise in the ground, otherwise it will look silly – ponds rarely occur on humps, and most usually in hollows. If you are going to rob the lawn to make the pond, ensure that the area of water will be in proportion, and try if you can to relate it to other features such as a rock garden or even a curve in the lawn's boundary.

When designing your pond, do not forget that you cannot step into it without damaging the liner. Make sure, therefore, that you make it of a size and shape that will allow you access to its entire surface.

■ Take a length of hose, a rope, or a few dozen small plastic pots and mark out the shape of the pond on the soil or grass. If you use this method you can adjust the shape until you have got it just right. Take a look from an upstairs window; it is surprising how much better you can judge proportion from above.

■ Decide, too, at this early stage how you want the surrounds of the pond to look. Do you want a rock garden to come right down to the water's edge? Perhaps you would like an informally paved path right round.

## POND SIZE

Try to make the largest pond you can, and make sure it is deep enough. Small, shallow ponds are almost useless, as they can freeze to the bottom, killing fish, they are likely to become soupy with algae, and the range of plants you can grow is very limited.

---

### CALCULATING LINER SIZE

*A pond up to 2.75sq m (3½sq yd) in area should be no less than 38cm (15in) deep. From 2.75 to 11sq m (3½ to 14sq yd) it should be 45cm (18in) deep, between 11 and 22sq m (14 and 28sq yd) the depth should be 60cm (2ft), and anything over that size should have 75cm (2½ft) depth of water – the maximum that is necessary, even for a small lake.*

*To work out what size of liner you need, measure the length and width of the pond at their widest points. For a circle, measure the diameter. Add twice the maximum depth of the pond to each measurement. Then: Area of liner = (maximum length + twice maximum depth) × (maximum width + twice maximum depth). For a circular pond, the area is (diameter + twice the maximum depth)².*

---

Do not dig straight down at the sides, but make them sloping, with a shelf 22cm (9in) deep and 30cm (1ft) wide round the rim of the pond. On this you will be able to stand pots of marginal plants so that their root balls are just covered with water. The shelf makes no difference to the area of liner required.

## LINING AND FILLING THE POND

When excavation is complete, make sure no sharp objects such as stones or roots are liable to abrade the liner, and make doubly certain by first lining the hole with a layer of sand about 2.5cm (1in) deep.

Now lay in the liner so that it is evenly spread, and weigh it down with bricks or stones placed outside the rim of the excavation. Let water in gently, moving the stones to allow the liner to settle, and gently but firmly pulling out most of the creases that form. A few creases are inevitable.

When the pond is full, let it settle for a day or so and then trim off the surplus lining, leaving a flap about 15cm (6in) wide. This can be anchored and disguised using rocks, paving stones, or whatever you decided earlier.

It is essential to let the pond stand empty for a few days to allow the water to detoxify. Most water supplies deliver unwanted chemicals – chlorine and so on – and you should give them a chance to clear.

### PLANTING THE POND

Your very first planting job will be to introduce oxygenating plants. Make sure there are plenty, and allow them ten days or so to begin to do their work. If you plant too few you will find you are battling against algae, including the dreaded blanket weed.

Next, plant your water-lilies and other aquatics, and then, as the very last thing, introduce any fish you have decided to keep, but at far less than the stocking rate you might have thought appropriate. Introduce too many fish too soon and the ecological balance of your pond will be spoilt. Fish produce droppings, which are acted upon by bacteria to produce nitrates. These nitrates are then used by the plants in the pond as food, which prevents them from building up to poisonous levels. If the bacteria have not had time to build up to an effective population they will not be able to break down the droppings quickly enough and your pond will not be healthy.

### OXYGENATING PLANTS

**A selection for your pond:**

*Callitriche autumnalis*
*Callitriche verna* (starwort)
*Ceratophyllum demersum*
*Eleocharis acicularis* (hairgrass)
*Elodea canadensis* (Canadian pond weed)
*Hottonia palustris* (water violet)
*Myriophyllum verticillatum*
*Myriophyllum spicatum*
*Ranunculus aquatilis* (water buttercup)

# plant
# *selections*

*Euphorbia griffithii*
*'Fireglow'*

### BULBS

There are all sorts of fancy **tulips** that can tempt you from the pages of bulb catalogues: Viridifloras with green bands central to the petals; Parrot tulips like twisted blobs of oil paint, and Frilled tulips – really Parrot types with fringes – confections that would put Ascot hats to shame. There can be little forgiveness for some of the names, too. 'Gay Presto' indeed!

But the Darwin tulips – those of the elegant, uncomplicated, square-based goblet shape – and their oval cousins, the Cottage tulips, are aristocrats among the flowers of late spring. You can grow them in substantial clumps, in formal arrangements, or even in closely packed drifts at the side of the lawn – where you should arrange for sweetly curved outlines and never a sharp corner.

### ALPINES

The rock garden now takes on a stronger palette entirely appropriate to the greater intensity of light. At one month from the summer solstice the light is almost at its brightest, and we tend to forget this and try to perpetuate the soft colours of spring.

Mat-forming hybrids of **Phlox subulata** in anything from softest pink to the most flaring magenta take over from the aubrietas, and **helianthemums**, whose Mediterranean appearance is the real thing, introduce heady orange and the flame tones of red, as well as a leavening of cream and soft yellow.

Helianthemums are not plants to be planted and then ignored. When their flowering finishes next month, do not let them relax, but cut them hard back. They will put on bushy new growth and flower again on the new wood late in the summer. This treatment will also keep them green and compact instead of allowing them to become a sprawl of woody stems just waiting to entangle the heels of potentially litigious visitors.

### HERBACEOUS PERENNIALS

In the more 'woodsy' parts of the garden, one of the true blues among ground-hugging plants keeps modestly low but impresses by the freedom with which it bears its round, light royal-blue flowers. **Omphalodes cappadocica** is one of the minor glories of later spring which, if not included among the more obvious stars, renders their performance less rich. Lighter

blue and almost as self-effacing, are the spring **veronicas** – *V. teucrium* 'Royal Blue' and *V. gentianoides* – perfect in front of the soft pink, 60cm (2ft) *Pyrethrum* 'Eileen May Robinson'.

**Euphorbias** dance to a different drum. Their odd flowers mass together to create effects that are simultaneously warm and cool. Nothing else does this in quite the same way. *Euphorbia griffithii* 'Fireglow' has cool green foliage and heads of bracts in a muted, warmish orange-red that is nevertheless conspicuous. *E. myrsinites* is of a greenish, staring yellow that should be offensive but is anything but. There is somehow a softness that saves it from vulgarity.

### TREES AND SHRUBS

In colder areas, **rhododendron** time arrives, having been delayed until the later frosts are no longer a danger. The Hardy Hybrids – red 'Doncaster', 'Cynthia' and 'Lord Roberts'; purple-blue 'Blue Peter' and many others – should be chosen with infinite care, as they become large and have little to recommend them for the rest of the year, but among rhododendrons that flower now there are so many species and varieties that there are some for everyone.

Late spring is **hawthorn** time – so much so that in old England it was called 'May' and you were supposed never to 'cast a clout' (discard winter clothing) until 'May be out' (hawthorn in blossom). Hawthorns and other thorns are excellent value for smaller gardens, especially those with pink or red flowers, and have, of course, their fruits with which to decorate themselves later in the year.

The **beauty bush**, *Kolkwitzia amabilis*, covers itself in lipped, pink flowers in late spring and early summer. There is a selected form called 'Pink Cloud' that is worth seeking out, but beware: unscrupulous hands may attach such a label to ordinary forms and charge you more. Not that the 'ordinary' versions of this lovely plant are to be despised, but a deal is a deal. You can grow smaller clematis into this shrub; try the tulip-shaped flowers of the Texensis group of clematis. My favourite is 'Gravetye Beauty', a sensation in ruby red that will dress the beauty bush in rich finery in late summer and early autumn. This is no mean device for enlivening shrubs with but one season of flower and not much to offer in the foliage line.

The utterly delicious **Mexican orange blossom**, *Choisya ternata*, is increasingly becoming known for its hardiness. Its glossy, dainty foliage is attractive all year round and because it is evergreen it must be out of cold winds, but for a plant whose home is south of the Tropic of Cancer, it is truly remarkable. It will produce its main crop of sweetly scented, white flowers now, but there will hardly be a month in which it does not carry a few blooms.

petunias and their ilk can play their part in integrating house and garden and in making you feel that you are really justified in putting away your woollens.

To do justice to the magical time that bridges spring and summer is impossible within the confines of this space. Perhaps, appetite whetted, you will go and see for yourself what riches there are. Do not, however, fill your garden with this month's delights. Be selective, choose the best for your tastes and gardening conditions, and difficult though it may be, remember that there are eleven other months.

*(left) The 'English' bluebell is native to much of Europe*

*(below) As the danger of frost passes, hanging baskets may be put out with impunity*

### WILD FLOWERS

Not everything in the garden needs to be exotic. While few of the wild flowers native to the country in which one gardens tend to be good garden plants, some do, and in Britain the native bluebell – *Hyacinthoides non-scripta* – is reliable, safe, and one of the most romantic flowers of all. It is by nature a plant of the woodland floor, and such positions suit it well, but it will grow perfectly happily in a considerable amount of sun. However, the best way of all to enjoy it is to see it assert itself among the freshly unfurled leaves of hostas. Its own foliage lies almost flat, but in borrowing that of other, well-chosen subjects, it becomes a plant of many guises.

### TENDER PLANTS

Towards the end of the month you can begin to indulge your passion for tender plants. Hanging baskets of lobelias, 'geraniums',

# plants
### IN
## *flower*

**KEY**

\* = evergreen    spp = species
vars = varieties

**NOTES**

*Laburnum* is poisonous.
The flowers of *Paulownia tomentosa* fail in cold
areas.
*Cotoneaster* and *Sorbus* are grown mainly for
berries or fruit and foliage.

## UNDERPLANTING AZALEAS

If you are wondering what on earth to do for the rest of the year with the evergreen (Japanese) azaleas that finished flowering in the first week or so of this month, make a note to plant lilies among them in future. They will have their bulbs in the cool and their heads in the sun – just what they need. You can also remember that Texensis clematis can sprawl over your azaleas to give them the appearance of bearing brightly coloured tulip flowers late in the year.

| TREES | colour | flower type |
|---|---|---|
| **Cercis siliquastrum** | Rose pink | Pea shaped, on main branches and trunk |
| **Crataegus** spp and vars (Thorn) | Pink or white | |
| **Davidia involucrata** (Handkerchief tree) | White | 'Handkerchiefs' |
| ***Embothrium** vars | Red | Clusters |
| **Halesia carolina** | White | Like snowdrops |
| **Laburnum** vars | Yellow | Panicles |
| **Malus** – many vars | White, pink or red | Like apple blossom |
| **Paulownia tomentosa** | Lilac | Like foxgloves |
| **Prunus** vars (Cherry) | Various | |
| **Sorbus** – many vars | White | |
| SHRUBS | | |
| ***Berberis** spp and vars | Yellow or orange | |
| **Ceanothus** spp and vars | Mainly blue | Many-flowered heads |
| ***Choisya ternata** | White | Scented |
| **Cornus florida** | White, pink or red | Bracts |
| **Cotoneaster** spp and vars | White | |
| **Cytisus** spp and vars (Broom) | Various | Pea shaped |
| ***Daphne** – dwarf spp | Purplish pink | Small, scented |
| ***Erica** spp and vars | Various | Bell shaped |
| **Genista** spp | Yellow | Pea shaped |
| ***Helianthemum** vars | Various | Flat, each lasts one day |
| **Kerria japonica** | Yellow | Single and double forms |
| **Kolkwitzia amabilis** (Beauty bush) | Pink, yellow centre | Lipped |
| **Paeonia** spp and vars (Tree peony) | Various | Large to very large, single to fully double |
| **Potentilla fruticosa** vars | Various | Dog-rose shaped |
| ***Pyracantha** spp and vars | White | Small, clustered |
| ***Rhododendron** spp and vars | Various | |
| **Rosa** vars (early climbing and shrub) | Various | |
| **Syringa** vars (Lilacs) | Various | |
| **Viburnum carlesii** and vars | White, flushed pink | Highly scented |
| **plicatum** and vars | White | 'Lacecap' heads |
| **Weigela** vars | Pink, white or red | Foxglove-like |

## CLIMBERS

| | | |
|---|---|---|
| **Clematis montana** vars | *White to pink* | *Medium-sized, scented* |
| large flowered | *Various (first flush)* | |
| **Lonicera** vars (Honeysuckle) | *Yellow-pink* | *Scented* |
| **Wisteria** vars | *Lilac, white, purple or rose* | |

## PERENNIALS

| | **colour** | **height** |
|---|---|---|
| **Anchusa 'Loddon Royalist'** | *Pure blue* | *45cm (18in)* |
| **Brunnera macrophylla** (Perennial forget-me-nots) | *Blue* | *45cm (18in)* |
| **Dicentra spectabilis** (Bleeding heart) | *Pink, white locket shaped* | *30cm (12in)* |
| **Euphorbia griffithii 'Fireglow'** | *Orange-red* | *60cm (24in)* |
| **wulfenii** | *Yellow-green* | *80cm (32in)* |
| **Geranium macrorrhizum 'Ingwersen's Variety'** | *Soft pink* | *30cm (12in)* |
| **Geum 'Lady Stratheden'** | *Yellow, double* | *30cm (12in)* |
| **'Mrs Bradshaw'** | *Brick red, double* | *30cm (12in)* |
| **Incarvillea delavayi** | *Rose, gloxinia shaped* | *40cm (16in)* |
| **Omphalodes cappadocica** | *Blue, somewhat like forget-me-nots* | *20cm (8in)* |
| **Polygonatum multiflorum** (Solomon's seal) | *Greenish white* | *80cm (32in)* |
| **Primula** – candelabra spp | *Red, pink, orange, yellow, mauve-purple or white* | *45–60cm (18–24in)* |
| **Tiarella cordifolia** | *White, in fluffy heads* | *20cm (8in)* |
| **Trollius** spp and vars | *Yellow, orange* | *45–60cm (18–24in)* |
| **Veronica gentianoides** | *Light blue* | *60cm (24in)* |

## BULBS

| | | |
|---|---|---|
| **Endymion non-scriptus** (syn **Hyacinthoides non-scripta**) (English bluebell) | *Blue, white* | *45cm (18in)* |
| **Fritillaria camschatcensis** | *Black* | *25cm (10in)* |
| **pallidiflora** | *Yellow, spotted red* | *45cm (18in)* |
| **Geranium tuberosum** | *Purple* | *22cm (9in)* |
| **Scilla campanulata** | *Blue* | *45cm (18in)* |
| **Tulipa batalinii** vars | *Various* | *30cm (12in)* |
| Darwin types | *Various* | *45cm (18in)* |
| **sprengeri** | *Scarlet, the last tulip* | *40cm (16in)* |

## CLEMATIS COMPANIONS

Many of the large-flowered clematis hybrids have two flushes of bloom, one in late spring and early summer, the other in late summer and early autumn. Among these is the well known 'Nelly Moser', perhaps the most popular clematis of all time, and deservedly so (see p.57).

And yet, one sees it so often being grown so that its lovely flowers, lilac-pink with a carmine bar down the centre of each sepal (there are no petals on clematis), fade badly in the sun. This plant should be placed out of direct sunlight and allowed to thrive in cool conditions, particularly those afforded by a shady wall.

Such a feature is always regarded as difficult to furnish with plants, but it need not be. *Clematis* 'Nelly Moser' will climb there happily on a trellis, and will be even happier if given congenial companions. The climbing rose 'Maigold', which flowers just once in the year, will produce its bright, softly golden flowers at the same time as the first flush of the flowers of the clematis. Later 'The New Dawn', another climbing rose but this time a repeat-flowering one, will take over and will then match its flesh-pink to the tones of the clematis, picking up the carmine and softening it. The second clematis flush should find the rose flowering too.

## ROCK GARDEN

**Aethionema** spp
**Aquilegia** spp
\***Armeria** spp
\***Dianthus** spp
\***Dryas octopetala**
**Erigeron** spp
\***Erinus alpinus**
**Gentiana acaulis**
**Gentiana verna**
**Geranium sanguineum**
**Iris innominata** and hybrids
**Linaria alpina**
\***Lithospermum oleifolium**
\***Omphalodes luciliae**
\***Phlox douglasii** vars
\***Phlox subulata** vars
\***Potentilla nitida**
\***Potentilla verna**
**Primula** spp
\***Saponaria ocymoides**
\***Saxifraga** – silver group
**Tunica saxifraga**

# JUNE

What is so rare as a day in June?
Then, if ever, come perfect days.
JAMES RUSSELL LOWELL

*Early summer days can be truly perfect, with skies of a powder
blue as yet unsullied by dust or wearied by having to get up early
every morning. The longest day of the year comes this month, and
after a short pause the nights begin to 'draw in'. And yet this is not
high summer, but only its beginning. The season has not yet
learned its craft and is all too wont to lose concentration and
relapse into greyness and torrential rain.*

*This is no bad thing for the gardener who, knowing that dry times
are to come, welcomes the freshening downpours that keep the
colours of the earlier perennials clean and bright. Delphiniums
and oriental poppies have a jewel-like quality in their best blues
and sweetest pinks, and lupins make the best of their summer
dresses before the senior matrons of the border take precedence.*

*On the whole it is not a colourful time for shrubs. There is an
early summer 'gap', during which the grand array of spring-
flowering shrubs are concentrating on making and ripening new
growth and those that have yet to flower wait, for the most part,
until pollinating insects have done with the herbaceous flowers.*

*Flowers, we may think, were created for our pleasure, but it is not
so. They exist solely and single-mindedly to induce pollination, so
that seed may be set and the species preserved.*

*It is hard, though, to think of such things during a balmy early
summer evening, when scents are borne on the lightest airs, bees
hum their soporific drone, and birds play a little music before
bedtime. This is a good month during which to recall that the best
garden tool is a deck chair, and that time taken to savour the
early summer garden can never be wasted. Is that not after all
what you made the garden for?*

# tasks
## FOR THE
## *month*
## 1

## CHECKLIST

- Start watering during dry spells, but check the local by-laws and any general restrictions
- Keep pests and diseases under control
- Plant out hardy fuchsias and well-hardened half-hardy annuals
- Deadhead spring-flowering bulbs
- Cut back oriental poppies
- Prune evergreen hedges, broom and *Clematis montana*
- Feed tulips and hyacinths
- Maintain the spraying programme for roses and, later in the month, start deadheading
- If you have used polyanthus for spring bedding, lift them and replant in a cool, moist spot for the summer
- Tie in climbers and wall shrubs

## MAINTENANCE

### WATERING

It is worth remembering that something like 50 per cent of the water lost by the top 22cm (9in) of soil during a prolonged drought has actually been lost during the first five days. Do not leave watering until plants start to show distress. If you do so, you will be setting them

### WARNING

- *Despite the need of your plants for water, if hosepipe and other watering bans or regulations are in force, observe them scrupulously. You may notice others in the neighbourhood who are not doing so, but they are likely to be the poorer for it in the long run* ■

back more severely than you might think and will cause them to suffer from retarded growth and reduced crops of flowers. As you are gardening for flowers, it is important not to let this happen.

### PESTS

Early summer is the time when vigilance and self-discipline pay off in the war against pests. It is young plants and the young wood of older ones that are especially vulnerable. Later on, tissues toughen up and become unpalatable to many insects as they become progressively loaded with bitter tannins. If you regard this as the anti-pest month you will find it pays off when you do not have to take remedial action later.

### CUTTING BACK

Oriental poppies should be cut down as soon as they

finish flowering. There is no point in letting them set seed. Take sharp shears and cut back the leaves by one half. This makes for neatness and also encourages the formation of new shoots from the base. Untidy poppies spoil the effect of the plants behind that are to follow.

### LILY DISEASES

Lilies often suffer from virus diseases. These are mostly carried by aphids, so it is a good idea to spray the plants against them. A fungicide spray will also prevent the onset of botrytis and stem-rot moulds.

### EVERGREEN HEDGES

Many gardeners, impatient with untidy evergreen hedges, prune them drastically in early to mid-spring and then learn to regret it. Depriving evergreens of their leaves gives them a check from which it takes them a long time to recover properly. Wait until this month, when, although still further growth will have taken place, it will be soft and easily clipped. A dense, well-furnished hedge will result, rather than a gappy, coarse one.

## PRUNING CLEMATIS AND BROOM

Towards the end of the month, *Clematis montana* varieties will require pruning. They should only be pruned hard early in the year if they have become thoroughly out of hand, in which case you will have to sacrifice a year's flowers, as flowering takes place on the wood made in the previous year. Now that flowering is over, cut out the shoots on which the flowers were borne. This causes the plant to put all its energy into the growths that will flower next year. (For other *Clematis* see p.22.)

Forms of the common broom (*Cytisus scoparius*) can be pruned back once they have flowered, and this applies to many of them this month, but take care not to cut into the old wood, as it has no growth buds. The only broom you can subject to 'renewal' pruning (severe cutting back to buds in the old wood) is the pineapple broom, *Cytisus battandieri*, which flowers at the end of this month and during next. The operation should be done after flowering and will induce new shoots from the base as well as from the buds. Check that the basal shoots are broom; many specimens are grafted onto laburnum, whose foliage is similar when young.

## WALL SHRUBS AND CLIMBERS

As climbers and shrubs trained on walls grow, check them over and tie in the new growths as necessary, rubbing out surplus young shoots that are likely to grow away from the plane of the wall. Unfortunately they do not look at all good if you bend them round to tie them in and never grow properly.

## MOWING THE LAWN

Modern thinking concerning mowing leads to the conclusion that it is better to leave the clippings on the lawn than to remove them. This depends on your point of view, as it presupposes frequent mowing in order to keep the clippings small. However, if you subscribe to the view that most lawns are overfed, yours will give rise to small clippings anyway, even if your mowing is not so frequent. The clippings will feed the lawn by being returned to it. Collected clippings are almost impossible to compost properly and make a very bad mulch, as they almost always contain weed seeds and attract moulds.

## PLANTING

### FUCHSIAS AND ANNUALS

I do not recommend planting shrubs and perennials during this and the next two months. If you can be sure to keep them watered and are not going away for longer than a short weekend, by all means plant anything irresistible that you find growing in a container. Other than that, restrict planting to half-hardy annuals and hardy fuchsias. The fuchsias should be planted with their crowns 5cm (2in) below soil level. This unusual practice is lethal to other shrubs but provides fuchsias with an opportunity to make strong, basal growths.

*BLIND BULBS*
*Did you write down the week in which the last flowers faded on the bulbs you naturalised in grass? If you did, you should be in the* qui vive *for the seventh week thereafter, during which you can safely mow the grass. Do it earlier and the bulbs will come up blind (flowerless) next year.*

*DRIED DELPHINIUMS*
*You can enjoy delphiniums for months rather than weeks if you cut them, hang them in a dry, airy, cool shed in the dark, and then use the dried flowers in arrangements. They hold their colour better than most air-dried flowers.*

**EVERGREEN HEDGE PLANTS**

*Berberis* (some)
*Buxus* (box)
*Ilex* (holly)
Lavender
*Lonicera nitida*
Privet
*Pyracantha*
*Rhamnus*
*Taxus*
*Thuja*

# plants
## OF THE
## *month*
## *1*

## LUPIN
### Russell Lupins

This race of multicoloured lupins must stand in the front rank of herbaceous perennials. Along with delphiniums and oriental poppies, they are the mainstay of early colour in the border, with aquilegias and the euphorbias that started last month acting as support. Russell lupins have recently been so improved upon as regards health, vigour, brightness of colour and ease of raising from seed that the modern strains can be regarded almost as a new race of plants.

| | |
|---|---|
| type | Herbaceous perennials |
| flowers | Dense spikes in many colours, including bicolours |
| foliage | Deeply cut into 'fingers'; rich green |
| height | 90cm–1.2m (3–4ft) |
| spread | 60cm (2ft) |
| hardiness | Hardy |
| planting | Plant seed-raised plants, as those raised from cuttings may be infected with virus. Modern seed strains come almost true to colour |
| position | Plant among other herbaceous plants so that the spikes emerge from among them. Early-flowering perennials should always have later ones in front of them |
| soil | A good, well-manured border soil |
| propagation | From seed sown in a garden frame in early spring. Soak in tepid water for 24 hours before sowing |
| varieties | Choose modern seed strains, either mixed, such as 'Band of Nobles' or single colours or bicolours |

## RODGERSIA
### *Rodgersia podophylla*

Rodgersias are shade-loving plants that prefer ample moisture. They are primarily grown for their large, dramatic leaves, which in some species have a metallic-bronze finish that is most attractive. The feathery flowerheads, though not always freely borne, strike a bold note on an early summer's day.

| | |
|---|---|
| type | Herbaceous perennial |
| flowers | Feathery heads of white |
| foliage | The finest in the genus. Large leaves have deep, irregular lobes that give them a jagged appearance. They are bronze when young, becoming green |
| height | 90cm (3ft) |

*RODGERSIA PODOPHYLLA*

| | |
|---|---|
| spread | 1.2m (4ft) |
| hardiness | Hardy |
| planting | Plant open-ground rodgersias in autumn. Container-grown plants are best planted in early spring or autumn |
| position | Part shade |
| soil | Moist but well-drained, leafy soil |
| propagation | By division in early spring, re-planting the divisions immediately into their final positions |
| alternatives | *R. pinnata* has large, pinnate leaves with bronze burnishing and pink flowers. *R. aesculifolia* is the best species for flowers, which may be white or creamy pink |

## MAGNOLIA
### *Magnolia wilsonii*

It is often forgotten that the magnolias of spring are by no means the only ones. The summer magnolias differ in that they tend to produce a few flowers at a time over a long period, rather than having one enormous flush of bloom, but they make up for it by the delicacy and charm of the individual flowers.

| | |
|---|---|
| type | Large deciduous shrub |
| flowers | Pendulous, white with crimson stamens |
| foliage | Typical magnolia paddle-shaped leaves |
| height | 2.5m (9ft) after 10 years |
| spread | 2m (7ft) after 10 years |
| hardiness | Vulnerable to severe frosts in late spring |
| planting | Best planted in late spring |
| position | Part shade |
| soil | Reasonably lime-tolerant. Prefers a soil to which organic matter has been added |
| pruning | None |
| propagation | By air layers or by semi-ripe cuttings taken in late summer and rooted under mist |

*HEMEROCALLIS 'ALAN'*

## DAY LILY
### *Hemerocallis* Varieties

The day lilies are among the most accommodating of all garden plants. They will grow in almost all conditions and soils, stand up to competition, flower over a long season, propagate easily, provide a wide palette of colours – and yet are not nearly as widely grown as they deserve.

| | |
|---|---|
| type | Herbaceous perennials |
| flowers | Large, lily-like, in all colours but blue, mauve and purple |
| foliage | Iris-like, but not stiff |
| height | Varies from 30–90cm (1–3ft) |
| spread | Clump-forming, 30–90cm (1–3ft) |
| hardiness | Hardy |
| planting | Plant in spring or autumn |
| position | Any apart from deep shade |
| soil | Any reasonable soil |
| propagation | By division just after the foliage starts to emerge – usually early spring. However, try to avoid disturbing the clumps until flowering starts to decline. This usually takes several years |
| alternatives | Lilies are far less easy than hemerocallis and often much less rewarding, but should nevertheless be attempted, especially those with scent, which is the one important quality almost entirely lacking in day lilies |

# tasks

## FOR THE

## *month*

## 2

**PLANTS FOR SIMPLE LAYERING**

The great majority of woody plants can be layered. Layering is especially important in the following genera, which are difficult to propagate by other means:

*Calycanthus*
*Chionanthus*
*Cornus*
*Hamamelis*
*Kalmia*
*Magnolia*
*Paeonia* (tree peonies)
*Photinia*
*Rhododendron* (including deciduous azaleas)
*Stachyurus*
*Stewartia*

**CHECKLIST**

☐ Make layers of appropriate woody plants
☐ Thin early spring-sown hardy annuals to 15–20cm (6–8in) apart
☐ Survey your garden for areas of sun and shade

## PROPAGATION

### LAYERING

Layering is a propagation technique in which the shoot to be propagated is rooted while still part of the parent plant, and is not separated from it until rooting is well advanced.

It is a slow but reliable method of propagation for quite a wide range of plants, most of them woody. It is often regarded as crude, to be scorned by those who are good at taking cuttings, but that is a mistaken viewpoint. Layering is the method of choice for certain shrubs, among them deciduous azaleas, magnolias and many rhododendrons, that are not easy otherwise without specialised equipment. It should be noted, however, that a full two years may elapse before they are likely to have rooted.

### Simple layering
Simple layering is only possible (1) if a branch can be brought towards the ground, or (2) if it can be brought sufficiently low for a pot of soil to be brought into contact with it.

■ *Method 1*
Let us take *Magnolia × soulangeana* as an example. It and the many magnolias that share its general habit regularly have branches that sweep near to the ground, ideal for simple layering.

■ Gently draw one such branch down to the ground, until the middle of one of its new shoots touches the soil. Label the shoot and let it go, having marked the point on the ground.

■ Dig the soil over to loosen it and reduce it to the consistency of a seedbed after firming with the heels (the soil should be just moist, neither too dry nor too wet). If it is light, add some peat or leaf mould; if too heavy, add the organic matter but also work in a bucketful of sand.

■ Go back to the shoot and, at the point where it touched the soil, make a diagonal slit in its underside in the direction of the tip and about one third through the shoot.

■ Make a hole at the layering point in the soil and bend

the shoot down into the hole, so that it is comfortably curved but not under strain.

■ Peg the shoot in position with a wire hoop and then fill the hole with soil, firming it down afterwards. The tip of the stem, with its foliage, should be left pointing upwards, as nearly vertically as possible.

■ If there is strain on the branch of which the layer is part, drive a tent peg in beneath it and guy the branch down, but do not allow such strain that the branch is damaged.

### NOTE

■ *This is the perfect month for initiating layers. The great majority of woody plants are growing fast, and the new tissues have not yet become brittle. They are also well charged with the growth hormones that allow them to make roots adventitiously – that is to say, on parts of the plants where roots do not normally grow* ■

### PLANNING

### SUN AND SHADE

You constantly read about the requirements of plants for shade, part shade, or full sun. Note that the expression 'part sun' is never used – I am unsure why not. Part shade is of two kinds: full shade for part of the day, such as that cast by buildings or dense shrubs, and the dappled shade provided by overhead trees. There is also a third, which is more theoretical but nonetheless important. 'Equivalent shade' is an expression of the sun's strength in different regions. Plants that need part or even full shade in warmer areas may need full sun where the climate is cooler. (It is worth noting in passing that almost all gardening operations on the North American continent are carried out at latitudes lower than those of the British Isles and that summer shade may be needed in America where none is necessary in Britain.)

It is not easy to estimate the sun and shade characteristics of the garden when you are planning your garden at the traditional time – midwinter. Neither can you be remotely precise at the main planting times – spring and autumn. It is now, when the sun is hot and high in the sky, that you should note carefully the places that are in full shade, shade for part of the day (and which part), and dappled shade.

*USEFUL REMINDERS*
*Do not be self-conscious about writing yourself notes, nor about placing stakes in the ground with messages on them. You will bless your own foresight when, in the appropriate season for action, you come across a label informing you that this is the centre of 2sq m (2½sq yd) of full shade from 11am to 2pm at the hottest time of year. You can, of course, label with numbers referring to your trusty notebook.*

**PLANTS FOR SERPENTINE LAYERING**

*Clematis*
*Hedera*
*Jasmine*
*Vitis*
*Wisteria*

### Transplanting
The layer will root over the next year or so, and you should plan to leave it undisturbed until the autumn of the year after it was layered, or even until the spring after that. However, if signs of strong growth are seen early next summer, sever the connection to the parent plant as a preparation for transplanting. It is never wise to separate the new plant and transplant it in the same operation.

### Serpentine Layering
Plants with long, whippy stems can provide more than one layer from a branch.

- Take branches of the current year's growth and peg them down at intervals, choosing leaf joints as the lowest points on the serpent.

- Remove the leaves on these joints and make a slanting cut just below the joints before burying them.

- As the angle of curve is not as great as in simple layering, it is often a good idea to prop each slit open with a pebble. Stems *will* root without wounding but they take a good deal longer and are not as certain.

- *Method 2*
With this method, a pot of soil is used instead of a hole in the ground for subjects without a branch that can be brought sufficiently far down. The pot is raised on suitable supports and the layer pegged into it. There is no difference in principle from method 1. It is most useful for layering *Camellia reticulata* varieties, which are very difficult indeed from cuttings.

# plants

## OF THE

## *month*

## 2

## HOSTA

### *Hosta* 'Thomas Hogg'

Hostas are above all foliage plants. Their leaves are so variable in size and colour, and their habit so neat and ground-covering, that they are more in demand than almost any other border plants. It is not generally realised that, with the exception of those with white or cream variegation and just a few others, they are sun-tolerant when in a rich, organic, moisture-retentive soil. Many hostas are first-class flowering plants.

| | |
|---|---|
| type | Herbaceous perennial |
| flowers | Like spikes of small, lilac lilies. This variety is one of the earliest to flower |
| foliage | Dark green with glossy undersides and broad, cream margins |
| height | 60cm (2ft) |
| spread | 50cm (20in) |
| hardiness | Hardy |
| planting | Plant at any time if from containers; autumn is best for bare-rooted plants |
| position | Part shade |
| soil | The richer and more organic the better. Lime-tolerant |
| propagation | By division in autumn or spring |
| alternatives | There are many variegated hostas, but few flower as prolifically or as early |
| special comment | Hostas are martyrs to slugs, so precautions should be taken or bait laid against them |

## ROSE

### *Rosa* 'Eyepaint'

Rose categories are not as definitely separated as is usually thought. Some old-fashioned roses, especially the Hybrid Perpetuals, closely resemble Hybrid Teas and some modern bush roses can perform the function of shrub roses in a garden.

| | |
|---|---|
| type | Cluster-flowered (Floribunda) rose. Generally agreed to be more realistically thought of as a shrub rose. Unnamed seedling × 'Picasso'. McGredy, 1976 |
| flowers | Large clusters of small, scarlet, white-eyed, single flowers with white reverses |
| habit and foliage | Like a shrub rose: very vigorous, strongly branching, bushy |
| height | Tall |
| spread | Wide-spreading |
| hardiness | Hardy |
| planting | Usually planted bare-rooted in winter, anytime if pot grown |
| position | Prefers full sun |
| soil | Well manured, tolerant of poorer soils than other floribundas |
| pruning | Shorten back long branches in autumn, then prune for shape in early spring. Do not prune hard |
| propagation | By budding |
| alternatives | Modern shrub roses such as 'Nevada' and 'Marguerite Hilling' |
| special comment | Prone to blackspot: spray regularly from early spring onwards |

*ROSA 'EYEPAINT'*

## ROSE

### *Rosa* 'Ruby Wedding'

This is the month during which the roses begin their summer-long display after the start provided by some early ones. The Large-Flowered (Hybrid Tea) roses are the mainstay of the rose garden.

| | |
|---|---|
| type | Large-flowered (HT) bush rose. 'Mayflower' × unnamed seedling. Gregory, 1979 |
| flowers | Crimson. Medium double, not full. Slight scent |
| habit and foliage | Short, bushy growth, medium-green foliage |
| height | Medium |
| spread | Medium |
| hardiness | Hardy |
| planting | Usually planted bare-rooted in winter but may be planted anytime from containers |
| position | Prefers full sun |
| soil | Well manured, on the heavy side, not too acid |
| pruning | Prune hard in early spring to outward-pointing buds |
| propagation | By budding |
| alternatives | Few combine its outstanding qualities |
| special comment | One of the very best roses for floristry, having few thorns, well-shaped blooms, and lasting well in water |

## ROSE

### *Rosa* 'Intrigue'

After the start initiated by some early-flowered roses, now is when the rest begin their summer-long display. Along with the large-flowered (Hybrid Tea), the Cluster-flowered are the mainstay of the garden.

| | |
|---|---|
| type | Cluster-flowered (Floribunda) rose. 'Grüss an Bayern' × unnamed seedling. Kordes, 1979 |
| flowers | Many blooms to a cluster, very dark red. No scent |
| habit and foliage | Bushy growth, mid-green foliage |
| height | Medium |
| spread | Medium |
| hardiness | Hardy |
| planting | Usually planted bare-rooted in winter but may be planted anytime from containers |
| position | Prefers full sun |
| soil | Well manured, on the heavy side, |

| | |
|---|---|
| | not too acid |
| pruning | Hard pruning for exhibition blooms; otherwise fairly light for quantity of flower |
| propagation | By budding |
| alternatives | There are few floribunda roses with this luxuriantly deep colour |

 ## WATER-LILY

### *Nymphaea* 'Escarboucle'

Water-lilies have been immensely popular since the Marliac nursery, in south-western France, discovered how to breed and develop hybrids during the second half of the nineteenth century.

| | |
|---|---|
| type | Hybrid water-lily |
| flowers | Medium-sized, good red |
| foliage | Floating leaves, purple, turning to dark green |
| spread | 1–1.3sq m (1–1½sq yd) (small to medium) |
| hardiness | Hardy |
| planting | Plant water-lilies in late spring |
| position | In sun. Do not plant near turbulent water, outlets of watercourses or fountains |
| soil | Plant in good, heavy soil, topped off with gravel. Do not use artificial fertilisers or fresh manure |
| propagation | By division in late spring, discarding the old, tough, main root and replanting the younger parts of the rhizome |
| alternatives | Other red lilies – 'Attraction' (medium-sized plant), 'Conqueror' (strong grower), 'Laydekeri' (miniature), 'Froebeli' (small) |

# *practical* project

### A GREENHOUSE
### PROPAGATION
### UNIT

How you make the best use of your greenhouse is largely a matter of personal priorities, but one thing is certain – greenhouses are not cheap and you should try to find ways of using yours to your utmost advantage.

Many people buy greenhouses and then find that their gardening interests change and that they no longer want to grow dozens of fuchsias and scores of 'geraniums'. They may also find that growing a variety of vegetables under glass has several snags, and that it is far from economical to devote the house just to one crop.

If your main interest is in the ornamental side of outdoor gardening, you are among the majority of gardeners, and if you have developed an interest in propagating, you are following the path down which all the best gardeners have passed. You are just the sort of person for whom the development of the greenhouse, or at least part of it, as a propagation unit is the ideal course of action.

There are several ways of organising such a unit but, again keeping an eye on the most advantageous use of the greenhouse, two main components are likely to take priority: a mist unit, for cuttings of the more difficult woody plants, and one or more heated frames for raising difficult seeds.

As space is at a premium, the greatest possible flexibility is wise, so the frames will be removable and can be stored when not needed.

## THE MIST UNIT

A mist propagation unit consists of one or more atomising jets that play on the cuttings on the open bench. They are controlled by a device called an 'electronic leaf', which detects the level of moisture or operates on a time interval. The advantages of the system are:

- Cuttings can be rooted that are difficult or impossible by other methods
- Rooting is quicker and more certain
- Cuttings can be taken earlier and later
- Handling and management are made easier
- Wilting and scorching are greatly lessened
- There is much less need for shading, so more light can reach the cuttings. This and the above factor make for rapid root growth

You will need a mains electricity supply and mains water at no less than 25lb/sq in. You can buy kits, but it is cheaper to make your own system.

### Staging
- Firstly, make sure the staging is very strong, and if it is not, build it anew so that it can take the weight of 7.5cm (3in) depth of wet sand and a full load of seed trays and their compost. It should have a board rail all the way round no less than 10cm (4in) deep.

- The base should be strong, and perforated at

### DIFFICULT CUTTINGS MADE EASIER BY MIST

*Actinidia*
*Berberidopsis*
*Camellia*
*Campsis*
conifers
*Fothergilla*
*Ilex* (holly)
*Leptospermum*
*Lithodora*
*Magnolia*
*Parthenocissus*
*Rhododendron* (including Azalea)
*Sarcococca*
*Syringa* (lilac)
*Wisteria*

soil-warming cable

thermostat

**cross section showing soil-warming cables**

5cm (2in)

2.5cm (1in)

staging base

seed frame  mist nozzle  maturing cuttings

intervals with holes for drainage. It is not satis-factory to lay sheet plastic over wooden slats, but stiff, corrugated plastic will do very well.

### Heating

Bottom heat is essential.

■ Lay in a soil-warming cable, using the length prescribed by the makers for the base area of your unit. The cable will be laid on a bed of sand 2.5cm (1in) deep in a series of loops.

### WARNING

■ *You* must *use all the cable – it is dangerous to attempt to shorten it* ■

■ The cable is controlled by a thermostat. The optimum temperature is a constant 18–21°C (65–70°F). The cable is eventually covered with a further 5cm (2in) of sand.

■ A water pipe, running under the staging base, branches at intervals at right angles so that a branch is led up through the base to terminate about 45cm (18in) above the sand in a mist nozzle, consisting of a small aperture through which the stream of water impinges on a striker plate which atomises it. The nozzle is adjustable.

■ The water is controlled by a solenoid valve in the water line, which in its turn is controlled by the electronic leaf, of which there are several different types.

### SEED FRAMES

Using a separate soil cable and thermostat, a further length of staging can be converted into bottom-heated frames for germinating seed. They will greatly extend your seed-sowing season and enable you to start sowing in late winter – particularly important for trees and shrubs, which need as long as possible in their first year to become established. Your rates of germination will be greatly increased, and you will be able to obtain early germination of dormant seed that has had to be chilled beforehand.

■ If you are capable of making a cold frame for outdoor purposes, you will have not the slightest difficulty in making one or more seed frames. Two are better than one, as you can then move the pots from a tightly closed one to another that is slightly open as the seeds germinate, before taking them out onto the open bench.

■ While germination is taking place, the frames are best lightly shaded with material of no greater density than muslin.

■ If you wish to use the space taken up by the frame for other purposes, there is no problem with making it removable, as it can simply rest on the sand bed and inside the rails of the unit. Because it does not have to stand up to weather, it can be of relatively light construc-tion, and clear plastic can be used instead of glass.

*A TIMELY TIP*
*Next month sees the start of the season for semi-ripe shrub cuttings. They are the ones that will benefit most from your mist system, so try to have it up and running by the end of this month so that you can monitor the characteristics of the electronic leaf and check the general running of the system before taking any cuttings. When it is running well without any pots of cuttings, the sand should be moistened at each firing of the leaf but should just begin to dry before the next. Adjust as necessary when cuttings are present. They should be constantly coated with moisture but the system should not create general wetness.*

# plant
# *selections*

### ● HERBACEOUS PERENNIALS

During the midsummer month (which by any standards is really its first one), herbaceous **peonies** enjoy the peak of their season – the earliest bloom at the end of spring; the latest in high summer.

They are not as widely grown as one might expect, largely due to a lack of understanding of their needs, but also because they are thought to contribute little outside their flowering period. This latter idea is hardly based on reality, as the pink or deep maroon shoots of newly emerged peonies are superb counterpoint to the narcissi of mid-spring.

To succeed with herbaceous peonies the crowns should be planted between 2.5–5cm (1–2in) inches below soil level. Any more inhibits flowering. They prefer a heavy soil to a light one, but take to acid and alkaline soils with equal aplomb. They are happy almost anywhere apart from deep shade, tolerate competition, and flower for half a century with just about no attention whatever.

Peonies have a palette restricted to the red tones of the spectrum and to white, but that allows for all kinds and combinations of pink, rich purple shades, and startling whites, as well as flamboyant, clean reds. The flower shapes – single, double and Imperial (semi-double, in which the centres of the flowers are filled with petaloid stamens) – allow for permutations of colour and flower style that provide a very wide choice of varieties.

**Hemerocallis**, known as day lilies for their extremely long succession of flowers that individually last but a day, have much in common with peonies. They, too, are less widely grown than they deserve, and they show an even greater toleration of widely differing growing conditions.

Day lilies can grow perfectly happily in the wettest, boggiest conditions and can thrive lustily on the driest, sunniest bank. They can live as isolated specimens, in large, jostling drifts, or even in grass, and soil content is of small concern to them. Just as with peonies, long-term neglect suits them well, and they should only be moved or divided when flowering starts to fall off, which is usually only after many years.

Their colour range is wider than that of peonies. They are, of course, a totally different style of plant, with iris-like leaves and lily-like flowers; resemblances are limited to their generally easy-going natures. Reds tend to a brick tone, but there are some fine, clear scarlets and deep crimsons, while the yellows are cool and clean or warm and rich. There are peach, apricot, salmon, mahogany, and many shades of pink, but blues, lilacs and lavenders are absent.

The ineffable blues of **delphiniums** are one of early summer's glories. Unfortunately, far too many seed-raised plants are seen whose colours are muddied by brownish purple. Named varieties – 'Loch Leven', 'Blue Nile', 'Cristella' and others – provide a purity of blue that is seldom seen in plants other than these and **Meconopsis**, the blue poppies of the Himalayas that start into stately flower in the peatier parts of the garden this month.

Against these and the gentler oriental poppies (some of the orange ones are just too strident), the flat heads of **achilleas** strike a different colour note as well as lending a difference of texture to the bed with their flat heads all of a plane. The contrast with the upright spikes of delphiniums and lupins is most marked. However, there is a coarseness about them that demands that they be used with discretion, but the clearest of the yellow varieties have great value.

*A BORDER ACHILLEA*

The **diascia** season – a long one, lasting well into early autumn – starts this month. This is a genus that is virtually new to gardens. In the early 1970s there was but one hardy species and no varieties; now South Africa and the hybridists (of whom your author was the first) have yielded up about another thirty.

Their nemesia-like flowers, almost always in some shade of clear, soft pink, are unlike anything else among perennials. They have a special value when set at the front of a border, keeping it continuously colourful right through the parade of arrivals and departures in the taller ranks. Try very soft cuttings (see p.122). They root easily as long as you pinch the tops out, even before they have rooted.

## ROSES AND SHRUBS

Repeat-flowering roses, too, set out on their long flowering season. Of the Hybrid Teas and Floribundas there is little ignorance – everyone knows a rose when they see one – but shrub roses are neglected in favour of their more glamorous cousins. There is these days a wide selection, and a well thought-out choice of just a few makes a fine framework around which the other roses can congregate.

This is a soft, 'cottagey' month in the garden, one where light scents, delicate colours and simplicity rule. The more regal, sophisticated, evening sorts of effects are appropriate to the later, high summer. So it is just right that **philadelphus**, the scented, white mock orange in all its guises – single, double, small and large – should be at its best just now. It does little for the rest of the year, but this is a month of rest from flowering for the shrub world as a whole, and the fairly nondescript bushes earn their keep.

**Deutzias**, again mostly white, although some are lilac, enjoy their fleeting moment of glory this month. There are still some **late rhododendrons** about, although a hot spell will shorten their show, and **weigelas**, some **lilacs** and a few **viburnums** continue to play their part. **Clematis** and **jasmines** are needed now, and **wisterias** glorify it.

## ALPINES

On the rock garden, little **cranesbills** (the true geraniums), alpine **hypericums**, and shrubby **penstemons** lead the field. It is hard not to love the cranesbills, especially such gems as *Geranium sanguineum lancastriense* (now *G.s. – striatum*), whose softest pink, darker-veined flowers come from just one sandy island close to the coast of northern England – Walney Island, and 'Ballerina', a man-made hybrid whose dark purple veining on lilac just, but only just, stays short of a sophistication that would disqualify it from a home in what is essentially the domain of wildings.

*DELPHINIUMS AND LUPINS*

# plants
IN
*flower*

**KEY**

\* = evergreen    spp = species
vars = varieties

**NOTES**

*Daboecia cantabrica* requires lime-free peaty soil. ***Magnolia sieboldii*** and ***Kalmia latifolia*** need lime-free soil.
***B. globosa*** is hardy in southern areas.
***Cistus*** do well in hot dry spots and ***Escallonia*** vars are good for coastal districts.

## FUCHSIA FORMALITY

If you like formal bedding schemes using fuchsias, try standards in varieties whose flowers are in the pink, red or white range with little or no purple, and set them among light pink petunias. The petunias should have been chosen or sown specially for the purpose. A strain such as 'Super Cascade Blush', an improved $F_1$ hybrid that comes true to colour, is ideal. Edge the bed with *Senecio bicolor cineraria* (syn. *Cineraria maritima, Senecio cineraria*), whose felt-white leaves emphasise the silvery effect you will have achieved, even though the motif colour is pink. This scheme will stay in full decorative order until the frosts, and all you have to do is weed it and keep it tidy.

| TREES | colour | flower type |
|---|---|---|
| **Liriodendron tulipifera** | Greenish yellow | Like tulips |
| **Robinia pseudoacacia** several vars | White | Pea shaped |
| **Styrax japonica** | White | Like snowdrops; all along undersides of branches |

| SHRUBS | | |
|---|---|---|
| **Berberis** deciduous vars | Yellow | |
| **Buddleia globosa** (Orange ball tree) | Orange | |
| ***Carpenteria californica** | White | Large, flat |
| ***Cistus** spp and vars | Various | 5–10cm (2–4in) wide |
| ***Convolvulus cneorum** | White | Typical of convolvulus |
| **Cornus kousa chinensis** | White | Bracts |
| **Cytisus** spp and vars (Broom) | Various | Pea shaped |
| ***Daboecia cantabrica** | Purplish red or white | Heather-like |
| **Daphne 'Somerset'** | Mauve-pink | Clusters, scented |
| **Deutzia** spp and vars | White; some are lilac-pink | Bell shaped |
| ***Escallonia** vars | White, pink or red | Small, bell shaped |
| ***Hebe** many | White, red or purple | Spikes |
| ***Helianthemum** vars | Various | |
| ***Hypericum 'Hidcote'** | Yellow | Large, round |
| ***Kalmia latifolia** | Soft rose | Small, clustered |
| **Magnolia sieboldii** | White | Chalices |
| **Philadelphus** vars | Mostly white | Scented |
| **Potentilla fruticosa** vars | Various | Dog-rose shaped |
| ***Prunus lusitanica** (Portuguese laurel) | White | Plumes |
| ***Rhododendron** the hardy hybrids | Various | |
| **Rosa** many | Various | |
| **Viburnum opulus** | White | Flat heads |
| 'Sterile' | White | Round heads |
| **Weigela** vars | Pink, white or red | Foxglove-like |

| CLIMBERS | colour | flower type |
|---|---|---|
| **Clematis** large flowered | Various | |
| **Jasmine** hardy types | White | Scented |
| **Lonicera** (Honeysuckle) | Yellow and pink | Scented |
| **Wisteria** vars | Lilac, white, purple or rose | Scented |

## PERENNIALS

| | colour | height |
|---|---|---|
| **Achillea** spp and vars | White, yellow | 60–90cm (24–36in) |
| **'Galaxy Hybrids'** | Cream, buff or pink | 45–60cm (18–24in) |
| **Alstroemeria** | Various, including yellow and orange | 60cm (24in) |
| **Astilbe** vars | Red, pink or white | 60cm (24in) |
| **Astrantia major** | White, tinged green | 60cm (24in) |
| **Campanula lactiflora** | Blue or white | 1.2m (48in) |
| **latifolia** | Blue or white | 1.2m (48in) |
| **persicifolia** | Shades of blue | 90cm (36in) |
| **Centaurea dealbata** | Pink | 60cm (24in) |
| **Centranthus ruber** | Pink, red or white | 80cm (32in) |
| **Coreopsis** vars | Yellow | 60–75cm (24–30in) |
| **Delphinium** vars | Blue, mauve, purple or white, tall spikes | 1.2–1.5m (4–5ft) |
| **Dianthus** many vars | Variations of pink | 20–40cm (8–16in) |
| **Eremurus bungei** | Yellow spikes in orange | 1.5m (5ft) |
| **Geranium endressii** vars | Pink, veined | 30cm (12in) |
| **'Russell Pritchard'** | Magenta pink | 30cm (12in) |
| **Hemerocallis** vars | Various | 30–60cm (12–24in) |
| **Heuchera** vars | Pink or white | 30–45cm (12–18in) |
| **Iris germanica** (Bearded iris) | Various | 75–100cm (30–40in) |
| **Leucanthemum × superbum** vars | White | 45–80cm (18–32in) |
| **Lysimachia punctata** | Yellow | 75cm (30in) |
| **Oenothera missouriensis** | Large, lemon yellow | 20cm (8in) |
| **Paeonia** herbaceous vars | Red, pink, white | 75cm (30in) |
| **Papaver orientale** | Red, pink, orange or white | 75cm (30in) |
| **Primula** candelabra and bog spp | Various | 45–90cm (18–36in) |
| **Trollius** spp and vars | Orange or yellow | 45–60cm (18–24in) |
| **Verbascum** vars | Yellow or pink | 1m (40in) |

## BULBS

| | | |
|---|---|---|
| **Allium** vars (Ornamental onion) | Various | 20–45cm (8–18in) |
| **Camassia** spp | Blue or cream | 30–70cm (12–28in) |
| **Iris** Pacific Coast Hybrids | Yellow or purple | 45cm (18in) |
| English vars | Blue, purple or white | 60cm (24in) |
| **Lilium martagon** vars | Purple or white | 90cm (36in) |

## FILL THAT GAP

Annuals play an increasing part as the month matures. It is a sad state of mind into which advanced gardeners retreat that tells them that annuals are somehow *infra dig*. The best gardeners think nothing of the sort and glee-fully tuck them in wherever there is a gap or wherever they add to the colour display. If you have pulled up the spring bedding – forget-me-nots, wallflowers and so on – do not be in too much of a hurry to put 'proper' plants in their place, and do not be intimidated by 'experienced' gardeners. Stick to your guns and your garden plan, determine to grow them again next year, and meanwhile put in something bright in the way of annuals that tone in with your overall colour scheme.

## EVENING ANNUALS

Nictotianas, stocks and mignonette are among the scented annuals that no garden should be without. There is nothing more pleasant than that first time when the per-fume of evening annuals reaches you as you settle down for a pre-dinner drink on the terrace. You will experience it many times during the summer, but the magic is never quite as complete again.

## ROCK GARDEN

**Achillea** spp
* **Androsace sarmentosa** vars
**Aster alpinus**
**Campanula** spp
* **Dianthus** spp and vars
* **Edraianthus** spp
**Erigeron** spp
**Erodium** spp
* **Geranium** spp
* **Gypsophila repens**
* **Helianthemum** vars
**Hypericum** spp
* **Leontopodium alpinum** (edelweiss)
**Linum** spp
* **Penstemon** spp
* **Phlox** spp and vars
* **Sedum** spp
* **Thymus serpyllum** and vars
**Veronica** spp

# J U L Y

I should like to enjoy this summer flower by flower . . .
ANDRE GIDE

*Among shrubs at any rate, early summer is like half-time in a football match. Those that bloom in spring on the wood made the previous year are separated from those that flower in high summer on the wood of the current year by an interval, during which a show is put on to keep our attention. The break over, summer swings into action.*

*It is the peak of the year for herbaceous perennials. They clamour for the attention of pollinating insects and it is all too easy to have planted them so that they are all clamour and far too little harmony. This is a month during which lack of planning becomes all too apparent and results in many a wince as magenta screams at scarlet and dark crimson argues bitterly with light purple.*

*We may scoff at those who meticulously draw up plans on paper for their plantings. Indeed, some inspired gardeners seem to manage beautifully on instinct and* ad hoc *associations. But the wise person knows how short memory is and that foresight is the key to consistent success. When you see* Lychnis coronaria *'Atrosanguinea' in a public garden, planted against neutral green, and then try to recall its colour at planting time in autumn, are you likely to remember that it was tooth-gratingly magenta, or will your memory, full of thoughts of a lovely day out, recall it as rich red? Again, the value of an active notebook is evident.*

*This is a somnolent month, but the solstice is past, the first signs of the decline of the year are just discernible, and as you enjoy the comfort of the summer weather you will feel, if you are truly attuned to nature, the stirrings of a primeval imperative. For our ancestors complacency was lethal; there was much to do to ensure survival during the cold to come. That is why, in midsummer, gardeners sit up suddenly and say, 'Can't sit here all day, you know. There's lots to be done'.*

# tasks
## FOR THE
## *month*
## 1

## CHECKLIST

- Prune wisteria, and shrubs that have recently finished flowering
- Cut back delphiniums and lupins
- Water hanging baskets and make sure the compost stays moist at all times
- Mulch young heather plants
- Pinch out the tips of ivy-leaved geraniums to make them bush out and flower freely
- Continue to deadhead roses, always cutting back to a new shoot or a leaf joint
- Continue to tie in climbers
- Order daffodils and narcissi before the varieties you want have sold out
- Kill out ants' nests, especially where they occur among the roots of herbaceous perennials
- Deadhead and remove seedheads from rock-garden plants whose seed you do not want to save
- Lift tulips and hyacinths and store in trays in a cool shed for planting again in autumn

## MAINTENANCE

### PRUNING WISTERIA

From about the middle of the month is the time to prune wisterias. They produce very long, whippy growths which, if not checked hard, will give you a great deal of unruly foliage and few flowers.

■ Cut back all extension growths (ie side growths from the leaders) to two buds or about 10cm (4in).

■ At the same time, head back the leaders if they are growing beyond their allotted space.

■ In winter, cut the leaders back again if necessary.

Some people advocate pruning less hard in summer and then shortening the

laterals again in winter. It is a counsel of perfection, as it combines pruning for growth with pruning for flowers, but pruning them once at this time of year will ensure ample crops of flowers and save you an extra job. Wisterias need no encouragement to grow.

### PEST CONTROL

All populations of pest insects vary in their resistance to different pesticides. If you persist with just one spray, the most resistant will survive and breed, so that you end up with an infestation of resistant pests. To avoid this, vary the treatment from time to time. This regime stands a good chance of mopping up the entire population.

### CUTTING BACK

You should have cut back oriental poppies last month, but if you have not done so it is not too late. It is time now to cut back delphiniums and lupins, again to encourage fresh shoots from the bases. You may also end up with a second, smaller flush of flowers.

### PRUNING SHRUBS

Do not lose sight of shrubs that have recently finished flowering. This is the time to prune them, cutting out thin, poor wood and shortening shoots that have become over-long. The overall object is to cut out the wood that has just flowered, so as to encourage new wood on which next year's flowers will be borne, but you should also keep an eye towards general shape and avoid dense, tangled bushes.

However, if you find that your purpose is impeded by the presence of a bird's nest, leave the shrub alone for a year. Next year hang strips of metal foil from the branches in spring and any inclination on the part of the bird to return will be lessened. We cannot on the one hand advocate the benefits of wild life in the garden and then on the other cast creatures aside when they get in the way.

### BLUE HYDRANGEAS

If your blue hydrangea varieties are not turning out to be blue, try a proprietary hydrangea colourant powder or purchase alum crystals from the chemist and rake them gently into the soil over the root area. If the flowers still refuse to turn blue there is no point in persisting and you should turn to pink or white varieties.

---

## NOTE ON PEAT

- *It is difficult to decide on maintenance measures that involve peat if you are un-decided about the ecological consequences of its use.*

   *Peat is not a non-renewable resource and the world's accessible reserves are such that, at the present rate of extraction, they will regenerate well before they are worked out. Much of the peat used in gardens would never have formed but for early man's cutting down the forests so it is by no means always a natural phenomenon and as a wild life resource is but a shadow of the forest it replaced. For the flower gardener, peat is one of the most useful soil condition-ers it is possible to find* ▪

---

### HEATHERS

Heathers should not suffer from drought if you have planted them properly, unless it is while they are still young. They should be planted in odd-numbered groups of three or more so that the groups interlock, and at distances that will cause them to make a continuous, unbroken carpet. During the first three years or so, before they have met and grown together, there is a danger of drought because of the bare earth between them, so it is wise practice to mulch with composted bark or preferably a 50/50 mixture of moist sphagnum peat and composted bark. If you have not done so already, it may not be too late yet as long as the ground is still moist.

## PLANTING

### RESERVE FOR PLANTING

This is not a good month for planting, as there is too much danger from drought and we tend to take our holidays during the warm weeks. However, do plant out whatever half-hardy annuals you have left, and set your biennials in a nursery bed – a corner of the vegetable garden will do well – preparatory to their being planted out in their final places in autumn.

If you see something irresistible in the garden centre, buy it by all means, but only if you are sure you can keep it in good condition. My own practice is to ask if a 'sold' label with my name on it can be put on the plant, or if it can otherwise be kept at the nursery or garden centre until I am ready to plant it in the autumn. In this way the plant benefits from the staff's routine attention during the hot and dry weather.

*HOUSE AND GARDEN*
*Do not forget to cut flowers for the house. House and garden form a continuum in summer. Your doors and windows are open for a good deal of the time and you tend to sit half-in and half-out while it is warm. Flowers brought from the beds and arranged in the house enhance this effect, and there is an interplay between arrangements and flowerbeds that is immensely pleasing to the eye. Sweet peas can be cut again and again and are the better for it; nicotianas come in colours that complement sweet peas. Try cutting orange crocosmias and arranging them with branches of the summer-flowering Ceanothus 'Gloire de Versailles'. It has powder-blue flowers of about the same tonal value as the orange of Crocosmia masonorum, and as blue and orange are what are termed 'perfect complements' (others are yellow/violet and green/red), the combination is a happy one.*

# plants
## OF THE
## *month*
## *1*

## ROSE
### *Rosa gallica* 'Versicolor'

This rose, also known as 'Rosa Mundi', is one of the most popular of the old roses and has been in gardens since the early part of the seventeenth century, if not before. It flowers only once, but in doing so should be regarded in the light of the performance of other garden shrubs, rather than of that of modern roses. As a shrub, it is among the most vivid and unusual of all.

| | |
|---|---|
| type | Old shrub rose of the Gallica group |
| flowers | Lightly double, light crimson, splashed and striped with pale pink. Fragrant |
| habit and foliage | Light green. The stems are almost thornless. A shrub capable of spreading by its own suckers |
| height and spread | About 1.5m (5ft) high and a little wider |
| hardiness | Hardy |
| planting | Usually planted bare-rooted in winter but can be planted anytime when container grown |
| position | Prefers sun |
| soil | Best in a good garden soil, but tolerant of almost any soil, even poor or chalky ones |
| pruning | Shorten long growths by one-third to one-half in autumn. Remove a few of the oldest growths from the base in early spring to prevent overcrowding of the shrub and cut out weak or diseased shoots |
| propagation | Detach and transplant rooted suckers in late winter. Take semi-ripe cuttings under mist in late summer or hardwood cuttings in a frame in late autumn |

## SUN ROSE
### *Cistus* × *purpureus*

The cistuses, known as sun roses, are aromatic shrubs from the Mediterranean region and beyond, where the summers are hot and dry. They are the ideal shrubs for light or stony soils in full sun, or on dry, arid banks, and remain in flower throughout this month, having started during the last. Most species have white flowers, but a few are pink or cerise; this plant is a hybrid between a white-flowered species (*C. ladanifer*) and one with rose-pink to purple booms (*C. creticus*).

| | |
|---|---|
| type | Evergreen shrub |
| flowers | Large, round, rose-crimson with a |

| | |
|---|---|
| | dark maroon basal blotch to each petal. Each bloom lasts one day |
| foliage | Dark, matt green, fairly narrow, wavy, aromatic |
| height | 2m (7ft) (the maximum) after 10 years |
| spread | 1.5–2m (5–7ft) after 10 years |
| hardiness | Not hardy in cold districts |
| position | Full sun |
| soil | Any soil except wet or heavy |
| pruning | None |
| propagation | By semi-ripe cuttings in summer |
| alternatives | *C. ladanifer* is the same size and shape and its flowers are white with the same maroon blotches. The two go well together. *C. pulverulentus* is cerise and the flowers are less rounded |

## CARPENTERIA
### *Carpenteria californica*

A medium-sized Californian shrub, sometimes known as the tree anemone. It needs all the sun that is available and is not reliably hardy in cold areas.

| | |
|---|---|
| type | Evergreen shrub |
| flowers | Large, white, decorated with bosses of golden stamens |
| foliage | Leaves lanceolate, glossy green |
| height | 2m (7ft) after 10 years |
| spread | 1.5–2m (5–7ft) after 10 years |
| hardiness | Hardy when sheltered from cold winds and given all available sun |
| position | Best against a warm wall, although it will grow and flower happily as a free-standing specimen in a mild, sunny climate |
| soil | Any good garden soil |
| pruning | None |
| propagation | By simple layering during summer or by soft or semi-ripe cuttings under mist or in a heated propagator. Do *not* propagate from seed, as the forms produced are almost certain to be inferior. Always buy vegetatively propagated plants |
| varieties | 'Ladham's Variety' and 'Bodnant' are especially large-flowered forms but unfortunately scarce |

## LILY
### *Lilium* species and varieties

Nowadays there are many kinds of lilies and an almost bewildering array of hybrids and

*ONE OF THE MANY HYBRID LILIES*

varieties from which to choose. Generally speaking, however, bulb catalogues offer lilies that can be grown with relative ease in the open garden. Provided that they are kept sprayed against mildews and pests, they provide a rich display, often of exotic colour, as summer reaches its height.

| | |
|---|---|
| type | Bulbs |
| flowers | Trumpet, open-trumpet or split-trumpet shaped, or turks-cap type with reflexed petals. Upward or side-facing, or hanging |
| foliage | Varied |
| height | 60cm–1.2m (2–4ft), depending on variety |
| hardiness | Most lilies that are generally available are hardy |
| planting | Bulb merchants usually despatch lilies in late winter or early spring. They should be planted immediately upon arrival or as soon as conditions permit. Plant with a pad of sand under the base of the bulb |
| position | The bulb should be in cool shade, with the flowers reaching into sun. The best way to achieve this is to grow them among low shrubs such as Japanese azaleas or among herbaceous perennials |
| soil | Soils should be on the light side and contain plenty of organic matter. Drainage must be good |
| propagation | Dry bulb scales |
| varieties | There are literally hundreds of species and varieties such as turks-cap and trumpet. Colour ranges from cool white to flaming orange so selection must be a matter of taste |

# tasks

## FOR THE

## *month*

## 2

*A DIBBER FOR CUTTINGS*
*Use an unsharpened pencil as a dibber for cuttings. Its flat end will make quite sure that you do not have any 'hung' cuttings.*

*CUTTINGS COMPOST*
*Firm the compost well (but not too much) before inserting the cuttings. If you do not, you will leave hollows in which water will stand, alternating with ridges that will quickly become dry.*

## PROPAGATION

### SEMI-RIPE CUTTINGS OF TREES AND SHRUBS

As the month progresses, more and more shrubs will start to ripen the growth they have made this year. Just now, this will apply to shrubs that flowered in spring; later, those that bloomed in early summer will start to firm up, and next month will see shrubs, such as eucryphias, with flowers and ripening shoots present at the same time. Here begins the busiest time of the year for keen propagators.

### Advantages

The shoots of trees and shrubs are full of growth hormones and remain so until they become hard and woody – the condition we term 'ripe'. When a shoot is severed from a plant, its hormones induce it to produce roots and endeavour to establish existence as a separate entity. The hormones are not evenly distributed along the shoots, but are concentrated at the tips and at the leaf joints.

If we take a shrub cutting when it is soft, it will tend to rot before it can establish roots. Soft cuttings of alpine shrubs are relatively easy, but the great majority of mainstream garden shrubs are better taken as semi-ripe cuttings in summer.

Hardwood cuttings (see p.134) root in a number of shrub and tree species, but the process is a long one. It is, however, completely independent of any specialised equipment. In the majority of shrubs, once the shoots have hardened they are reluctant to root. Semi-ripe cuttings are a compromise, in which the cuttings are sufficiently firm to stand without wilting until rooting can take place, and have enough growth hormone to root relatively quickly.

### Rooting conditions

The cuttings require artificial heat for optimum rooting, otherwise fluctuations of temperature between day and night tend to slow down the rooting process. However, most shrubs will root perfectly well in a garden frame as long as it faces the sun for warmth, but is shaded with white greenhouse shade paint to keep the strongest rays from burning the cuttings. The frame should be closed whenever possible to maintain a humid atmosphere, but ventilated if the temperature rises much above 24°C (75°F).

For the very best results, with which no other system can compare, a mist system is a first-class investment

and one that will last for twenty or more years with virtually no attention.

### Taking the cuttings

The ideal semi-ripe shrub cutting will bend to about thirty degrees from its main axis without snapping, but more than that will cause it to snap. If it bends to a right angle it is too soft; if it feels as though it is about to snap beyond twenty degrees it is probably too hard.

■ Cut the cutting from the plant at a point just *above* a leaf joint, making a slanting cut. You will trim it to just *below* the next joint, but by doing it this way you do not leave a stump on the shrub to attract disease.

■ Place it in a plastic bag with any others from the same shrub and repair to the shed to prepare the cuttings.

■ Having trimmed to just below the joint, remove the pair of leaves that spring from this joint, or the single one from the first joint and the one from the joint above, depending on whether the leaves are oppositely or alternately disposed.

■ With shrubs that are known to be difficult, such as magnolias, wound one side of the base of the cutting by carefully slicing off the bark for a length of about 0.5cm (¼in). This stimulates rooting.

■ Dip the end of the cutting into hormone rooting powder, tap off the surplus, and insert it to about one-third of its length into a 50/50 mixture by volume of moss peat and sharp sand.

■ Firm gently, making sure that the cutting is not 'hung', and has its base in position on the compost and not on an air pocket.

Trim cutting to below leaf joint

Remove lower pair of leaves

Correctly positioned cutting

'Hung cutting'

### Which shrubs?

It would be invidious to provide a list of shrubs that root by this method and at this time of year. There are so many factors that affect results.

Your success rate will improve with practice, and it has to be said that shrubs vary from year to year in their readiness to root and the precise time at which they are ready. After a very few seasons, you should, if you have a mist system, be able to achieve 100 per cent strike rate with 'tricky' subjects such as camellias, and a very reasonable rate if you do not. Keep a sharp eye open for cuttings in the right state of ripeness and experiment, particularly with any that you especially like and wish to increase either for yourself or for friends.

**R**EMEMBER

▪ *No gardening advice should be taken as if graven on stone. During the winter of 1977–78, I took fifty cuttings from a large branch of the ever-green* Magnolia grandi-flora *– at best a difficult sub-ject – that had fallen under the weight of snow. Every single one rooted and was potted up by autumn* ▪

## **D**IVIDE IRISES

*If you did not lift and clean iris rhizomes in early spring, you can do so as soon as flowering is over, dividing the rhizomes and replanting straight away. This applies not only to bearded irises but also to beardless and water irises. The Pacific Coast irises can be moved and divided immediately after flowering and at no other time, otherwise they die.*

## PLANNING

### GARDEN VISITING

There is so much going on in high summer that not much planning gets done. However, it is the very time of year when visits to gardens that feature herbaceous perennials and the uses of annuals among other kinds of plants are most valuable.

Garden visiting is at its peak in late spring, and this may have something to do with the general over-emphasis on plants that flower at that time of year. Take time off to go to gardens famous for their herbaceous or mixed borders and don't forget – take your notebook.

Take careful note now of any colour combinations you would like to change in the border.

In addition to your notebook, a small filing system for the garden is a good idea. If you open a file called 'border', the observations you make can go into it, to be recalled when it is time to move plants or order new ones.

*POTTING UP*
*Do not forget any softwood cuttings that may still require potting up*

*J U L Y*

# plants
## OF THE
## *month*
## 2

### BUSY LIZZIE
*Impatiens* hybrids

The well known busy lizzies are to be found in gardens of all kinds from the tropics, where they are shade-loving perennials, to the cold countries of the north, where they are grown as annuals in sun or shade. If you have wondered what to do when the leaves of the daffodils in your border have died down, here is your answer: plant busy lizzies.

| | |
|---|---|
| type | Tender perennials, treated as half-hardy annuals |
| flowers | Many colours in the pink-red-purple-range, also white, striped and doubles. Flowering starts early in the month and carries right through to the frosts |
| foliage | Light green on succulent stems |
| height | 10–20cm (4–8in). Heights and spreads vary very greatly with situation, climate and soil |
| planting | plant in late spring or early summer depending upon prevalence of late frosts |
| position | Best in part shade |
| soil | A good, general border soil, but busy lizzies will tolerate quite poor conditions |
| propagation | Sow in early spring in heat (22°C/ 73°F) and allow 4 weeks for germination. High humidity is essential, so wrap the pots or trays in clingfilm |

### CROCOSMIA
*Crocosmia* 'Lucifer'

Crocosmias are related to and often mistaken for the old montbretias. There are two distinct types, in which the flowers either droop or are held along the tops of the final curves of the stems. 'Lucifer' is of the latter persuasion and is one of an exciting race of crocosmias in vibrant colours that have been raised in recent years.

| | |
|---|---|
| type | Herbaceous perennial |
| flowers | Bright scarlet, tubular |
| foliage | Iris-like |
| height | 1.2m (4ft) |
| spread | 45cm (18in) |
| hardiness | Hardy |
| planting | Plant in spring or autumn |
| position | In sun |
| soil | Any good garden soil |
| propagation | By division in spring |
| alternatives | For smaller gardens, choose 'Bressingham Blaze' or 'Spitfire', both 90cm (3ft) tall |

### SEA HOLLY
*Eryngium* × *zabelii*
(*E. alpinum* × *E. bourgatii*)

Sea hollies are among the most attractive foliage plants for the summer border, as the bracts that surround every flowerhead are sharp and spiny and often of a different colour from the holly-like basal leaves.

| | |
|---|---|
| type | Herbaceous perennial |
| flowers | Blue, in tight heads; bracts silver-grey |
| foliage | The bracts build up almost to hide the basal leaves, which are green, whitish-veined and broadly holly-like |

*CROCOSMIA 'LUCIFER'*

*HYDRANGEA MACROPHYLLA 'VEITCHII'*

| | | |
|---|---|---|
| height | 75cm (2½ft) | |
| spread | 45cm (18in) | |
| hardiness | Hardy | |
| planting | Best planted in spring or autumn | |
| position | In sun | |
| soil | Reasonably good garden soil | |
| propagation | By division in early or mid-spring | |
| alternatives | *E. × oliverianum, E.* 'Violetta' (both blue) | |
| special comment | The bracts are sometimes termed 'piccadills', referring to their fancied resemblance to a type of collar that gave its name to London's Piccadilly | |

### HYDRANGEA
*Hydrangea macrophylla* 'Veitchii'

Hydrangeas are of two main kinds, 'lacecaps' and 'mopheads'. The former, of which *H.m.* 'Veitchii' is one, are the nearer to nature, with each flowerhead having a central zone of tiny, fertile flowers and an outer zone consisting of sterile flowers with large, colourful bracts. Mophead hydrangeas have round heads consisting exclusively of sterile flowers (the proper term is 'florets'). Lacecaps generally look better in a woodland setting, mopheads are more formal, but it is unwise to interpret this too rigidly.

| | |
|---|---|
| type | Deciduous shrub |
| flowers | Outer florets white, inner (fertile) florets blue or pink, depending on soil |
| foliage | Dark green |
| height | 1.5m (5ft) after 10 years |
| spread | 1.8m (6ft) after 10 years |
| hardiness | Young growths are vulnerable to severe frost |
| position | Part shade but open |
| soil | Any good, organic soil, the leafier the better. On acid, 'bluing' soils, in which free aluminium ions are present, blue hydrangeas will be blue; on alkaline soils they will be pink or purplish pink, depending on the degree of alkalinity and/or the availability to the plant of free aluminium. Iron is not the critical mineral |
| pruning | Deadhead in early spring, not before. Remove old branches at ground level in early spring to encourage new ones to arise from the base |
| propagation | By semi-ripe cuttings in summer (see p.90) |
| alternatives | 'Blue Wave' (blue), 'White Wave' (white, blue fertile florets), 'Mariesii' (pink in all soils) |

## BLUE HYDRANGEAS

**LACECAPS**
*H. macrophylla* **'Blaumeise'**
*H.m.* **'Blue Wave'**
*H. serrata* **'Blue Bird'**

**MOPHEADS**
*H. macrophylla* **'Altona'**
*H.m.* **'Générale Vicomtesse de Vibraye'**
*H.m.* **'Holstein'**
*H.m.* **'Maréchal Foch'**
*H.* **'Ayesha'**

# *practical* project

### MAKING AND

### PLANTING A

### ROCK GARDEN

*FIRM WITH YOUR FINGERS*
*If your compost is properly made,*
*you will be able to use stiff*
*fingers for ramming it between*
*and around the rocks. Do not use*
*a stick or any other rammer; you*
*will only overdo it and pack the*
*soil too hard. You cannot use a*
*rammer for planting in crevices –*
*in the final analysis it is the*
*strength and sensitivity of your*
*fingers that ensure the safety of*
*the plants.*

*ROCK SOLID*
*Firmly set rocks will not have air*
*pockets under them where mice,*
*woodlice and other pests can*
*hide. They also act as invaluable*
*stepping stones.*

*A GRAVEL MULCH*
*After final planting, cover the soil*
*in the pockets with 3cm (1½in) of*
*small gravel. This will prevent*
*soil splashing on the plants,*
*reduce evaporation, discourage*
*slugs, and keep weeds to a*
*minimum and your boots clean.*

Most specialist alpine gardeners started with a rock garden and became addicted to the world of jewel-like plants that opened up to them. There is nothing quite like alpine plants for arousing depth of interest and affection and for providing a widely varied flow of flower colour throughout most of the year, but their setting needs to be as sympathetic as possible.

This a good month during which to start to build a rock garden. It is not a process that should be rushed, and you may well plan to let it carry on into next month. That is no bad thing, as it will need some time to settle before it is ready for planting when the hot, dry weather is over. Meanwhile, you will not be trying to work with wet soil.

## CHOICE AND PREPARATION OF THE SITE

A rock garden should be sited in full sun. Its contours and rock outcrops will create enough shady or partly shady nooks. The position should be well drained, and the rock garden should, when finished, blend in with the rest of the garden and relate to other features.

■ Take your hose, rope, or pile of pots as you would for determining the shape of a pond (see p.62) and 'draw' the shape of the rock garden on the site. Do not be too meticulous, as it is certain to change as you build.

■ Dig the site over thoroughly, loosening the soil and removing every last trace of perennial weed roots.

■ Add to the soil liberal quantities of a mixture of moss peat (or substitute), sand and coarse grit in equal quantities and mix thoroughly. As a rough guide, there should be twice as much of the mixture as there is soil. The result will be an organic, very gritty compost which should crunch in the hand as if loaded with sugar. You will now have a large mound where previously there was even ground.

## CHOICE OF ROCK

You must be prepared to spend good money on rock. It is advisable to buy it by volume, not weight, and to avoid like the plague anything called 'rockery stone'. Purchase any kind of sandstone, limestone, millstone gritstone, and any of the well-respected stones. In Britain these include Cotswold, Yorkshire, and so on. If you are elsewhere, I am sure you will easily translate the advice into terms that apply loc-

ally. Dense granites are difficult to work with, but can be used effectively. Limestone pavement must *never* be bought by anyone, no matter how attractive it looks. It constitutes a precious, natural ecological environment that must be preserved at all costs.

## BUILDING THE ROCK GARDEN

Build from the bottom upwards. Before you even start, take time to go to a range of mountainous hills to see how rock lies in nature. You will find that it runs in strata (layers) that are usually somewhere near the horizontal, and that the strata are fissured more or less vertically. A rock outcrop is thus a mass of crevices. It is in the crevices that the choicest plants will grow, and your rock garden building will emphasise the creation of crevices and also of pockets for the plants that prefer to grow on reasonably flat soil.

■ The lowest stratum of rocks is laid so that each one slopes backwards and down into the soil mound.

■ Ram the compost hard beneath and round the first rock so that you can stand on it without its rocking.

■ Butt the next rock up against it with a fillet of compost between them in the manner of mortar.

■ Ram more compost into the crevice between them and, once again, under and behind the second rock.

■ Carry on like this until there is a stratum of rock following the outline you originally made – or as near to it as you wish to come.

■ The rocks of the second stratum should slope in the same way – it prevents run-off and channels the rain back into the soil. This layer can wander away from the line of the first, creating pockets as it does so, but in places can be almost vertically above the first. It can disappear here and there, too, to look as if it emerges from below. In fact, the first stratum can do this too. Some of the best rock gardens look as if they were outcrops of rock that were there long before the gardens that surround them.

■ Carry on adding rock strata, but do not fall into the error, by making the rock garden too high, of creating an artificial-looking lump.

Bear in mind at all times that it is a natural appearance that, above all, you are endeavouring to create.

The process of building, if done properly so that the rocks are solidly laid, will considerably reduce the original height of your mound of compost.

## PLANTING

The key to a really successful rock garden is to plant as you build. This does not mean that you do the greater part of the planting while building the rock garden, but that you set crevice plants in their homes as you make the crevices. You can safely do this in high summer, as the rocks themselves will help to prevent the plants drying out.

You need first to appreciate that plants of all kinds are far tougher than you think, and that this applies especially to alpines.

Take a crevice-loving plant, such as a silver saxifrage, water it, and remove it from its pot.

■ Where you have a rock ready for the next one to be placed beside it, put the plant with its roots next to the side of the first rock and its neck level with the front face.

■ Now butt the next rock hard up against the plant. The root ball will squash – and should.

■ Ram compost into the crevice so that the plant is thoroughly fixed in place.

A similar procedure is used for horizontal crevices. It is almost impossible to plant pot-grown alpines into crevices once building is over, although small seedlings and rooted cuttings can be winkled into place with some trouble. Water in the plants you have found homes for and then wait until cooler, damper weather arives before planting the pockets.

### SOME CREVICE-LOVING PLANTS

*Androsace sarmentosa*
*Armeria caespitosa*
*Aubrieta* **vars**
*Campanula cochlearifolia*
*Draba aizoides*
*Haberlea* **spp**
*Lewisia* **spp and vars**
*Moltkia petraea*
*Phlox douglasii* **vars**
*Phyteuma comosum*
*Potentilla nitida*
*Ramonda* **spp**
*Saxifraga* **spp and vars**
*Teucrium subspinosum*
*Vitaliana primuliflora*

**Side view**

**Front view**

**Established rock garden**

# plant
# *selections*

## SHRUBS

After the brief break in shrub flowering, which careful choice can easily disguise, shrubs burst back into activity this month.

Midsummer sees **hydrangeas** in full flower, although their real peak comes next month in colder areas. These magnificent shrubs come in many guises – species of many kinds as well as the better known 'lacecap' and 'mophead' hybrids. In larger gardens the enormous *H. aspera* subsp. *sargentiana* will find room to expand its 30cm (1ft) long, velvety leaves and attain its full height of well over 3m (10ft), but most of us have the space to enjoy one or two hybrid hydrangeas where we can give them a little shade and a leafy or peaty soil.

The blue foliage of a eucalyptus, of which about twenty species are now proving hardy in quite severe winter weather, provides just the right amount of shade, and its leaf colour is enhanced by blue hydrangea flowers (of whatever shape) below. I have grown *Hypericum* 'Hidcote' and the larger-flowered, less hardy 'Rowallane' among blue hydrangeas but disliked the effect, and greatly prefer it with pink ones such as the lacecap 'Mariesii'. One of the more gentle bamboos as far as invasiveness goes (some are absolute thugs) makes in its turn a perfect backdrop for the hydrangea. Try the one we have always known as *Arundinaria murielae* but must now apparently call *Thamnocalamus spathaceus*.

**Lavateras** are another group of shrubs that get under way this month and, like the hydrangeas, keep going well into autumn. *Lavatera olbia* is the ubiquitous one that you see as a large blob of purplish rose, usually in a corner of the garden and far too often clashing discordantly with red brick.

It can be kept in bounds by cutting it well back after flowering or in spring, as it is a subshrub, making all its soft top-growth in the current season. Many gardeners are thoroughly bored with it, but that is because its talents are too often allowed to be subordinate to its manners. If it is restrained by pruning and made to co-operate rather than lead a selfish existence, it can prove to be a component of beautiful combinations with grey foliage, such as that of sea hollies, cardoons or Scotch thistles.

*Lavatera* 'Barnsley' has been subjected to the most ill-informed debate among gardeners, who have either insisted on its origins in the town of Barnsley in Yorkshire or at Barnsley House, home of the renowned plantswoman, Rosemary Verey, in Gloucestershire. The latter was where it truly originated, and its subtle colouring, with the faintish blush of rose pink strengthening towards the centre of the flower and not a hint of purpling, is what one might expect from the garden of one who is well known for deploying soft colours well. It has rocketed to almost universal popularity in a remarkably short time but is unlikely to induce ennui, unlike its somewhat misrepresented cousin.

**Roses** continue to bloom during the high days of summer, and attention has to be given to removing the dead heads of flowers if their beauty is to persist and they are not to become tired-looking. Surely there can be no task more enjoyable than this? To stand among the scents and colours of roses on a summer's day calls for an excuse if one is not to feel assailed by conscience, and a gentle wielding of secateurs is not too taxing.

**Buddleias** and butterflies are inseparable. No matter in what country they find themselves able to grow, they will exert irresistible magnetism on a diadem of butterflies. That they are collectively called 'butterfly bushes' is no surprise, but beware! The darker the flower the more sought after it often is, and the less it attracts butterflies and moths. Many a gardener has been bitterly disappointed in seeing flowers on their *B. davidii* 'Black Knight' only to wait in vain for its jewelled accompaniment.

The finest of all the brooms flowers this month. *Cytisus battandieri*, the Moroccan or pineapple broom, is one of the very best of all silver-leaved shrubs, bearing its silver-plated leaves glossily through the year in mild places and from spring to autumn elsewhere. It is quite hardy, despite its origin, and when in full flower, draped with large, conical heads of tightly-packed pea-flowers in a clean, bright yellow, it is one of the most beautiful sights given to gardeners. On top of that, its unique scent, strongly redolent of pineapples (and therefore not so unique?) is simply delicious.

●

## HERBACEOUS PERENNIALS

At last the border takes on its full glory and there are flowers everywhere. **Phloxes** in many shades; purple, red and mauve **salvias; crocosmias** brilliant in orange, red and yellow; there is richness everywhere. The yellow **daisies** of summer – helianthus, heleniums and heliopsis – make delightful contrasts with dark purple **monardas** or even, if you are brave, the carpeting *Potentilla* 'Gibson's Scarlet'.

There is not much blue, mauve or purple in the high summer border; it is time for brightness. But of course you do not have to be brash. *Sidalcea* 'Rose Queen', softly pink

*ROSA MUNDI*

and almost retiring, may be more to your taste than the vivid vermilion of *Lychnis chalcedonica*, but if you have planned well and paid attention to tonal order, you may well be able to encompass both within your palette and your harmony.

●

## ALPINES

On the rock garden, or planted as ground cover for roses, provided that your soil is acid, the rock plant that has headed the popularity poll for decades covers its dark green self with flowers of pure Oxford blue. *Lithodora diffusa* (we knew it as *Lithospermum diffusum*) is not difficult to grow if given a moisture-retentive soil and sun, but is by no means easy to propagate. Cuttings taken precisely during the last week of this month and the first of next *may* all root – or they may not at all.

●

## CLIMBERS

**Clematis** continue to garland the garden in swags of exotic colour. If you have a warm wall you can persuade **passion flowers** to wheel their strange blooms into the light of a summer less powerful than that of their homeland. **Honeysuckles** persist, not only in blooming but in strangling everything within reach. The garden is wonderful in midsummer, but watchful gardening is as essential as ever.

# plants

## IN

## *flower*

**KEY**

\* = evergreen      spp = species
vars = varieties

**NOTES**

*Erica* varieties require lime-free soil.

**ROCK GARDEN**

*\*Acantholimon* spp
*Campanula* spp
*Cyclamen europaeum*
*\*Dianthus* spp and vars
*Epilobium* spp
*Gentiana septemfida*
*\*Geranium* spp
*\*Globularia* spp
*\*Gypsophila cerastioides*
*\*Helichrysum milfordiae*
*Hypericum* spp
*\*Lithodora diffusa*
*\*Moltkia* spp
*Oenothera caespitosa*
*\*Onosma* spp
*\*Penstemon* spp
*Platycodon grandiflorum*
*Prunella* spp
*Pterocephalus* spp
*Rhodohypoxis* vars (mid-spring
to early autumn)
*\*Santolina chamaecyparissus* 'Nana'
*Scabiosa* spp
*Scutellaria alpina*
*\*Sempervivum* spp

| TREES | colour | flower type |
|---|---|---|
| **Aesculus indica** (Indian horse chestnut) | Pink | Erect spires |
| **Catalpa bignonioides** (Indian bean tree) | White, yellow and purple markings | Like large foxgloves |
| **Koelreuteria paniculata** (Golden rain tree) | Yellow | Large panicles |
| **SHRUBS** | | |
| **Buddleia davidii** vars | Various | Long, conical spires |
| **Cytisus battandieri** | Yellow | Pea shaped, in large heads, pineapple scented |
| **\*Erica ciliaris, E. cinerea, E. tetralix, E. vagans** (Summer heathers) | Various | Bell shaped |
| **\*Eucryphia** spp | White | Saucer shaped |
| **Fuchsia** hardy types | Various | Typically fuchsia, small in species |
| **\*Hebe** many spp and vars | Various | Spikes of 'veronicas' |
| **Hydrangea** – many vars | Various | Mopheads or lacecaps |
| **\*Hypericum** 'Hidcote' | Yellow | Large, saucer shaped |
| **\*Lavandula** vars (Lavender) | Lavender, pink or white | |
| **Phygelius** spp and vars | Red, pink, yellow or cream | Long, tubular |
| **Romneya coulteri** | White | Large, poppy-like |
| **Yucca filamentosa** | Ivory | Tall columns of large bells |
| **CLIMBERS** | | |
| **Clematis** many vars | Various | |
| **Eccremocarpus scaber** | Orange or red | Tubular |
| **Passiflora caerulea** (Passion flower) | Blue-and-white | Unique |
| **Schizophragma hydrangeoides** | White | Hydrangea-like |
| **\*Trachelospermum jasminoides** | White | Large, jasmine-like, scented |
| **PERENNIALS** | colour | height |
| **Acanthus** spp | Mauve or purple-and-white | 1.2m (48in) |
| **Aconitum** spp and vars | Blue | 1.2m (48in) |
| **Agapanthus** vars | Blue or white | 90cm–1.2m (36–48in) |
| **Aruncus dioicus** | White | 1.8m (72in) |
| **Asphodeline luteus** | Sulphur yellow, fragrant | 90cm (36in) |
| **Coreopsis** spp and vars | Yellow | 60cm (24in) |

| | | |
|---|---|---|
| **Crambe cordifolia** | White | 1.8m (72in) |
| **Crocosmia** vars | Yellow, orange or red | 90cm–1.2m (36–48in) |
| **Echinacea** vars | Various | 60cm (24in) |
| **Echinops ritro** | Blue | 1.2m (48in) |
| **Eryngium** spp and vars | Mainly blue | 60–90cm (24–36in) |
| **Geranium 'Johnson's Blue'** | Blue | 30cm (12in) |
| **Gypsophila** vars | White or pink | 45cm (18in) |
| **Helenium** spp and vars | Yellow or russet | 90cm–1.5m (36–60in) |
| **Helianthus** spp and vars | Yellow | 90cm–2m (36–80in) |
| **Heliopsis** vars | Yellow | 1.2–1.5m (48–60in) |
| **Hosta** spp and vars | White, lilac or purple | 45–60cm (18–24in) on average |
| **Iris sibirica** vars | Blue or white | 90cm (36in) |
| **Kniphofia** vars | Yellow, orange or red | 1.2m (48in) on average |
| **Libertia formosa** | White | 65cm (26in) |
| **Ligularia** spp and vars | Yellow or orange | 1.2–1.8m (48–72in) |
| **Lychnis chalcedonica** | Vermilion | 1m (40in) |
| **Lysimachia** spp | Red-purple or yellow | 90cm (36in) |
| **Lythrum** vars | Red or purple | 1.2m (48in) |
| **Monarda** vars | Mauve, red, pink or purple | 90cm (36in) |
| **Nepeta mussinii** | Lavender-blue | 45cm (18in) |
| **Oenothera** spp (Evening primrose) | Yellow or white | 45–90cm (18–36in) |
| **Phlox paniculata** vars | Various | 90cm–1.2m (36–48in) |
| **Physostegia** vars | Various | 90cm (36in) |
| **Potentilla** vars | Scarlet, yellow or pink | 45cm (18in) or less |
| **Rheum palmatum** vars | White or red | 1.8m (72in) |
| **Scabiosa caucasica** | Blue or white | 60cm (24in) |
| **Solidago** vars | Yellow | 90cm (36in) |
| **Thalictrum** spp | Lilac or purple | 90cm–1.2m (36–48in) |

## BULBS

| | | |
|---|---|---|
| **Crinum × powellii** | Pink | 60–90cm (24–36in) |
| **Cyclamen purpurascens** | Carmine, sweetly scented | 10cm (4in) |
| **Gladiolus nanus** | Various | 45–60cm (18–24in) |
| large-flowered hybrids | Various | 90cm–1.2m (36–48in) |
| **Lilium** vars | Various, scented | Various |

## TONAL ORDER

The hot colours of high summer can be hard to place if you have no rules to go by. It is all too easy, on a soggy, cold, late-autumn day, when you have run out of options for planting and can wait no longer, to throw up your hands in frustration and just plant sharp reds, shrill yellows and thermal orange wherever you happen to have a few spaces left.

So much the better for your having made a plan – make it and stick to it and you will find foresight once again to have been your greatest ally. As far as rules go, the most reliable is the one governing tonal order. It is worth repeating: put light tones of light colours with dark tones of dark ones.

Of course, it all depends on where you stand. Take, for example, a red-hot crocosmia like 'Lucifer'. If you look at it as a light tone of a light colour, then a dark tone of a darker colour has to be *really* dark; and so it turns out. Set 'Lucifer' alongside a dark purple-blue salvia such as *S. nemorosa* 'Superba' or *S.* 'Lye End', and you will have a dramatic, perhaps an opulent combination, but a harmonious one. A light tone in the purple range, such as mauve, sets up a fairly dreadful clash with the scarlet of the crocosmia. Now, on the other hand, consider the red of 'Lucifer' as itself a medium tone of red. You must, if you are going to employ a higher (lighter) colour, choose a very light tone. A pale, creamy yellow, such as is found in *Sisyrinchium striatum*, or light sulphur, as in *Verbascum* 'Gainsborough' are just about right. You can, of course, choose as a companion for a strong colour such as this a lighter tone of itself, or perhaps what is strictly called a tint – in which it is mixed with white – in other words, in this case, a pure pink based on the scarlet side of red and with no trace of blue or orange in it. Some of the best pink phloxes, such as 'Balmoral' or 'Sandringham' are good companions for these brilliant scarlet reds.

## COLOUR TO SPARE

The midsummer garden should be bursting at the seams with colour. Most of it will come from perennials, but the hardy and half-hardy annuals will by now be playing their full parts. Try busy lizzies in low tubs by the door or the French windows (I shall for ever protest at 'patio doors'), as well as in places where spring bulbs or biennials have been removed.

# AUGUST

August creates as she slumbers,
replete and satisfied.

JOSEPH WOOD KRUTCH

*Whereas last month summer reached its fulfilment, now is a time
of transition. To begin with, colour and form seem held in a stasis
of time, and little changes. Colours are true and sometimes fierce:
reds flame purely, blues glow coolly, and green is as green can be.
Then, towards the month's end, a weariness can be seen to have
crept in. There is a hint of russet in the reds, a bleaching of
yellows, and blues show their age by a muddying of purple.
Among the greens, the keynotes of the garden since the spring
began, the golden buff of straw heralds the onset of autumn.
How you react to these changes depends on your personality, your
mood, and your view of the horticultural year. A pessimist, or
one who sees the year linearly, can hardly bear to part with
summer's glory. Someone for whom the year is an expression of
circular time, however, will find himself able to look forward to
autumn cyclamen, fall foliage colour, and even beyond, to
snowdrops in the spring.
Isolated thus from the bustling past and the running down of the
year that is to come, this month has much to offer in the well-
planned garden. To those who think in seasons, rather than
months, it is too easily lost between 'summer' and 'autumn' and
allowed no character of its own. Yet it can be the most individual
of months, redolent of all the quiet satisfaction that goes with an
unaccustomed afternoon nap taken while on holiday.
There are many plants which are now at their flowering peak, but
many more that have carried on from earlier in the summer or
even, in some cases, from late spring. They all join together in a
last glorious crescendo of richness and colour before the quiet
melody of autumn gently takes over.*

# tasks
## FOR THE
## *month*
## 1

### CHECKLIST

- Keep the lawn neatly edged
- Make provision for watering if you are away from home
- Feed perpetual-flowering roses in order to keep the display up to standard for the rest of the season
- Pinch out the shoot tips on all fuchsias except species in order to promote further flowering stems
- Water biennials growing in nursery beds
- If you are a dahlia or chrysanthemum fancier, disbud to produce exhibition blooms. Otherwise don't bother
- Nip off seedpods of sweet peas
- Order and plant autumn-flowering bulbs as soon as possible if you have not done so already
- Dig up and burn any dahlias with stunted or mottled foliage, which probably indicates a virus infection
- Cut back gladioli after flowering, but leave at least five leaves on each plant to feed the corm

## MAINTENANCE

### LAWN CARE

With the borders in such magnificent fettle, it is shabby, to say the least, to leave the lawn untended to the extent of neglecting the edges. During the summer they are bound to have become broken down in places where careless feet have slipped, and you are almost certain to find that there are grasses growing out of the soil-face below the grass edge.

■ Put aside your edging tool, take to your hands and knees, and weed this area; do not just cut it. When you have done that, take the edger and trim up in the usual way.

■ To repair a broken-down lawn edge, cut a piece out of the lawn to include the spoiled edge. The size of the piece will depend on how bad the damage is, but will usually be about 30cm (12in) square.

■ Lift it with a spade or turfing iron so that the sod is level across the bottom.

■ Turn it round through 90° so that the clean-cut edge fits level with the rest of the lawn edge.

■ Firm the sod and then fill in the hole with sandy, peaty compost, the top 1cm (½in) of which should contain lawn-grass seed.

■ Firm and water, and top up again with compost if necessary.

*POND CARE*
*Remove any blanket weed from the pond by twisting it round a twiggy stick. Then resolve to plant more oxygenating plants and water-lilies next spring.*

## NOTE

▪ *It is in high summer that you become conscious of worn patches on the lawn. Do not let them become worse. Fence them off with string, instruct the family to keep off, aerate the patch, fork over the top couple of inches, smooth, sow lawn seed, and water. Leave it until later and the seed will not germinate. Put up a little sign saying 'GUR'. When you tell non-golfers it means 'ground under repair' they will be most impressed with your efficiency* ▪

### WATERING

If you go on holiday, or just take a trip for a few days, here are some hints for taking care of the watering needs of your plants:

▪ For tubs and urns, lay a flat stone or slate on the soil. Take a coffee tin and pierce the bottom with the finest point you can find – a strong needle, held in pliers, will do

the best job. Fill the tin with water, put the lid on, and stand it on the stone. The seepage of water will be very slight but enough to prevent drying out, as it will not evaporate from beneath the stone.

You can make versions of exactly the same idea anywhere in the garden or greenhouse where there are special plants or newly planted ones. The point is that it is much kinder to ask a neighbour to fill the tins than to hand them the responsibility for your best plants.

▪ There are ultra-fine trickle hoses on the market (sometimes called seep hoses) that operate from reservoirs – usually large, clear plastic containers – and can be wall-mounted. The higher you mount the reservoir, the faster the seep rate, and vice versa. You can ask the neighbours to fill this up, too.

▪ To ensure peace of mind about a whole border, water it thoroughly before you go and mulch with composted forest bark. Even if there is then a drought, you would have to be away much longer than the average annual vacation to return to trouble.

## PLANTING

### BULBS

Bulb specialists will be despatching a number of varieties late this month ready for immediate planting.

▪ There is much confusion about the name 'autumn crocus'. Colchicums are often referred to as autumn crocuses, but they are not crocuses at all. The term should really be reserved for those *Crocus* species that flower in autumn.

▪ Plant autumn crocus in any good garden soil, including the most calcareous ones, and choose species and varieties that will flower from next month until early winter.

▪ Colchicums appear late next month and during the one after. They like a rich soil and are excellent among shrubs.

▪ Madonna lilies should be planted only just below the surface in a well-drained soil, preferably but not necessarily limy, in full sun.

▪ Rhodohypoxis are tiny bulbs whose curious little flowers are only about 5cm (2in) high. They need lime-free soil and are ideal in tubs and other containers where they can be covered in winter to keep off excess rain and frost. They are winter-dormant.

▪ *Scilla autumnalis* flowers next month. *S. peruviana* blooms in early summer, but has to be lifted and transplanted now.

▪ Sternbergias, 10–12cm (4–5in) in height, flower in two months' time and bear starry yellow blooms.

**BULBS TO PLANT**

*Colchicum* (Autumn crocus)
*Lilium candidum* (Madonna lily)
*Rhodohypoxis*
*Scilla autumnalis* and *S. peruviana*
*Sternbergia*

# plants
## OF THE
## *month*
## 1

### ARUM LILY
*Zantedeschia aethiopica*

The white 'arum lilies' so beloved of florists are first-class plants for moist areas of the garden. The variety 'Crowborough' is hardier than the type.

| | |
|---|---|
| type | Herbaceous perennial |
| flowers | White, like large lords-and-ladies, borne from early summer to early autumn |
| foliage | Leaves bold, shaped like spearheads |
| height | 90cm–1.2m (3–4ft) |
| spread | 60–70cm (24–28in) |
| hardiness | 'Crowborough' is hardy away from really cold areas once it is established |
| planting | Best planted in spring |
| position and soil | Ideally, this plant should have its crown at soil level in a really wet, muddy spot, or can even be covered by one or two inches of water. Where possible it should be thickly mulched in winter. 'Crowborough' will grow in a good, rich border soil as well as in a wet place |
| propagation | By division in spring or from seed |
| alternatives | None |

### CALIFORNIAN POPPY
*Eschscholzia caespitosa*

Californian poppies are unrivalled among summer flowers for brilliance of colour and length of flowering. From early summer to mid-autumn they provide a blaze of orange, yellow, red and pink. Their open-cup-shaped, poppy-like blooms are silky in texture and sit daintily over the finely cut foliage.

| | |
|---|---|
| type | Hardy annuals. In mild areas they will behave as semi-evergreen perennials |
| flowers | Silky poppies, usually self-coloured and single, sometimes semi-double, and in at least one strain bicoloured in scarlet and yellow |
| foliage | Light, greyish green, finely divided |
| height | 25cm (10in) |
| spread | 15cm (6in) |
| planting | Sow where the plants are to grow. In areas where they are perennial, cut the plants back in spring to encourage new growth but take care, as the stems are brittle |

| | |
|---|---|
| position | Full sun |
| soil | Any good garden soil |
| propagation | From seed |
| varieties | There are several seed strains, either of mixed or self colours. The classical eschscholzias (pronounced esh-olt-sias) are of a startlingly pure orange |

### COSMOS
*Cosmos atrosanguineus*

There is no other plant like this rather tender perennial. Apart from its highly unusual colour, its scent, quite astonishingly like that of dark chocolate, puts it in a class of its own. It is one of the few Mexican plants that grows happily in cool-temperate gardens, and it shares the appearance of its flowers with those other Mexican natives, the dahlias.

| | |
|---|---|
| type | Herbaceous perennial |
| flowers | Deep maroon, like small, single dahlias, produced until autumn |
| foliage | Leaves pinnate, with 5–7 leaflets |
| height | 45–60cm (1½–2ft) but sprawling |
| spread | 60cm (2ft) |
| hardiness | Hardy in mild areas. Elsewhere it should be lifted for the winter and the tuber stored until spring |
| planting | Plant in spring with the tuber 15cm (6in) deep. Do not expect growth to start until spring is almost over. In mild areas where it can be left in the ground over winter, protect with a mulch |
| position | Full sun |
| soil | Moisture retentive |
| propagation | By division of the tubers or from seed |

### FUCHSIA
*Fuchsia* hardy varieties

Taking all gardeners together, you would probably find that fuchsias were the most popular plants of all. However, it is the tender ones that attract the most attention, even though there is a rapidly increasing range of 'hardy' varieties that will grow happily out of doors. Hardiness in fuchsias is a matter of degree, and in general even these are best lifted for the winter in cold areas, but where the climate is mild, maritime, or both, they can be left outside. They may be cut to the ground in winter but will usually shoot again in spring.

*Zantedeschia aethiopica*

*FUCHSIA MAGELLANICA*

| | |
|---|---|
| **type** | Semi-evergreen to deciduous sub-shrubs |
| **flowers** | Various, typically fuchsia. The point of growing them out of doors is to exploit their very long flowering season |
| **foliage** | Lightish, rich green, leaves small |
| **height and spread** | Varies according to variety and climate |
| **hardiness** | Hardy species fuchsias are hardy within 8km (5 miles) of a mild coast and become progressively less so further away. 'Hardy' varieties follow much the same pattern, but vary greatly in their ability to stand up to the winter |

| | |
|---|---|
| **planting** | Plant in mid- to late spring |
| **position** | Cool but sunny. Fuchsias do not appreciate excessive heat. They will grow and flower in part shade but are much less hardy than when in sun |
| **soil** | Any good garden soil |
| **pruning** | Usually unnecessary when grown outside; frost will do the pruning for you. If you overwinter the plants indoors, cut them back, but not too hard, before planting |
| **propagation** | Soft cuttings taken from new spring growths will root readily |
| **varieties** | Many |

# tasks
## FOR THE
## *month*
## 2

## CHECKLIST

- [ ] Collect ripe seed
- [ ] Sow any seed which must be fresh in order to germinate
- [ ] Cut back violas and pansies so that cuttings shoots will be made next month
- [ ] Make notes of all necessary changes to your beds and borders
- [ ] Keep up your garden visiting

## PROPAGATION

### COLLECTING SEED

One of the main advantages of collecting your own seed is that you can sow some of it right away and you are not at the mercy of the despatch systems of the seed houses who, although highly responsible and very much in the business of providing you with seed that will germinate readily, are not in a position to do anything about the habit seeds have of going dormant if they are stored for long.

On the other hand, many annuals refuse to germinate at all unless they have gone through a period of dry storage. You may think this odd, as there are no warehouses in nature, but plants from places whose climates are dry out of the growing season are adapted to 'knowing' that the dry period has happened.

In order, therefore, to hedge your bets, you can take half of each batch of seed and sow it as soon as harvested, keeping the other half for sowing in spring if the autumn seed should fail. This you can do with the amount of seed you can collect yourself; the portions in commercial packets are often – but not always – too small for such treatment.

### Species and varieties

There are certain seeds that you should not harvest. Among them are all those from named varieties – with certain exceptions. The exceptions are seed strains that come 'true'. The word 'variety' is an unsatisfactory one, but then so is 'cultivar'. This word is supposed to mean the sorts of varieties that have to be propagated by cuttings, division and so on, as they will not come 'true' from seed, but the botanists have made a mess of its definition, which is why I am using 'variety' with slightly different meanings according to context.

Sweet peas are often described as varieties, whereas they are really seed strains that come true from seed. You can harvest their seed and sow it with reasonable expectations of getting the same flower colours as the parents. However, if you have a nice, hot summer and a camellia variety sets seed, it will not come true. If it has large, formal double, white flowers for example, the chances are that many of the seedlings would have very small, single, red ones and the rest would be poor when compared with the parent.

Sow seed of a species, however – a plant with a Latin name and no fancy suffix – and it will come true, although in every species in earth there are small differences between individuals. Thus you get what are termed good 'forms' of species, and they can only be propagated by vegetative means (cuttings, division and so on).

### Collecting the seed

Keep an eye open for seed that is almost ready to disperse: you cannot collect it once it has scattered. As with everything else that has to do with being a good gardener, foresight must be employed.

The mechanisms whereby plants disperse their seeds are almost infinite in their variety and wonderful in their ingenuity. To collect seed you must get to know them and be ahead of the game. Violas, for example, split their little, round pods into five-pointed stars. You cannot harvest the seed until this happens, as it will not be ripe, but once the pods have split the slightest touch can see the seeds pinged as far as 2m (7ft) or more. You have to get there just at the right moment.

Geraniums (cranesbills, not the pelargoniums) have a spring-release mechanism that sends their seeds anything up to 7m (24ft). Some euphorbias have pods that stay the same for weeks and then, one hot day, they start to explode without warning.

Seed collection demands plenty of paper bags, labels, patience, craftiness and system.

■ Always collect seed on a dry, warm day as it will not store if at all damp, but remember that the plant tries to scatter its seeds on just such days.

■ To collect fine seed, cut off the entire flowerhead and shake it into a paper bag. A small pinch of seed can contain enough to cover your entire garden with plants, so do not bother collecting too much.

■ With explosive seed capsules, choose a hot day, cut off the entire flowerhead and put it into a paper bag with the neck tied firmly. Put it in a hot place and wait. If the seed is perfectly ripe, it will soon start to jump about as the capsules go off inside.

■ All seed should should be thoroughly cleaned of all debris before storage. Take no notice of people who tell you to lay in a range of sieves – seed is too diverse in its sizes for that to work. Use your hands, sheets of paper, and whatever you do, don't sneeze.

■ Store seed in paper bags or small cardboard boxes, but never in tins. The storage place should be dark and above all cool, even cold, although free from frost. Seed life is badly shortened by warmth and destroyed by damp.

Collecting

Cleaning

Storing

## PLANNING

### TWO-PART PLAN

The most important planning you can do this month is in two parts:

■ Go over all your beds and borders, notebook in hand, and write down everything you want to change. This is the time of year when the most flowers are out, and you can also see the gaps created where you have been too enthusiastic with your spring flowers.

■ Go and visit gardens, notebook in hand, and learn where you went wrong,

what you did right, and what you are going to do next.

If you have taken over a new garden (or one that is new to you) and there are no beds or borders yet, plan them now if you have not done so already. The best time of year for acquiring and planting herbaceous perennials is autumn, but the plants are not in flower then, therefore you should draw up your design now, while you have the plants to refer to. Precise colour lives better in your memory than on the page of a book or catalogue, and the intangible qualities of plants – poise, presence, elegance and so on – are better seen at first hand than read about.

*EXPLOSIVE SEEDHEADS*
*Any explosive seedhead already firing seeds may be grasped firmly in the whole hand and thrust into a paper bag. You will trap enough for your needs, even if some gets away.*

*CLEANING SMALL SEED*
*When cleaning small seed, do not try to blow the debris away. The blast needed to remove bits of capsule will see your seed gone for ever as well.*

# plants
## OF THE
## *month*
## 2

## AGAPANTHUS
### *Agapanthus* hybrids

*Agapanthus* is the generic name for the plants known as 'blue African lilies'. They lend a distinct air of the exotic to the garden, and anyone who has seen agapanthus growing by the roadside in the Aberdare Mountains of Kenya might be surprised to find them thousands of miles into cooler territory. However, they are much hardier than has always been supposed, and some recently raised varieties are very hardy indeed.

| | |
|---|---|
| type | Herbaceous or semi-evergreen perennials |
| flowers | Shades of blue, occasionally white. They are lily-shaped and held in terminal umbels, onion-fashion |
| foliage | Clumps of long, strap-shaped, rich green leaves |
| height | 60cm–1.2m (2–4ft), according to variety |
| spread | 60cm (2ft) |
| hardiness | Variable; most herbaceous kinds are hardy |
| planting | Plant in spring or autumn |
| position | Full sun. They are often mistakenly planted in shade |
| soil | Any good, fertile soil that is not dry. Drainage must be good |
| propagation | From seed except for named varieties, which should be divided in spring |
| varieties | Many, but the 'Headbourne' hybrids are particularly reliable |
| special comment | Do not plant agapanthus near a wall, fence or hedge, even when facing the sun, as they will lean towards the light and their shape will be spoilt. Just a *little* leaning can, on the other hand, be attractive |

## FLAME CREEPER
### *Tropaeolum speciosum*

The flame creeper from Chile is a plant that can infuriate you if you cannot grow it, and enthral you if you can. To succeed, a cool, moist climate is almost essential: this plant does not appreciate heat and dryness. To grow it well is to have achieved one of gardening's greatest delights.

| | |
|---|---|
| type | Herbaceous climbing perennial |
| flowers | Long-stalked, nasturtium-like, brilliant scarlet |
| foliage | Attractive six-lobed leaves on twining stems |
| height | To about 3m (10ft) |
| spread | 90cm (3ft) while in growth (very approximate) |
| planting | Plant in late autumn or mid-spring |
| position | Part shade |
| soil | Lime free, with peat or leaf mould. Add sand to heavy soils |
| propagation | Lift the rootstocks in mid-spring and divide. This operation requires care, as the roots arising from the rhizomes should be damaged as little as possible |

## PHLOX
### *Phlox paniculata* varieties

Border phloxes are among the backbone plants of the late-summer border. As long as the stocks are kept free from eelworm or the nematodes (which means planting young plants raised from root cuttings and not divisions off old plants – never accept a phlox from an unknown source), they will prove to be *the* border plants of this month: tall, cleanly coloured and, even from a considerable distance, richly fragrant.

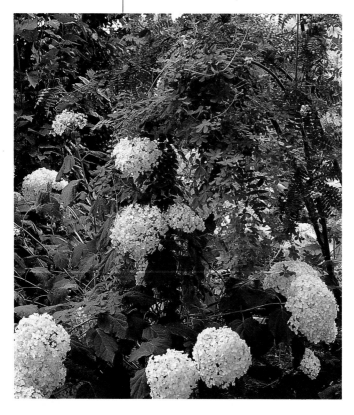

*FLAME CREEPER WITH HYDRANGEA 'MME. MOUILLIERE'*

| | |
|---|---|
| type | Herbaceous perennials |
| flowers | Wide, flat heads in most colours apart from yellow and orange |
| foliage | Two varieties have variegated leaves: 'Norah Leigh' and 'Harlequin' |
| height | 1.2m (4ft) |
| spread | 60cm (2ft) |
| planting | Plant in autumn or spring |
| position | Full sun. Although tall, phloxes require minimal staking |
| soil | Any well-manured border soil |
| propagation | Take root cuttings in midwinter, cutting pencil-thick roots into pieces about 3cm (1¼in) long and laying in a sandy, peaty compost. Wait before potting up until three weeks after the appearance of the shoots. |
| varieties | Many. Some, such as 'Mount Fuji' (which, as a white phlox or just as a phlox, is in a class of its own), are particularly long-flowering and carry on well into next month |

## POTENTILLA

*Potentilla* shrubby hybrids

The shrubby potentillas begin flowering in late spring and early summer and many of them flower right through to the middle of autumn. They are stalwart shrubs, of just the right size for small gardens, and need almost no attention. However, gardeners sometimes plant too many of them, and they are not noted for adding much in the way of excitement to the garden in winter.

| | |
|---|---|
| type | Deciduous shrubs |
| flowers | Like small dog roses; yellow, white, orange, red and pink. Flowers with the last three colours, especially red, fade in sunlight and are best planted in part shade |
| foliage | Small, divided leaves, grey-green to green, more or less downy |
| height | 90cm (3ft) after 10 years (if pruned occasionally) |
| spread | 90cm (3ft) after 10 years (if pruned occasionally) |
| hardiness | Hardy |
| position | Sun for white and yellow species and varieties, otherwise part shade |
| soil | Any garden soil |
| pruning | Cut hard back with shears every four or five years |
| propagation | By semi-ripe cuttings in early |

*POTENTILLA FRUTICOSA 'ELIZABETH'*

| | |
|---|---|
| | autumn. They will root in a garden frame and can be potted up the following spring. 'Red Ace' is subject to Plant Breeders' Rights and may not be propagated for sale without the permission of the licence holder |
| varieties | 'Red Ace' and most orange varieties, such as 'Tangerine' fade badly in the sun. 'Abbotswood' and 'Tilford Cream' are good whites; 'Elizabeth' and 'Katherine Dykes' are among the best yellows. 'Daydawn', which is a peachy colour, does not fade much if planted in a little shade |

# *practical* project

### PRESERVING AND DRYING FLOWERS

**FLOWERS FOR AIR DRYING**

*Achillea*
*Allium*
*Delphinium*
*Echinops*
Everlastings
Heather
*Hydrangea*
Lavender
Love-lies-bleeding
*Salvia*

Foresight is once again the key to one of the more subtle pleasures of gardening. While you are surrounded by the very tangible reality of flowers in summer, it takes quite an effort of imagination to project yourself into winter, when there are few flowers about, and certainly none so stately and regally colourful as those of summer.

To be able to preserve flowers so that they can be enjoyed during the long, dark days is to some extent to enable summer to be prolonged into winter. Dried arrangements last a long time, they do not need any attention, they do not mind changes of temperature, and they go with any decor. Furthermore, if you knock a vase over you will not have sticky water staining the carpet, and if you go away you will find them just the same as when you left them.

There are three principal methods of drying and preserving flowers. With a knowledge of them all, you will be able to make a wide range of arrangements.

## AIR DRYING

With some exceptions, most flowers cannot be air dried as they fall apart, but the method is ideal for grasses, most seedheads and some conifer foliage.

- Collect the material when it is thoroughly dry. The right time for gathering varies considerably, but in the main it is either just as the flowers have started to open or after they have turned brown or otherwise changed colour or texture in late summer or autumn.

- The place you choose for your drying should be dark. A cellar is ideal, or a darkened shed, but there must be good air circulation. It should preferably be cool, but people who live in damper areas find it needs to be warmer, otherwise the air cannot take up the extra moisture.

- Tie the stems in bunches and hang them upside down from the ridge of the shed or garage, or the ceiling of the cellar. For flowers such as love-lies-bleeding or grasses with weeping heads, which would be spoilt by being upside down, stand the stems upright in a preserve jar.

Air drying is unsuitable for preserving anything but the youngest foliage, as older leaves will become wrinkled and brittle and fall away in shreds. Arrangements of dried flowers do look better with some attendant foliage, and if you buy dried and dyed flowers from florists and gift shops your arrangement will certainly need a little foliage to take away the bought-in image. This is best preserved using glycerine.

## PRESERVING WITH GLYCERINE

Glycerine is a highly viscous fluid that plants are capable of taking up into their tissues when it is mixed with water. It is good not only for foliage but also for seedheads and for flower calyces, such as those of bells of Ireland (*Molucella laevis*), which become brittle if air dried. Mature foliage in general, and leathery, tough evergreens are ideal subjects for glycerine preserving.

- The glycerine mixture should be hot. Do not heat the glycerine, but add it to twice its volume of hot water. If it is not thoroughly mixed, the material will fail to absorb it, as it will if the stems are left too long after being cut.

- You will only need a small amount of the mixture – about enough to fill by one-third a standard preserve (jam) jar – but you should check it every day to see if it needs topping up. Place the leaves in this with the stalks immersed. As they absorb the glycerine the texture of the leaves will change, taking on a silky, even oily feeling, and it will become supple. The colour changes: sometimes the foliage immediately turns brown, while in other cases the green darkens towards a more olive shade. Deciduous foliage goes through these sorts of changes in a few days; with evergreen material it may take a month.

- The degree to which green colour is preserved depends on the amount of light. The more light, the less green is preserved, and you can, with a little experience, adjust the light to produce just the effect you require.

- Monitor the material as it takes up the glycerine, paying particular attention to its not absorbing too much. Leave it in too long and you will find that the tissues leak and an oily film forms on the surface which soon attracts moulds.

- Once the outermost tips have changed texture, remove the plant material, wipe it gently to remove all traces of the mixture, and store it in a cardboard box with a few holes in the lid until you want to use it.

You cannot preserve immature foliage by this method, or deciduous leaves whose colours have started to turn in autumn.

## DRYING WITH DESSICANTS

Dessicants are chemical substances with high capacities for absorbing water. The best one for use in drying flowers is silica gel, which consists of crystals very like those of unground sea-salt.

Silica gel can be re-used. When it becomes saturated with moisture, it can be dried in a warm (not hot) oven for half an hour or so. It is a clean material to use, and does not stick to your hands or to the flowers. You cannot preserve many flowers at a time in this way and silica gel is not cheap, so it is a method for specimen blooms in perfect condition.

- Flowers should be cut while open but before insects have had a chance to pollinate them. Pollination marks the end of the function of petals, and they immediately begin to loosen and will drop off in the arrangement if you pick them in this state.

- With some flowers – roses and dahlias especially – the stem develops a weakness just below the bloom. Cut the stem so it is about 2.5cm (1in) long then insert a short length of florist's wire. This will keep the stem straight and support the flower after it is dried.

- Use a biscuit (cookie) tin and pour in just over 1cm (½in) of crystals so that the bottom is evenly covered. Now take a rose, for example, and lay it gently on the crystals so that it is looking up at you. The wire in the stem will maintain the resulting bend in the stem and keep the rose in position. Lay in further roses but do not let them touch one another.

- Now, slowly and carefully, build up the layer of crystals around the roses. They should not be covered with crystals until they are firmly supported all round. You must not bruise the flowers nor distort their shape. Finally, cover with another 1cm (½in) of crystals and close and seal the lid.

- About ten days later, open the lid and gently move away some of the crystals until you can feel a flower. It should have changed to a crisp, papery texture. If it has, remove it very carefully and then deal with the rest.

Flowers preserved in this way can be kept for several weeks when sealed into a box with a handful of crystals in the bottom. They will be saved from distortion if you insert their wires into dry florist's foam.

Deciduous leaves that have changed to their autumn colour will preserve well by the dessicant method. They go beautifully with the generally autumnal palette presented by dried flowers.

### FOR DRYING WITH DESSICANTS

**FLOWERS OF:**
*Ageratum*
*Althaea* (hollyhock)
*Astilbe*
*Camellia*
*Chrysanthemum*
*Dianthus*
*Freesia*
*Japanese anemone*
*Lilium*
*Narcissus*
*Nymphaea* (water-lilies)
*Paeonia*
*Rose*
*Solidaster*
*Syringa* (lilac)
*Tagetes*
*Zinnia*

### FOR DRYING WITH GLYCERINE

**CALYCES OF:**
*Ballota*
*Helleborus*
*Hydrangea*
*Molucella*
*Stachys*

**SEEDHEADS OF:**
*Clematis*
*Pulsatilla*
**Grasses**

**FOLIAGE:**
**both deciduous and evergreen leaves are suitable**

*BEAUTIFUL BERRIES*
*To preserve berries, do not wait until they ripen as they will quickly shrivel. Gather them while still green, and they will ripen on the twig while actually part of an arrangement.*

# plant
*selections*

*Hydrangea aspera is one of the most natural-looking species and grows happily in part shade*

### SHRUBS

*Calluna vulgaris*, the **common heather**, is only 'common' on moorland in western Europe, a sliver or two of North Africa, and Iceland. It arrived in Nova Scotia as seeds on the heather used by settlers as packing for their belongings, and has spread to gardens everywhere in the temperate world.

It is one of the glories of late summer and continues to make a magnificent contribution all the way through to late autumn, when the last few varieties flower. When varieties are selected with foliage ranging through many shades of green, grey-green, grey, silver, gold and russet, heather can play a year-round part in the garden with which very little else can compete.

**Clematis** of the kind that need to be cut back every early spring to within 30cm (1ft) of the ground look wonderful when growing over the heathers, but need to be chosen with care lest their colours, manifest at the same time of year, should clash. Clear red (such as the texensis clematis 'Gravetye Beauty') or a fairly pure blue ('Elsa Späth') will enhance, rather than quarrel with the heather flowers.

Possibly because of a loss of the identity of this month in the general concept of 'summer', some of its own particular treasures are all too often overlooked and can even acquire unjustified reputations for difficulty, merely because they are seldom seen. **Eucryphias** are a case in point – superb evergreen shrubs with crops of white flowers of a ravishing purity set against deep, almost black-green leaves.

They are thought of as being on the tender side, yet most are anything but. I have seen *Eucryphia* 'Nymansay' flourishing and flowering beautifully in some of the coldest parts of Britain, as well as in the mildest, kindest places in Ireland. It will, in time, grow tall, but no more than many slow-growing conifers, and clothes itself to ground level with small, stiff, prettily shaped leaves. Late summer sees large flowers, the white equivalent, if you like, of *Hypericum* 'Hidcote', equally coming down to the ground.

In Leicestershire, England, between which and Moscow there is not a single hill to break the howling viciousness of the east winds, the owner of a beautifully shaped 'Nymansay' told me that growing heathers right up to its 'skirts' gave it the coolness at the root as well as the protection from having its soil frozen that was the secret of its success.

Blue is always welcome, no more so than at this time of year, when delphiniums are a memory and the eye might just yearn for relief from the yellows and reds that are so typical of the month. Two small shrubs, for which the smallest garden surely has room, provide it for a few of the weeks of high summer.

***Caryopteris × clandonensis*** is a rounded shrub not much more than 90cm (3ft) high, especially when given the preferred treatment, which is to cut it back quite hard in spring. This keeps it bushy and encourages it to make a dense mass of small, greyish, aromatic leaves and generously to produce its clusters of bright blue flowers. There are four or five different varieties, of which 'Arthur Simmonds' is marginally the best.

It shares a liking for dry soil in sun with the hardy plumbago, ***Ceratostigma plumbaginoides.*** This possessor of one of the more fearsome names among plants is again a 90cm (3ft) charmer. Its leaves are also small, but glossy, and its flowers are a little larger, just like those of plumbago, but almost royal blue.

**Ceanothus** are larger shrubs whose contribution to the presence of blue in the garden cannot be over-praised. There are species and varieties to grace every month from spring to early autumn, and the Delilianus group of ceanothus are especially to be sought after for

*Alchemilla mollis, penstemons, lupins and astrantias, demonstrating that the late-summer border can look as interestingly fresh as any day in spring*

the high-summer period. *C.* × *delilianus* itself is a medium-sized, deciduous shrub with soft blue flowers all summer long, and the others are cast in the same mould. 'Gloire de Versailles' has large flower clusters that last until autumn, 'Henri Desfosse' is deep, violet blue, and 'Indigo' is, as you might imagine, even deeper in colour.

**Yuccas** are, like eucryphias, misunderstood. It is a fallacy to equate an exotic appearance with tenderness or difficulty of cultivation. Many yuccas are indomitably hardy, though their agave-like foliage, like so many outward-pointing swords, suggests the margins of deserts and scrub wherein coyotes might lie up by day. In fact, such a picture is not that inaccurate, as the south-eastern United States are their main area of distribution, but they are subject to hard frosts in nature and it is only the weight of snow that is likely to do much harm.

I do not suggest you try yuccas too far from the moderating effects of a maritime location or, failing that, shelter from the coldest winds, but I do suggest that they be grown more widely. Their enormous, white flowers in stately spikes are one of the special treats of the warmest part of the year.

## HERBACEOUS PERENNIALS

Above all, it is perennials that dominate the late-summer scene. Those with long flowering seasons that started earlier in the summer are caught up by those whose proper season is just pre-autumn, and the combination leads to the richest time in the garden for concentrations of flower power. It is an awe-inspiring time, representing in cultivation the full, urgent thrust of botanical nature, as the plants call out for one last reproductive effort before their options close down.

## THE YEAR'S CLIMAX

Add to all this the burgeoning of **annuals**, the continuing activity in the **water-lily** production line, the formation of elegant, golden flowerheads among **ornamental grasses**, the maturing of **hydrangeas** from cool misses into sumptuously-clad matrons, and then stop to think. How ever did you fail to realise that, if spring is when the flower garden year really starts, high summer is its climax?

# plants

IN

# *flower*

**NOTES**

**Clethra alnifolia** vars and **Berberidopsis corallina** require lime-free soil. **Berberidopsis** is moderately hardy. **Lapageria rosea** is on the tender side and should be grown in the shade. **Myrtus** spp are not hardy in cold areas.

## CONIFER AND HEATHER CLICHÉ

If you possibly can, try to avoid a plant association that is now utterly passé: the conifer-and-heather bed. Few plantings are quite as satisfying to lovers of natural-looking gardens than undulating carpets of heathers, and the summer heathers – particularly the host of varieties of *Calluna vulgaris* – make an overwhelmingly important contribution to the lime-free garden with their wide range of foliage colours, sizes, habits of growth and late summer flowers. A gnarled specimen of *Pinus sylvestris* 'Beuvronensis', never attaining more than 90cm (3ft) in height in a long life, is perfect among them, as are some of the dwarfer willows, trees that represent those you might reasonably expect to find on the moorland among the heathers. But geometrically conical spruces, tightly columnar junipers, and chamaecyparis like large bathroom sponges combine with heathers to create the ultimate in horticultural kitsch. Worse, after you have seen several such plantings all within the bounds of one suburb, they become boringly predictable.

| SHRUBS | colour | flower type |
|---|---|---|
| **Caryopteris × clandonensis** | *Blue* | *In neat heads* |
| **Ceanothus × delilianus** and vars | *Blue* | *Conical heads* |
| **Ceratostigma willmottianum** | *Blue* | *Like those of plumbago* |
| **Clerodendrum bungii** | *Purplish red* | *Heads like mophead hydrangeas* |
| **trichotomum fargesii** | *White, in maroon calyces* | *Very fragrant* |
| **Clethra alnifolia** vars | *White or pink* | *Small, in terminal clusters, sweet scent* |
| **Genista tinctoria** | *Yellow* | *Broom-like* |
| **Hibiscus syriacus** vars | *Various* | *Mallow-like* |
| **Indigofera** spp | *Pink or purplish rose* | *Pea shaped* |
| **\*Itea ilicifolia** | *Greenish white* | *Long 'tassels'* |
| **Leycesteria formosa** | *White with purple bracts* | *Hanging clusters* |
| **\*Myrtus** spp (Myrtle) | *White* | *Starry* |
| **Olearia** spp | *White* | *Daisies* |
| **\*Yucca** spp | *White* | *Spires of large bells* |

Also: **Abelia, Buddleia, Colutea, Convolvulus cneorum, Cytisus, Desfontainea, Erica, Escallonia, Fuchsia, Hebe, Hydrangea, Hypericum, Lavandula, Ligustrum, Magnolia grandiflora, Perovskia, Phygelius, Potentilla, Romneya, Roses, Ruta, Spartium, Spiraea, Tamarix, Teucrium, Vinca**

## CLIMBERS

| | colour | flower type |
|---|---|---|
| **Berberidopsis corallina** | *Crimson* | *Rounded, hanging from long stalks* |
| **Campsis** 'Mme Galen' | *Salmon-red* | *Large trumpets* |
| **Clematis** many vars | *Various* | |
| **Lapageria rosea** | *Rose* | *Large, waxy trumpets* |
| **Lonicera** (Honeysuckle) late vars | *Various* | *Fragrant* |
| **Mutisia oligodon** | *Salmon pink* | *Like gazanias* |
| **Pileostegia viburnoides** | *Creamy white* | *Hydrangea-like* |

## PERENNIALS

Most of the perennials that flowered last month carry their peak of flowering over into this. The following are perennials that generally appear this month but *not* last. In their turn, many of them continue into early autumn.

| | colour | height |
|---|---|---|
| **Anaphalis triplinervis** | *White everlastings* | *45cm (18in)* |
| **Anchusa** vars | *Blue* | *90cm (36in)* |
| **Anemone × hybrida** vars | *Pink or white* | *1.5m (60in)* |

| | | |
|---|---|---|
| **Catananche caerulea** | Lavender blue or white | 60cm (24in) |
| **Cimicifuga racemosa** | White | 90cm (36in) |
| **Galega × hartlandii** | Lilac or lavender | 1.5m (60in) |
| **Limonium platyphyllum** | Lavender or pink | 30cm (12in) |
| **Lobelia** hybs | Bright red | 90cm (36in) |
| **Penstemon** many | Shades of red, pink or white | 75cm (30in) |
| **Platycodon grandiflorum 'Mariesii'** | Large blue bells | 45cm (18in) |
| **Polygonum** spp | Crimson or pink | 25–75cm (10–30in) |
| **Rudbeckia** spp and vars | Yellow or orange | 60cm–1.3m (24–52in) |
| **Salvia turkestanica** | Bluish white with rose bracts | 1.2m (48in) |
| **Sedum spectabile** and vars | Red or pink | 45cm (18in) |
| **Stokesia laevis** | Blue | 45cm (18in) |
| **Tradescantia** vars | Blue, white or rose | 45cm (18in) |
| **Zantedeschia aethiopica** | White arum lily | 60cm (24in) |
| **Zauschneria californica** (now **Epilobium canum**) | Scarlet | 30cm (12in) |

Also: **Achillea, Agapanthus, Anthemis, Astilbe, Astrantia, Campanula, Centaurea, Centranthus, Coreopsis, Crinum, Crocosmia, Dianthus, Dictamnus, Echinacea, Echinops, Eryngium, Geranium, Geum, Gypsophila, Helenium, Helianthus, Heliopsis, Hemerocallis, Heuchera, Hosta, Kniphofia, Leucanthemum superbum, Liatris, Ligularia, Lychnis, Lysimachia, Lythrum, Monarda, Nepeta, Oenothera, Phlox, Physostegia, Potentilla, Scabiosa, Sidalcea, Solidago, Thalictrum, Veronica.**

| BULBS | colour | height |
|---|---|---|
| *****Cyclamen europaeum** | Pink, fragrant | 10cm (4in) |
| **Galtonia candicans** | White, tinged green | 1.2m (48in) |
| **Nerine bowdenii** | Pink | 30cm (12in) |

## ROCK GARDEN

| | |
|---|---|
| *Ceratostigma plumbaginoides* | *Geranium* spp |
| *Crassula sarcocaulis* | *Oenothera* spp |
| *Cyclamen europaeum* | *Polygonum* spp |
| *Dianthus* spp and vars | *Sedum* spp |
| *Gentiana* – Asiatic | *Silene schafta* |
| | *Tunica saxifraga* |

## LIVING ACCENTS

At a time when there is so much colour about, it is all too easy for the garden to take on an over-stuffed look, rather like a Victorian drawing room. It is a good idea to stand back and, with as objective an eye as you can muster, take stock of the structure of the garden. Is it standing up to the great surge of late summer colour? Or is it submerged by it?

If the answer to the first question is an honest affirmative, it probably means that you have got two important aspects of your garden design right: the balance of greenery and flowers, and the provision of accents. The former point hardly needs to be be-laboured; the latter is one whose importance is all too often neglected.

Accents are easy to provide by using artefacts – fountains, gazebos of different kinds and even 'statuary' for which an entirely lamentable fashion has emerged in recent years. What is not so easy, and is far more rewarding, is to create accents using plants.

At this time of year, an illustration of this is easy to find. Yuccas, which are fairly con-spicuous at all times, now become command-ing features when they erupt in fountains of large, creamy bells. The tall spikes of flowers are the perfect complement to the clumps of sword-like leaves, and the plants are in tune with almost any style of garden, formal or informal, small or large.

## ARTFUL TIDINESS

Towards the end of the month, deadheading becomes a necessity. It was an occasional obligation last month, something constantly at the edge of consciousness in the first weeks of this, but now it takes over as the key to the good appearance of the flower garden. No matter how carefully you have planned and planted for late-summer associations of flower colour and form, browned, distorted flowerheads will ruin your efforts as would curry stains on your best Ralph Lauren. This is really only the beginning. As next month pro-gresses, you will find the job increasingly demanding and less and less restricted to flowers, until it culminates in the great autumn cut-back of perennials.

Nevertheless, keep an open eye for flowerheads that are not so much dead as extra-mature. Watch for the calyces left after flowers have dropped, the changing textures and colours of hydrangeas, and the interest-ing brown of the spent stems of astilbes. Be tidy, but avoid being too meticulous. You are aiming for your gardening to be artistic rather than twee, and you should be alert to beauty in whatever form it takes. There are a full six months of the true gardening year to come. Whoever coined the phrase 'putting the gar-den to bed', so often used as summer comes to a close, was indeed a philistine.

# SEPTEMBER

Summer ends, and Autumn comes, and he who
would have it otherwise would have high tide
always and a full moon every night.

HAL BORLAND

*Last month in temperate latitudes was the throbbing height of
summer, but carried with it a tendency to create a desire for its
end. Guiltily, we begin to look forward to cooler conditions, to
soft rain and damper breezes. They may not come during the first
few days of this month, yet for some reason those days bring
sudden changes. The ranks of the great colour parade of past
weeks thin dramatically and new plants take the stage, but in
considerably fewer numbers.*

*As the month progresses, early autumn's mature palette casts a
veil of russets and dusky reds over the garden, enlivened here and
there by white and an occasional splash of old gold. The
background is still green, but a darker, more sombre, middle-aged
range of tones, flashed here and there with amber.*

*Towards the end, grandmotherly purples, mauves, and discreetly
understated reds enjoy a major celebration, but the equinox brings
the first gales, the soil softens rapidly under the first serious rains
of autumn, and the fireside begins to beckon. Suddenly, the
evenings are long again, and gardening books are taken from
shelves as plans are laid for future springs and summers.*

*But you have no urgency in that direction, have you? For you
have been planning all along. And because you know what this
time of year is capable of, you are by no means surprised when a
lower, but still hot sun persists in delivering strong and poignant
reminders of the summer just gone. That is when the month casts
its subtle spell; when stillness and warmth take over under the
rich, slanting light, and you join the bees and the last butterflies
among the theatrical flowers of autumn.*

# tasks

## FOR THE

## *month*

## 1

# CHECKLIST

- Clear paths of weeds
- Check your stocks of garden chemicals
- Prune rambler roses
- Transplant evergreen shrubs
- Plant spring-flowering bulbs
- Cut back dead and dying foliage in the pond, and stretch netting over the pond to catch falling leaves
- Clear tired annuals and compost them. Prepare windowboxes, tubs and beds for next month's planting of spring bedding
- In the herbaceous border, cut back seeding stems unless you wish to retain them for seed or flower arrangements
- Move tender perennials into the greenhouse before frost strikes
- Lift gladioli and sort out the old and new corms. Store the new ones in a frost-free shed

## MAINTENANCE

### CLEARING PATHS

The path weedkillers for which it is claimed that they keep all growth down for an entire season certainly do so, but it depends on what you mean by a 'season'. Applying one in spring will give you a full six months of weed-free paths and drives, but it is unrealistic to expect it to last for a whole year.

The more effective of these agents combine pre-emergent with contact weedkillers. They are highly efficient, but spring applications will to a large extent have been leached away. Weed seeds are bound to have found their way into the cracks between paving or among the gravel during the summer, and you should give an application of weedkiller again now to give cover until next spring.

**SPRING-FLOWERING BULBS TO PLANT**

*Aconitum*
*Allium*
*Anemone*
*Chionodoxa*
*Crocus*
*Erythronium*
*Hyacinth*
*Narcissus*
*Scilla*

### GARDEN CHEMICALS

A general word on chemicals. They are not evil substances to be avoided at all costs and are only deleterious if they escape into the environment as a result of being used to excess. Weedkillers, insecticides and fertilisers that are applied excessively find their way into the water supplies, kill flying insects, harm other wild life, and take up energy reserves in their manufacture.

Used sensibly and to an extent that ensures their efficacy but no more, they are essential tools in the preparation and maintenance of a good flower garden. Without them, all the organic cultivation in the world will not keep weeds to a level people in full-time work have time to control, nor will it counteract the unnatural concentrations of insect pests caused by the crop pattern of the countryside and townscapes.

Organic cultivation greatly assists the strength of plants and their ability to combat pests and diseases, but its definition does not exclude inorganic aids. In maintaining your ornamental garden, you can combine the generous use of organic materials with the judicious use of chemicals and leave the environment none the worse.

### Care and disposal of chemicals

Where you *can* do untold damage is in the methods you use to get rid of surplus or unwanted chemicals. They must never, ever, be poured down drains. The advice sometimes given to dig a hole and pour surplus chemicals into it is unintelligent in the extreme. Firstly, buy discriminately and only in small quantities; secondly, contact your local authority if you have any you wish to dispose of, no matter how small the quantity.

## WARNING

■ *You should never use a pesticide in the year after it was bought. They nearly all deteriorate and weaken. If you spray pests with a weakened pesticide, the strongest will survive to breed, reinfest, and build up a resistant strain that will then travel to other gardens* ■

This month and next, see to your stocks of chemicals. Are they properly and safely stored? Do you really need all the ones you have? Is it not time you got rid of all the old stock? Contact the appropriate officer of your local authority and ask advice on disposal. Then think green, with the emphasis on the 'think'.

### PRUNING RAMBLER ROSES

Now is the time to prune rambler roses. Do this by cutting back flowered stems and tying in the best of the current year's shoots.

### THE POND

Cut back dead and dying foliage to prevent it decaying in the pond and fouling the water. Towards the end of the month, stretch netting over the pond to catch falling leaves – for the same reason. During thundery spells, increase the force of the jet from the garden hose by placing your thumb over the end, and spray the water surface to increase oxygenation.

## PLANTING

### TRANSPLANTING EVERGREENS

Early autumn is one of the times – late spring is the other – when evergreen shrubs that resent movement at other times of the year can be transplanted with the minimum of risk.

With some exceptions, evergreens are difficult to transplant successfully because they do not become dormant in the winter but carry on losing moisture from their leaves, moisture which has to be drawn from the soil by the roots. If the roots are damaged, as they almost always are in transplanting, there is bound to be stress on the plant.

From the middle of this month to the beginning of

next, the soil is warm enough for vigorous root growth to take place, and the air is cool enough to keep water loss down to an acceptable level. The colder your garden, the earlier you should move the shrubs. This does not apply to rhododendrons, azaleas, young camellias and most members of the heather family (Ericaceae), whose roots make fibrous mats that can be lifted in their entirety. They can be moved at any time of year except in extremes of weather. Hollies, laurels, and other evergreen shrubs with woodier, more wide-spreading root systems must be moved only during these narrow windows of opportunity.

Every effort should be made to dig out as much of the root system as possible intact and with the soil still attached. When replanting follow the method for planting shrubs on p.150.

Shrubs are moved for several reasons, but unfortunately the most usual one is because the initial planting was too crowded. The majority of gardeners – not the few – make the mistake of trying to fill their gardens too soon. If you are restrained when planting and allow shrubs to have room to grow properly you will save on pruning, combating disease and, eventually, the labour of transplanting.

### SPRING-FLOWERING BULBS

This month is the time to plant spring-flowering bulbs. It is important to get them settled earlier rather than later, as they soon start to make roots. Tulips, however, can be planted next month so that they do not produce precocious shoots that are likely to be frosted.

## TRANSPLANTING EVERGREEN SHRUBS

*Dig a trench around the shrub – beyond the extent of its branches*

*Use a spade to cut under the root ball – dig out as much of the root system as possible*

*To make moving the shrub easier, a pole strapped to its base allows for lifting with an assistant*

## TOP TIPS FOR PLANTING BULBS

*If you make the planting hole for each bulb three times the height of the bulb and make sure the bulb is sitting firmly on the bottom, the planting depth will be just right.*

*If you are thinking of naturalising bulbs in grass, plant them between one-and-a-half times and twice the normal depth. This will ensure that the inevitable compaction caused by foot traffic and mowers does not harm the bulbs.*

*For a more natural look to bulbs in grass, take a double handful of bulbs and throw them away from you. Plant each where it lands. Any that land so that they touch should be separated, but resist the temptation to be tidy. Plant any outliers just where they land – they will help create the illusion.*

# plants
## OF THE
# *month*
# *1*

### CHRYSANTHEMUM
#### *Dendranthema* 'Grandchild'

*Chrysanthemum* has been split by the botanists into several new genera, and the plants we have always known so well as 'chrysanths' now fall within the genus *Dendranthema* and include the Reflexed, Incurved, Intermediate and other classes. We have to learn new names, such as *Argyranthemum, Chrysanthemopsis,* and *Arctanthemum,* but *Dendranthema* is destined to become the most familiar.

| | |
|---|---|
| type | Pompon chrysanthemum: semi-hardy herbaceous perennial |
| flowers | Small, button-like, pink, darker at centre |
| foliage | Small, neat |
| height | 45cm (18in) |
| spread | 30cm (1ft) |
| hardiness | Hardy in fairly mild areas. Elsewhere, lift and store during winter |
| planting | Best planted in spring. Planting should be shallow |
| position | Full sun |
| soil | A good, fertile, well-manured border soil |
| propagation | Take cuttings 5cm (2in) long in spring |
| alternatives | 'Mei Kyo' (purple and pink), 'Mavis' (similar to 'Grandchild' but lighter colour), 'Golden Treasure' (orange-gold), 'Imp' (crimson) |

*DENDRANTHEMA 'GRANDCHILD'*

### JAPANESE ANEMONE
#### *Anemone × hybrida* (syn. *Anemone japonica*) 'Honorine Joubert'

This is the Japanese anemone that makes such a splendid contribution to the autumn garden. The more usual forms are rose pink, but there are variations in this colour and some fine whites including 'Honorine Joubert'. They can be invasive and are best planted as adjuncts to large shrubs that have flowered earlier in the year.

| | |
|---|---|
| type | Herbaceous perennial |
| flowers | Large, flat, white |
| foliage | Broad, vine-like, dark green |
| height | 1.5m (5ft) |
| spread | 90cm (3ft) |
| hardiness | Hardy |
| planting | Plant in spring or late autumn |
| position | An open, sunny position |
| soil | Moisture retentive, limy or acid. Japanese anemones do not, on the whole, thrive on sandy, dry soils |
| propagation | By division in early spring, or root cuttings taken in midwinter and rooted in pots in a garden frame |
| alternatives | There are about twenty other varieties, of which the best are 'Queen Charlotte' and 'Louise Uhink' (pink) and 'White Giant' ('Géant des Blanches') |

*SCHIZOSTYLIS COCCINEA*

## SCHIZOSTYLIS
*Schizostylis coccinea*

This South African plant is often listed among bulbs but, although a member of the Iris family, its roots are a fibrous mat and not a bulb. It is not entirely hardy, as you might expect from its origins, but it is almost so, and will grow in all but the coldest areas as long as it is given the right conditions. It is pronounced 'skitso-steyelis' rather than the prevalent 'sheyezo-steyelis'.

| | |
|---|---|
| type | Herbaceous perennial |
| flowers | Rich, bright crimson, resembling a lily or a gladiolus |
| foliage | Upright, slender, iris-like |
| height | 60cm (2ft) |
| spread | 30cm (1ft) |
| hardiness | Hardier than often thought, but not for the coldest areas. Spreads freely where it is really mild |
| planting | Plant in spring |
| position | Full sun, but needs a good deal of moisture |
| soil | Any good soil except sand or shallow soils over soft limestone |
| propagation | By division in spring. Each portion should carry four to six shoots |
| varieties | A choice of varieties, starting with the pink 'Tambara' in late summer, and finishing with 'Viscountess Byng' in late autumn, provides a long flowering season and colours from soft rose to richest crimson |

## RUDBECKIA
*Rudbeckia* 'Goldsturm'

One of the boldest splashes of rich yellow that can be found to offset the red-purple palette of early autumn will be found among the perennial rudbeckias. They are related to *Echinacea* and share its elevated flower centre and slightly drooping petals.

| | |
|---|---|
| type | Herbaceous perennial |
| flowers | Large, bold, deep yellow daisies with chocolate-brown to black centres |
| foliage | A little coarse, deep green |
| height | 90cm (3ft) |
| spread | 60cm (2ft) |
| hardiness | Hardy |
| planting | Plant in spring |
| position | Full sun |
| soil | Any good garden soil that is fairly moisture retentive |
| propagation | By division in spring |
| alternatives | 'Goldquelle' is earlier, 'Golden Glow' is tall, coarse and brassy |
| special comment | A first-class foil for Michaelmas daisies |

# tasks
## FOR THE
## *month*
## 2

**TENDER PLANTS FOR
TAKING CUTTINGS**

*Abutilon*
*Argyranthemum* 'Jamaica Primrose'
*Brachyglottis*
*Callistemon*
*Cestrum*
*Euryops pectinatus*
*Felicia*
*Fuchsia*
*Gazania*
*Grevillea*
*Hebe andersonii* 'Variegata'
*H.* 'Alicia Amherst'
*H.* 'La Seduisante'
*Mandevilla*
*Osteospermum*
*Penstemon*
*Plumbago auriculata* (heel)
*Salvia*

## CHECKLIST

- ☐ Take soft or semi-ripe cuttings from tender plants
- ☐ Take cuttings from fuchsias and conifers
- ☐ Divide herbaceous perennials and alpines
- ☐ Sow sweet peas and hardy annuals such as godetias and calendulas in a sunny, sheltered spot in the open
- ☐ Plan your planting of roses

## PROPAGATION

### CUTTINGS FROM TENDER PLANTS

Almost all tender perennials and quite a few tender shrubs growing outdoors can be propagated this month from cuttings, with the specific aim of obtaining replacement plants should there be winter losses.

Some of the cuttings, such as those from osteospermums, will be quite soft. It may seem odd to be taking cuttings that are soft or only just semi-ripe at this time of year, but propagation possibilities are far more flexible than many people think, and as long as the material is in a condition in which it will root, little else matters.

As you are not looking for a large increase, the method used might as well be kept as simple as possible. For such plants as osteospermums, *Euryops pectinatus* and the more tender penstemons, a pot of 50/50 by volume of sand and peat on the kitchen windowsill will do perfectly well. After inserting the cuttings, take two hoops of wire, stand them in the compost, invert a plastic bag over them, draw it tight round the bottom of the pot, and you have a mini-propagator.

Cuttings of the more tender hebes, such as 'Alicia Amherst', 'La Séduisante' and *H. andersonii* 'Variegata', will root in boxes of pure sand in a cold frame and will be sturdy plants with quite large root systems by spring.

### FUCHSIA STANDARDS

Fuchsia cuttings can be taken now for growing into standards. The cuttings will be semi-ripe but can be rooted either under mist or in a heated propagator. They will root quickly and should be potted on as soon as

possible and kept growing in heat.

As they grow, the leading shoot of each is encouraged to make swift progress by pinching out each sideshoot as it forms. The sideshoots are made in the angles of stem leaves, and these are left on. You should take care to remove just the sideshoots and not the leaves that subtend them, otherwise the plants will have no foliage with which to make food by the action of light.

## NOTE

- *One of the great advantages of a mist propagation system (see p.78) is that you can take cuttings at almost any time of the year. It is a mistake to let it stand idle, as your investment will not be earning to its maximum capacity. A great many conifer cuttings, taken this month under mist, will root slowly over the winter and be ready for potting in spring* ■

### DIVIDING PERENNIALS

Just as in spring, you can now propagate flowered herbaceous perennials by division, using much the same method as you did then. However, you should not break the plants down into divisions as small as those you can make earlier in the year, as they need substantial roots to see them through the winter and into spring growth.

### DIVIDING ALPINES

The same goes for alpines. However, although I know it

to be so in theory, this book is based on personal experience, and I have to admit that in over a decade as an alpine nurseryman, during which time I propagated many hundreds of thousands of plants, I cannot recall ever having divided alpines in autumn. For whatever reason seemed right at the time, all the divisions were done in spring, so it would ill behove me to advise anything different. Mainly, I suppose, it was because to break down an alpine into commercially small pieces was not a good idea in autumn. There is probably no reason at all why larger divisions should not be made in autumn, apart from the general tendency of alpines to have root systems that are more wandering, longer, and less relatively compact than those of the larger plants of the border.

## PLANNING

### ROSES

This is your last chance to plan the planting of roses, as you should make out your orders and get them posted, otherwise you will be at the back of the queue.

You should decide what you want the roses for, rather than going through a catalogue and picking out the ones that catch your eye. Roses fulfil many roles in gardens, and your planning will dictate which parts your roses will be called upon to play. It is a good idea to have an overall idea of the types of roses and their uses.

### Bush roses

These are the hybrid teas and floribundas. They are best grown in beds of their own, as they are different from other kinds of plants. Because of the way they are pruned, they behave in much the same way as summer-flowering herbaceous plants, but fail to mix happily with them. With bush roses, colour is paramount, and no matter what care you give to the selection of flower size and quality, you will always find yourself working out colour schemes and finding roses to fit them. This is perfectly valid, but bush roses are isolationist in their demands.

### Modern shrub roses

Shrub roses in general fit much more readily into mixed plantings, chiefly because they are shrubs like any others and not annually renewed, stiff frameworks entirely for the display of flowers. They have characteristics of shape, habit and foliage that give them value even when not in flower.

A shrub rose of a given colour can perform as the centrepiece for a group of different kinds of plants based on that colour, and you may need only half a dozen or so to lend coherence to quite a large border.

### Old-fashioned roses

These are shrub roses raised before the modern, perpetual-flowering hybrid teas and floribundas had been developed. They have all the advantages of modern shrub roses but many flower only once, in midsummer, and others repeat fairly poorly. They have wonderful fragrances, delightfully shaped, 'cabbagey' blooms, and pretty foliage, and many are not nearly as subject to disease as modern roses.

The old rose colours are quite different. They are on the whole more modest, less flamboyant, given to velvety maroons and even dove grey, and they should be regarded as shrubs in their own right. It is entirely illogical, for example, to grow a deutzia that flowers in early summer only and has no scent, and at the same time to give no room to an old-fashioned rose that will bloom for two months in summer and give a fragrant elegance to the garden that nothing else can in quite the same way.

### English roses

These are a new race of roses, combining the virtues of the old-fashioned shrub roses with those of the modern bush roses. You can use them either on their own in a bed or as focal points in mixed plantings, or just grow them with other plants.

### Species, climbing and rambling roses

These have their own particular uses, and your planning will include them according to whether you want to grow roses over walls, fences, trees, or – if you have a very large garden – just as flowering shrubs for the wilder areas.

# plants
## OF THE
## *month*
## 2

### SEDUM
*Sedum* 'Autumn Joy'

The large-headed sedums, forms or hybrids of *S. spectabile*, are indispensable assets to the autumn garden, both early and late. They are superb butterfly plants with the exception of 'Autumn Joy' which, though the most cleanly coloured, avoiding the puce of others, is a sterile hybrid and does not attract butterflies.

| | |
|---|---|
| type | Herbaceous perennial |
| flowers | Large heads of tiny, starry flowers; rich pink, turning darker with age and eventually coppery red |
| foliage | Broad, grey-green, toothed, succulent |
| height | 60cm (2ft) |
| spread | 60cm (2ft) |
| hardiness | Hardy |
| planting | Plant in spring or late autumn |
| position | Full sun |
| soil | Any good garden soil |
| propagation | By division in spring |
| alternatives | *S. spectabile* 'Brilliant', *S.s.* 'Meteor'. 'Iceberg' is white |

### MICHAELMAS DAISY
*Aster amellus* 'Sternkugel'

The varieties of *Aster amellus* are sometimes included under the term Michaelmas daisy, but their flowering period starts in late summer and they are at their peak earlier than the true Michaelmas daisies (see below), which are at their best late in the month and well into next. *Aster amellus* are shorter, tough, fairly disease-resistant plants. They are also attractive to butterflies.

| | |
|---|---|
| type | Woody-stemmed herbaceous perennial |
| flowers | Many-rayed daisies, rich lavender-pink |
| foliage | Matt, dull green |
| height | 50cm (20in) |
| spread | 30cm (1ft) |
| hardiness | Hardy |
| planting | Plant in spring or late autumn |
| position | Sun or part shade |
| soil | Any good garden soil |
| propagation | By division in spring |
| alternatives | About a dozen varieties, including 'Brilliant' (deep rose pink), 'Moerheim Gem' (violet), 'Sonia', pale pink |

### MICHAELMAS DAISY
*Aster novi-belgii* varieties

These, the New York asters, and the *novae-angliae* (New England) asters are the true Michaelmas daisies. Wisely chosen, their display can last from the middle of this month until late autumn.

| | |
|---|---|
| type | Woody-stemmed herbaceous perennials |
| flowers | Many-rayed daisies in a variety of colours in the pink to purple range, including some good blues |
| foliage | Matt, dull green |
| height | 75cm–1.5m (2½–5ft) according to variety |
| spread | 45–65cm (18–26in) |
| hardiness | Hardy |
| planting | Plant in spring or late autumn |
| position | Full sun or part shade |
| soil | Any good garden soil, including moist |
| propagation | By division in spring |
| alternatives | There are many. It is advisable to buy from a specialist nursery and to ask for varieties known to be resistant to disease |

*SEDUM 'AUTUMN JOY'*

*ASTER NOVI-BELGII VARIETIES*

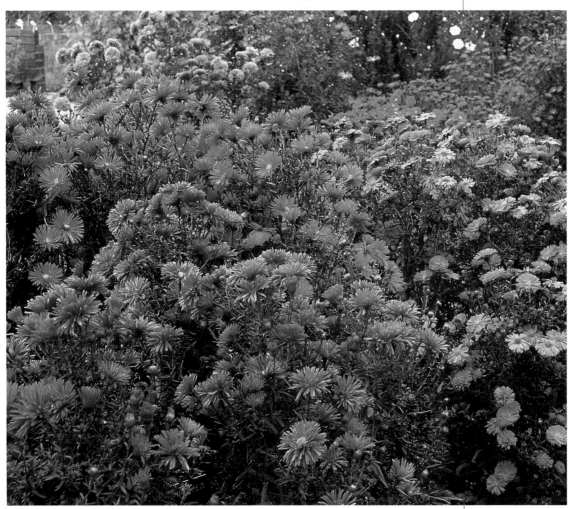

## PENSTEMON

*Penstemon* 'Raven'

Herbaceous, as opposed to shrubby, penstemons are late-flowering plants of the
greatest value. Generally speaking, those with
somewhat smaller, more slender flowers are
the hardiest, while the wider, larger, tubbier
ones tend to be less so. Some with very large
flowers are, frankly, tender. The hardier ones
(of which the bright red 'Garnet' is a fine
example) often remain green all winter in mild
areas and should not be cut down until spring;
otherwise they are herbaceous, dying down
later in the autumn but flowering well into
next month.

| | |
|---|---|
| type | Semi-herbaceous perennial (evergreen in mild areas) |
| flowers | Deep crimson, wide-tubular |
| foliage | Slender, bright green |
| height | 75cm (30in) |
| spread | 60cm (2ft) |
| hardiness | Will stand a considerable amount of severe winter cold but not cold, dry spring winds |
| planting | Plant in spring or late autumn |
| position | Full sun, shelter from cold winds |
| soil | Any good garden soil |
| propagation | By softwood cuttings in late spring |
| alternatives | 'Garnet' is deep red; 'King George' is crimson with a white throat; 'Myddleton Gem' is light red; 'Firebird' is scarlet; 'Sour Grapes' is greenish purple (plants labelled 'Sour Grapes' are often, in fact, 'Stapleford Gem') |

# plants

IN

## *flower*

**KEY**

= evergreen    spp = species
vars = varieties

**NOTES**

*Ceratostigma griffithii* and *Grevillea* 'Sulphurea' are tender. *Oxydendrum arboreum* requires lime-free soil.

| TREES | colour | flower type |
| --- | --- | --- |
| ***Magnolia grandiflora** | Creamy white | Very large, fragrant |
| **Oxydendrum arboreum** | White | Urn shaped, in drooping clusters |

| SHRUBS | | |
| --- | --- | --- |
| **Abelia × grandiflora** | White, pink tinge | Small, funnel shaped |
| **Aralia elata** | White | Small, in large plumes |
| **Ceratostigma griffithii** | Deep blue | Plumbago-like |
| **Elsholzia stauntonii** | Deep lilac | Pea shaped, in large bunches |
| ***Eucryphia** 'Nymansay' | White | Saucer shaped |
| ***Grevillea** 'Sulphurea' | Yellow | Tubular, like honeysuckle |
| **Lespedeza thunbergii** | Rose-purple | Pea shaped |
| **Perovskia atriplicifolia** | Lavender-blue | Tubular, lipped |

Also: **Buddleia, Calluna, Ceratostigma willmottianum, Clerodendrum, Colutea, Daboecia cantabrica, Erica** spp, **Fuchsia, Hebe, Hibiscus, Hydrangea, Hypericum, Genista tinctoria, Indigofera, Leycesteria formosa, Potentilla, Romneya, Yucca.**

| CLIMBERS | | |
| --- | --- | --- |
| **Polygonum baldschuanicum** (Russian vine) | White | Large plumes |
| **Solanum crispum** 'Glasnevin' | Purple or white | Like potato flowers |

Also: **Campsis, Clematis, Eccremocarpus, Jasminum, Lapageria, Mutisia, Passiflora, Pileostegia**

### EASY ON THE EYE

During early autumn, the borders behave rather like a crowd at the end of a football match. One moment they are at their fullest, bursting with colour and activity; the next sees them having almost imperceptibly thinned, and after a short while you realise that a steady drift home has become established.

Your eye once more becomes attuned, as it was in spring and early summer before the great rush of flowering that was to come later, to individual colour matches and contrasts, and to the importance of flower shape and size. The white, fluffy-centred *Leucanthemum superbum* 'Snowcap', a short-stemmed form of what used until recently to be *Chrysanthemum maximum*, growing intimately with the crimson, double, equally fluffy nasturtium *Tropaeolum majus* 'Hermione Grashoff', is just the sort of association that easily passes unnoticed in high summer but begins to catch the eye as other distractions disappear.

### MAGNOLIAS IN AUTUMN

*Magnolia grandiflora* is a tree magnolia. In its native south-eastern United States it grows very large, often to more than 30m (100ft), especially on the drier 'Hammocks' of the swamps. Like yuccas, it is hardy but cannot stand up to the weight of snow, and for that reason it never grows to large sizes in cool-temperate climates, where its branches break and flowering is attenuated. While still young, it is not so susceptible to breakage and will flower well, but only if you choose a variety that flowers at an early age. 'Exmouth' and 'Goliath' are the ones to look for; note the brown-felted undersides of the leaves in the former, but not the latter, whose leaves are green on both sides. The best long-term results with this magnolia species are with trees that have been trained from youth on sheltered walls that are not too hot. It will grow happily and for very many years on a good, rich soil and, provided that there is plenty of organic matter added, will thrive over chalk.

For sheer size of flower and delicacy of scent, *Magnolia grandiflora* has no rival in the garden in late summer and early autumn, and I would rather plant it than any of the somewhat hackneyed magnolias of spring, were I to be allowed only the one.

| PERENNIALS | colour | height |
|---|---|---|
| *Ceratostigma plumbaginoides* | Dark blue | 30cm (12in) |
| *Cimicifuga cordifolia* | White | 1.2m (48in) |
| *Aster amellus* vars | Various | 60cm (24in) |
| *Aster × frikartii* **'Mönch'** | Blue | 90cm (36in) |
| *novae-angliae* vars | Various | 60cm–1.5m (24–60in) |
| *novi-belgii* vars | Various | 90cm–1.5m (36in–60in) |
| *Penstemon* many | Various | 75cm (30in) |
| *Schizostylis coccinea* vars | Pink, white or red | 60cm (24in) |
| *Sedum maximum* 'Atropurpureum' | Deep pink | 45cm (18in) |
| 'Vera Jameson' | Pale pink | 25cm (10in) |
| *Campanula portenschlagiana* | Blue | 15cm (6in) |

Also: **Anaphalis, Anemone × hybrida, Centaurea, Centranthus, Coreopsis, Crocosmia, Dianthus, Eryngium, Geranium, Gypsophila, Helenium, Heliopsis, Hemerocallis, Heuchera, Hosta, Kniphofia, Lavatera, Liatris, Ligularia, Limonium, Lythrum, Monarda, Oenothera, Phlox, Physostegia, Polygonum, Potentilla, Rudbeckia, Salvia, Scabiosa, Silene schafta, Stokesia, Tradescantia, Veronica, Zauschneria.**

## BULBS

| | colour | height |
|---|---|---|
| *Colchicum* spp | Lilac, mauve or pink | 10–18cm (4–7½in) |
| *Crocus cancellatus* | Lilac, marked purple | 12cm (5in) |
| *cartwrightianus* | Purple | 8cm (3in) |
| *Scilla autumnalis* | Lilac | 10cm (4in) |
| *Sternbergia lutea* | Yellow | 12cm (5in) |

**ROCK GARDEN**

*Ceratostigma plumbaginoides*
*Colchicum spp*
*Crocus see bulbs*
*Gentiana* – Asiatic spp and hybs
*Lapeirousia cruenta*
*Sternbergia lutea*
*Zauschneria microphylla*

## THE NEGLECTED SEASON

The plant associations of spring have much in common with those of early autumn and those of neither season receive the attention lavished upon those of summer. Much is written about colour co-ordination, themes and harmonies, but almost always with the summer border in mind. When summer is over, there remain nine months before the next one. What a short-sighted view it is that takes no heed of the importance of plant associations during that long period!

## THE TIDY TIME

No matter what else is said about plant associations for September, remember that it is the *only* time in the whole year when bare, freshly cultivated soil among the plants looks positively attractive (because of the contrast with the busyness of August). Clean out everything tatty, dying or dead and do not be in too much of a hurry to fill in the spaces. Give yourself some thinking time.

## PLAN FOR BULBS

There are many such autumnal combinations that should be deliberately planned for a full year ahead. It is such long-range plans, when there is a considerable time lag between conception, ordering the plants, planting them and then their flowering, that are impossible to execute coherently unless you make use of a methodically kept notebook.

You will now be planting the spring bulbs. Yet on what grounds have you planned their deployment? Have you just seen nice ones in pictures at the garden centre or in the catalogue and thought in general, perhaps woolly terms that they would look good? Or did you, last spring when bulb time was at its height, go out and look at other gardens, public and private, notebook in hand?

For you cannot even set bulbs, stand back, assess the effect, and then rearrange them. You make holes, put them in, and cannot see them any more. They are gone until next spring. This is why you so often see dreary lines of otherwise lovely daffodils slavishly following the edge of a drive, and it is why scillas and crocuses, appearing in isolated clumps on rockeries, make you feel even colder by their naked vulnerability to the chilly winds, unsheltered by the friendly warmth of neighbouring plants.

# OCTOBER

There is no season when such pleasant and sunny
spots may be lighted on, and produce so pleasant
an effect on the feelings, as now in October.

NATHANIEL HAWTHORNE

*This month is true autumn, temperamental and hardly to be
trusted, but capable of the utmost charm as well as the most
dreadful rages. There are wild gales and lashing rain, but there
are also still, diamond days after crisp frosts, when views you
had forgotten about appear again with the fall of leaves,
sharpened by the sun's clarity in the rain-washed air.*

*Just as in spring there is a rush to flower before the deciduous
canopy closes overhead, now there is another, lesser scramble, as
it falls away. There is little to compare with the sight of freshly
opened autumn crocuses, leafless on the lawn's edge, standing like
footless wine glasses magically balanced by some mischievous,
overnight hand.*

*Colchicums flop foolishly after a few days, but are always
endearing.* Cyclamen hederifolium *can be found all over the
world where it can enjoy a cool, leafy spot. It is valued almost as
much for its marbled leaves as for its sturdy blooms that never
bow, even before the strongest winds.*

*This month is prized by many for the colours of the autumn
leaves, but in equable climates they can often be mediocre. They
can also be fleeting, swept away by gales before they can be
appreciated. It is therefore a mistake to give the autumn garden
over to a celebration of foliage colours.*

*Nevertheless, to dismiss them completely is as great an error.
Autumn's glory is a fuchsia's clear scarlet against the burnt-
orange leaves of a dogwood. It is deep, velvety-crimson nicotianas
beside a flaming Japanese Maple, inwardly lit nerines against the
last deep green of a shrub rose, and the rosy-lilac saffron crocus,
orange-red stigmas echoing its bed of fallen leaves.*

# tasks

## FOR THE

## *month*

## *1*

*PLANT SUPPORTS*
*Once herbaceous plants have finished flowering, remove, dry, clean and store their supports. If you used twiggy sticks, burn them before they can harbour fungus diseases.*

# C H E C K L I S T

☐ Continue to cut back herbaceous perennials
Remove all weeds from among their crowns
☐ Rake or pick up all fallen leaves from lawns and beds and compost them. Do *not* burn
☐ Later in the month, lift and store dahlias if necessary
☐ Protect young evergreen shrubs from wind
☐ Finish pruning rambler roses
☐ Plant spring bedding, containerised trees and shrubs, and bulbs, especially tulips
☐ Plant up your new rock garden

## MAINTENANCE

### WEEDING PERENNIALS

You are quite likely to find that pernicious weeds have seeded into your border and gained a hold among the crowns of the herbaceous perennials. You will not have noticed them because of the top growth, but now they become obvious. It is very tempting, when you have removed the greater part of such a weed, to give up and leave a little behind. This will cause you untold trouble, as the next time you notice it will be a full year later, by which time it may have killed out the plant, if not its immediate neighbours.

In such cases, lift the border plant and tease every last piece of weed root away from the roots of the plant. You will be surprised just how much there will probably be and how deep it has managed to run.

### BONFIRES VERSUS COMPOST

There has been much to-do about bonfires recently. Garden bonfires are unlikely to make the slightest

difference to global warming, and you should have no compunction about burning material that might cause disease, weed roots, dead wood, and so on. Thinking 'green' people will rightly maintain, however, that to burn material which can be made into good compost or mulch is – given the state of our increased knowledge of ecological balances, plain common sense and elementary home economics – verging on the criminal.

### DAHLIAS

If your climate is on the cold side, leave dahlias blackened by the first air frost for a few days until their tops have died right down.

■ Cut the stems to within 15cm (6in) of the ground.

■ Insert the spade into the soil about 30cm (1ft) from the centre of a plant and, with one hand on the spade and the other on the stem stumps, gently ease the tuber from the ground.

■ Discard any broken tubers and bring the sound ones under frost-free cover, where they should be turned upside down so as to drain the hollow stems.

## WARNING

■ *If you cut the stems too short, you risk damaging the points where new growth is made; too long and they are unlikely to drain properly and will get in the way* ■

■ Once drained, place the tubers right way up in boxes of moss peat that is just damp, leaving the crowns uncovered.

■ Inspect the tubers at intervals between now and spring, cutting any diseased parts back to sound tissues and dusting with sulphur.

■ Some tubers will shrivel. Put them in a bucket of water overnight and then dry them thoroughly before returning them to store.

## EVERGREEN SHRUBS

Take this point further and erect netting protection for young evergreen shrubs. The object is not to exclude the wind, but merely to slow it and reduce its wind-chill factor. If you also mulch them on a warmish day, you will retain soil warmth as well as moisture, and the plants will have just a little longer to make root growth.

## PLANTING

### BULBS

You should finish your bulb planting this month. Tulips can be left until quite late in the month, but everything else should be in as soon as possible.

### EVERGREENS

Evergreen shrubs are not, on the whole, easy to establish. Many losses, attributed to tenderness, are really caused by an insufficient understanding of their needs.

The survival of a plant is dictated by the fact that the water lost by its leaves must never exceed the water gained by its roots. This means that if you plant in autumn, you stand the risk of its dying because cold, drying winds draw the moisture from the leaves while the roots, made partly dormant by the soil temperature, cannot supply enough to compensate.

In spring, the danger to newly planted evergreens is twofold. There may be cold, continental winds that can be fiercely drying, and also there will be an increasing amount of warmth and sunshine to counteract the action of the roots.

The main solution to the problems of both seasons is to mulch as soon after planting as possible, using at least a 5cm (2in) depth of partly rotted organic matter or something like composted forest bark. The secondary remedy is to temper the wind to the young plant (see above), and the third is to water when it becomes necessary. Watering has little or no effect from now until mid-spring.

There is nothing like the same problem with deciduous trees and shrubs, some of which may in fact be less temperature-hardy than evergreens but do not have to cope with the loss of water to anything like the same degree. The drying caused by cold winds is termed 'physiological drought' and is a major killer in the garden.

### SPRING BEDDING

Plant out bedding for next spring. The plants used for bedding are mainly biennials, they have made their growth

but no flowers this year, and will flower and die next year.

### ROCK GARDEN

If you made a rock garden earlier and have been waiting for the soil to settle, you can plant it during the first half of the month, but you must be prepared from the outset always to inspect the plants after any severe frost. This is because the action of the frost will be to lift the plants partly from the soil, and the better and more gritty your soil, the more likely it is to happen.

A good top-dressing of pebbles is an excellent precaution against frost and has saved many an autumn-planted alpine. Do not forget that the majority of alpines are evergreen and used to being comfortably ensconced beneath snow. They are not accustomed by nature to drying, frosty winds in winter. The best precaution, again, is the mulch, as it prevents the freezing of the roots that prevents their taking up water to replace that lost by the leaves.

*SOIL TEMPERATURE*
*Plant growth stops when the temperature of the soil drops below 5°C (41°F). This is also the temperature at which the anomalous expansion of water begins, culminating in the formation of ice.*

**SPRING BEDDING PLANTS**

***Bellis*** (Double daisies)
***Campanula medium***
(Canterbury bells)
***Cheiranthus*** (wallflowers)
***Dianthus barbatus***
(Sweet Williams)
***Myosotis*** (forget-me-nots)
**Polyanthus**
**Winter-flowering pansies**

# plants
## OF THE
## *month*
## *1*

  CHRYSANTHEMUM
*Argyranthemum* 'Jamaica Primrose'

While not a true autumn flower – it blooms for most of the summer – 'Jamaica Primrose' is outstanding now before the harder frosts kill it. It is especially fine when allowed to thread its stems among grey foliage. Until recently it was classified as a chrysanthemum.

| | |
|---|---|
| type | Tender perennial |
| flowers | Large, yellow daisies |
| foliage | Green, ferny |
| height | 45cm (18in) |
| spread | 45cm (18in) |
| hardiness | Not winter-hardy, but will withstand light frosts |
| planting | Plant in spring after danger of frosts has passed |
| position | Full sun |
| soil | Not too rich, well drained |
| propagation | Take shoots a few inches long early in the month and root them in 50/50 sand and moss peat by volume. Pot up when rooted and overwinter in a frost-free greenhouse |
| alternatives | *Argyranthemum frutescens* (marguerite) has white flowers |

*ARGYRANTHEMUM 'JAMAICA PRIMROSE'*

## CYCLAMEN
*Cyclamen hederifolium*

By choosing well from the species of cyclamen, it is possible to have flowers for many months of the year. *C. hederifolium* (syn. *C. neapolitanum*) is valuable for its comparatively long flowering season and for its beautifully marbled leaves, which follow the first flowers and coincide with the later ones. Flowering may begin as early as midsummer, there are often blooms a month later, early autumn sees the species into full flower, and this month the combined beauty of flowers and foliage is at its peak. This sequence varies with latitude and climate, and may be compressed into early to mid-autumn.

| | |
|---|---|
| type | Tuberous perennial |
| flowers | Auricled (notched), recurved, rose pink to white |
| foliage | Oval, ivy or arrow shaped, smooth edged or wavy, matt green marbled with silver to varying degrees. The leaves of no two individuals are alike |
| height | 10–12cm (4–5in) |
| spread | Old tubers may bear up to fifty flowers and be 15cm (6in) or even more across |

| | |
|---|---|
| hardiness | Hardy |
| planting | Plant when dormant in mid- to late summer or at any time when purchased pot-grown 'in the green' |
| position | Partly shaded |
| soil | A good garden soil with well-rotted organic matter added |
| propagation | By seed preferably sown as soon as it is ripe. All species germinate at the same time of year as the leaves appear on adult plants |
| special comment | Mulching during the dormant period is important for this species, as it is surface-rooting from the top of the tuber |

## COLCHICUM
### *Colchicum autumnale*

Although colchicums are all too frequently called 'autumn crocuses', they are nothing of the sort, and the crocus species of autumn are entirely different. Crocuses have corms, colchicums have tubers; crocuses have three stamens, colchicums have six. They flower incredibly quickly from tubers in early autumn and then appear reliably every year thereafter, increasing freely as time passes.

| | |
|---|---|
| type | 'Bulb' – in fact tuberous |
| flowers | Long-necked, large goblets, rosy-mauve |
| foliage | Large, strap-shaped, produced after flowering |
| height | 15cm (6in) |
| spread | Clumps increase rapidly |
| hardiness | Hardy |
| planting | Plant when available in late summer or early autumn |
| position | Flowers best in full sun, but looks best beside shrubs or near small trees |
| soil | Any reasonable garden soil |
| propagation | By division of the clumps in late summer |
| special comment | The flowers of many colchicum species fall over a few days after opening. This happens in the best weather and is not a sign of pests or disease |

## NERINE
### *Nerine bowdenii*

The gorgeous nerines of autumn are like no other flowers. The petals contain cells that behave like crystals, reflecting and concentrating

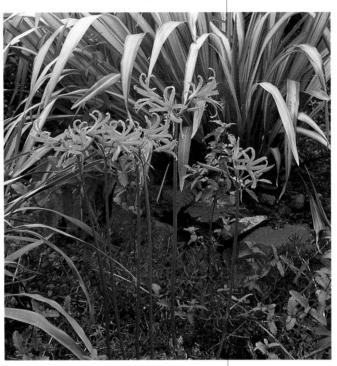

*NERINE BOWDENII*

the light so that they seem to glow from within as if made from cool jewellery. They take a year or two to settle down, but should then be left to increase undisturbed for many years, as they flower best when crowded.

| | |
|---|---|
| type | Bulbous perennial |
| flowers | Ice-pink, petals strap-shaped and undulating |
| foliage | Strap shaped |
| height | 60cm (2ft) |
| spread | 30cm (1ft) |
| hardiness | Hardy in most areas if sheltered from cold winds |
| planting | Plant in late summer, 15cm (6in) deep |
| position | The foot of a warm wall is the classic position for nerines, but it should not be hot and dry. In my own experience, the base of a shrub rose, where they received a little shade during the day, proved eminently successful, as did a formal bed in a tiny town garden |
| propagation | By division of established clumps, or removal of bulbils, in late summer. These should be transplanted to pots or a nursery bed |
| alternatives | Other species are best treated as greenhouse plants |

# tasks

## FOR THE

## *month*

## 2

**SHRUBS TO PROPAGATE**

Among the genera that can be propagated from hardwood cuttings in the open are:

*Azara* • *Buddleia*
*Campsis* • *Celtis*
*Deutzia* • *Diervilla*
*Escallonia* (in mild areas)
*Forsythia* • *Franklinia*
*Jasminum* • *Kerria*
*Laburnum* • *Leycesteria*
*Ligustrum* • *Metasequoia*
*Neillia* • *Philadelphus*
*Physocarpus*
*Platanus* • *Populus*
*Prunus cerasifera* vars
*Rhodotypos*
*Ribes* • *Salix*
*Sambucus* • *Santolina*
*Sorbaria* • *Spiraea*
*Stephanandra*
*Symphoricarpos*
*Tamarix*
*Viburnum* (deciduous)
*Vitis*
*Weigela*

## CHECKLIST

- Divide herbaceous perennials
- Take hardwood cuttings of shrubs and roses
- Take leaf-bud cuttings of mahonias
- Plan the planting of spring-flowering perennials

## PROPAGATION

### RENOVATING OLD BORDER PLANTS

At some time or other you are almost certain to find yourself with some real old stagers among the herbaceous plants. They form seemingly impenetrable masses of root that have about as much sympathy to handling as barbed wire, and you feel you should really divide them, but shirk the job – yet again.

■ If you have such a plant, dig it up and lay the root ball on ground – not on a path or on concrete, but soil that has not recently been dug.

■ As you are a good gardener, your spade will be clean and shiny, but it is worth honing it to a reasonable cutting edge with the sort of stone that is used for grass hooks and scythes.

■ Using all your weight through hands and foot, thrust the spade through the middle of the root ball, slicing down into the soil beneath.

■ Separate the two halves and cut them in their turn into halves.

■ Do nothing more at this stage other than to plant the four quarters as they are.

■ Not next spring but the one following, by which time the

quarters will have put on strong, new crowns and roots, dig them up again and divide them. This time, discard the older parts and just replant the young growths.

By following this process, instead of one old, failing plant, you will have about a dozen young, strong ones eager to make a fine floral display.

### SHRUBS FROM HARDWOOD CUTTINGS

Many deciduous shrubs, particularly, as it happens, the most popular ones, can be propagated by the simplest method of all, which is to take cuttings of fully ripe wood this month.

It is quite astonishing that amateur gardeners almost totally ignore this method, which calls for no special

equipment whatever, not even a frame in most cases. Take a spade, some coarse sand, your secateurs and a spare bit of ground, and you are in business.

■ A hardwood cutting is made from a fully ripened shoot of the current year's wood. The bark should be completely hard and will not wrinkle and pull away under pressure from your thumb. How long the cutting is will depend on the distance between the buds, but most are around 25cm (10in) or a little less. You can, of course, use prunings.

25 cms.

■ Cut straight across below a joint (bud), and then make a sloping cut just above a bud higher up. You will usually find the ends of the shoots too soft, and will discard the terminal bud. By always making the low cut straight and the high cut sloping, you will avoid the embarrassment of putting your cuttings in upside down.

■ Dip the bases of the cuttings in hormone rooting powder and tap off the excess.

■ Make a trench in your spare piece of ground, which should be in shelter, by driving the spade in vertically and rocking it forward. Use the sharp sand to make a layer about 2.5cm (1in) deep at the bottom.

■ Rest the bases of the cuttings on the sand at 15cm (6in) intervals and backfill the trench, firming with your foot. The lower two-thirds of each cutting should be in the soil.

■ Loosen the soil surface where you trod, otherwise puddling will occur.

■ Keep weeds down during the following spring and summer and leave the cuttings until autumn, when they can be dug up and planted in permanent quarters.

■ The cuttings are inserted, one to a pot, so that the stem section is just buried in the 50/50 peat/sand compost. Rooting is slow and should take place in a heated propagating frame or, best of all, in a mist unit.

■ You will know that the cuttings are rooted when, next spring, you see a robust new shoot pushing up through the soil of each pot.

■ When it is growing well, you can trim away the old leaf, as its work is done.

### ROSES FROM HARDWOOD CUTTINGS

Most roses other than bush roses (hybrid teas and

floribundas) and climbers can quite easily be propagated from hardwood cuttings. I have used the method to greatest effect with old-fashioned shrub roses and ramblers.

■ The cuttings should be taken as late as possible, towards the end of this month or even during next.

■ Hardwood cuttings of roses are not usually very long and will root if they are as short as 10cm (4in), although 15cm (6in) is better if shoots of that length can be found.

■ The tips are usually on the soft side and should be clipped off to a bud and discarded, but the cuttings may well have a few leaves even so late in the year. It is best to leave them alone and let them fall in their own time.

■ It is sometimes recommended that you remove the prickles, but it is not necessary and is only for your own comfort. Wear gloves and you should have no trouble.

■ The cuttings should be given the same length of time in which to root as other hardwood cuttings.

■ Hybrid teas and floribundas will root from hardwood cuttings, but the resulting plants tend to be weaker than those grafted onto commercial rootstocks. It can, however, be worth doing with a select few of the more vigorous varieties and with many modern shrub roses.

### MAHONIAS FROM CUTTINGS

You can propagate mahonias this month. Many people shy away from doing so because

they cannot see how to take cuttings from them. In fact, you take leaf-bud cuttings.

■ Each cutting consists of an entire, pinnate leaf, a section of the stem to which it is attached, and the bud in the axil between the leaf and stem. The leaf can be reduced in size by about one-third to prevent toppling.

> ## NOTE
>
> ■ *Some gardeners (I am among them) cut the stem section longitudinally in half, discarding the part without the leaf. I have to admit that I am not entirely clear why I do this, only that I always have, which is no good reason at all, but it gets good results* ■

■ The stems should be green and semi-ripe, as they are this month, and not brown and ripe, as are those of many other shrubs. The length of stem attached to the cutting should be about 5cm (2in).

### PLANNING

### PLAN FOR SPRING

The most valuable planning you can do this month is to bear spring in mind while you are tidying the borders. Almost all gardeners overemphasise summer in their flower borders, and spring among their shrubs. At the risk of labouring the point, one must say that good gardening is a matter of balance, and you should turn a critical eye on the borders and see if you should not plan to include more spring-flowering perennials.

**MAHONIA CUTTINGS**

**SPRING-FLOWERING PERENNIALS**

*Bergenia*
*Doronicum*
*Epimedium*
*Euphorbia*
*Helleborus*
*Pulmonaria*

# plants

## OF THE

## *month*

## 2

### DAHLIA
*Dahlia* 'Bishop of Llandaff'

This is the month during which dahlias seem to put extra energy into flowering, as if they somehow know that their long days of blooming are almost over. Ground frosts do not affect them much, but the first air frost will see them blackened and ready for lifting for the winter in the colder areas. In mild climates dahlias will overwinter in the garden. During these last weeks, dahlias are rendered the more conspicuous by the dying down of their hardier neighbours.

| | |
|---|---|
| type | Peony-flowered border dahlia |
| flowers | Brilliant scarlet, late summer onwards |
| foliage | Deep bronze-maroon |
| height | Varies according to conditions, 90cm–1.5m (3–5ft) |

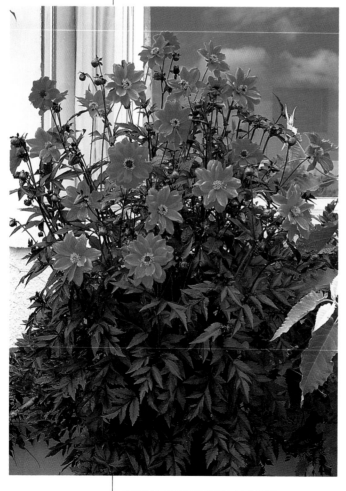

*DAHLIA 'BISHOP OF LLANDAFF'*

| | |
|---|---|
| spread | Also varies. Plants in full leaf cover up to 1sq m (1sq yd) |
| hardiness | In climates where the soil does not become frozen solid below about 2cm (¾in), and that only fairly occasionally, this and similar dahlias may safely be left in the ground all year. In colder climates they should be lifted after the first blackening frost and prepared for storage in a frost-free building |
| planting | Plant the tubers 10cm (4in) deep in spring when the dangers of hard frosts are past. Tie the stems loosely to stakes 30cm (1ft) shorter than their final heights |
| position | Full sun |
| soil | Any good, well-drained soil, enriched well in advance with well-rotted manure. Give a light dressing (100gm per sq m/3oz per sq yd) of bonemeal when planting |
| propagation | By division of the tubers in early spring. Place them in a shallow box containing a moist mixture of equal parts of moss peat and sand. After fourteen to twenty days, the eyes will swell. Divide the tubers by cutting with a sharp knife so that each division has at least one eye. Dust the cut surfaces with sulphur and plant out the divisions |
| alternatives | A recent introduction, 'Bednall Beauty' is shorter and more compact |

### CHINESE LANTERN
*Physalis franchetii*
(syn. *P. alkengi* var. *franchetii*)

Many flower arrangers love to grow this plant for its unique, bright orange seed pods that can be such a feature of the flower garden in autumn. They are delightful in a simple arrangement with honesty or complementing the berries of *Iris foetidissima*, or as part of a general autumn arrangement. Needless to say, they make a bright focal point in the garden.

| | |
|---|---|
| type | Herbaceous perennial |
| flowers | Insignificant, cream. It is the orange-red seed pods ('Chinese lanterns') for which the plant is grown |
| foliage | Lanceolate, mid-green |
| height | 60cm (2ft) |
| spread | 90cm (3ft) |
| hardiness | Hardy |
| planting | Spring or late autumn |

*PHYSALIS FRANCHETII*

| | |
|---|---|
| position | Full sun |
| soil | Any good border soil |
| propagation | By division in spring or root cuttings in winter |

## SAXIFRAGE
### *Saxifraga fortunei*

This plant is remarkably different from most garden saxifrages, but is still most at home among rocks and in a gritty soil. It is too tall and its leaves too large for a small rock garden, but a partly shaded place on a larger one is ideal.

| | |
|---|---|
| type | Deciduous (herbaceous) alpine (perennial) |
| flowers | White. Each has five petals; the two lower ones are three to four times as long as the upper three |
| foliage | Bold, rounded, glossy, brownish green, the undersides and leaf stalks conspicuously red |
| height | 40cm (16in) in flower |
| spread | 30cm (12in) |
| hardiness | Hardy |
| planting | Whenever available |
| position | Part shade, cool |
| soil | Leafy, gritty |
| propagation | By division in spring |
| varieties | 'Wada', large, purple leaves; 'Rubrifolia', leaves reddish brown |

## MONKSHOOD
### *Aconitum carmichaelii*

There are several species of monkshoods, all of which bear a 'family' resemblance, with hooded flowers in some shade of blue or near-blue and divided leaves. The roots are poisonous, hence the folk name 'Wolfsbane'. This species is the latest in flower and maintains its foliage well, although a certain amount of yellowing is inevitable in a plant that comes into leaf very early in the year.

| | |
|---|---|
| type | Herbaceous perennial |
| flowers | Upright, hooded, in spikes. Blue to violet-blue |
| foliage | Wide, divided leaves |
| height | 1.2cm (4ft) |
| spread | 30cm (1ft) |
| hardiness | Hardy |
| planting | Plant in late autumn or winter |
| position | Full sun, part or full shade |
| soil | Any good soil, preferably moisture retentive but well drained |
| propagation | By division in late autumn. 'Barker's Variety' comes true from seed |
| varieties | 'Arendsii', rich blue; 'Barker's Variety', good.blue, tall; 'Kelmscott', deep violet blue; *A.c. wilsonii*, over 1.5m (5ft) |

# plants

IN

## *flower*

KEY

\* = evergreen    spp = species

vars = varieties

| TREES | colour | flower type |
|---|---|---|
| *Magnolia grandiflora* | Creamy white | Very large, fragrant |

| SHRUBS | colour | flower type |
|---|---|---|
| *Erica carnea* early vars | Various | Heather |
| *Fatsia japonica* | White | Round clusters |
| *Mahonia × media* vars | Yellow | Long racemes |

Also: **Abelia, Calluna, Ceratostigma, Erica vagans, Fuchsia, Hibiscus, Hydrangea, Hypericum, Lespedeza, Potentilla**

## CLIMBERS

**Clematis, Eccremocarpus scaber, Lapageria rosea**

## PERENNIALS

**Anemone × hybrida, Aster amellus, Aster novae-angliae, Aster novi-belgii, Ceratostigma plumbaginoides, Heliopsis, Kniphofia, Liriope muscari, Polygonum, Rudbeckia, Scabiosa, Schizostylis, Silene schafta**

| BULBS | colour | height | remarks |
|---|---|---|---|
| *Colchicum agrippinum* | Violet, chequered | 10cm (4in) | |
| atropurpureum | White, becoming carmine-purple | 7cm (2½in) | |
| 'Autumn Queen' | Lilac | 15cm (6in) | |
| autumnale | | | |
| album plenum | Double, white | 15cm (6in) | Rare |
| pleniflorum | Double, mauve | 10cm (4in) | |
| cilicum | Rosy-lilac | 7cm (2½in) | |

### **P**LANTS FOR **O**RNAMENTAL **F**RUIT

This month is the peak of the season of 'mellow fruitfulness' and the well-planned garden will always have a good display of various fruits. In this context 'fruit' is not restricted to those that are edible, but includes any seed-bearing organs that are of ornamental value. There is a dramatic decline in flowering as compared with the previous month, and the colour factor is to a large extent taken over by fruits. This is also true of next month, which is, in climates where winters are not dominated by snow, the nadir of the flowering year.

Continentally-influenced climates will, from now onwards, to a greater or lesser extent remain flowerless until the general spring thaw, but milder, maritime or island climates will see a thread of flowering activity continuing until the year 'starts' again in early spring. In these latter locations, which include the British Isles, this month may be seen as the end of the main flowering phase of the year, next month as a transitional, almost blank time, and the following month as the start of low-key, winter flowering that is none the less often quite ravishing.

### Trees

*Crataegus* Although the hawthorns are among the best-known berrying trees, they are all too often planted without proper concern for the lasting and attractive qualities of their berries. Among the best for berries are *Crataegus laciniata*, which has large, coral-red fruits, and *C. × lavallei* 'Carrieri', whose leaves are among the last to fall of all trees, and whose orange-red berries last right through winter. Several forms of the common hawthorn, *C. monogyna*, bear heavy crops of red fruits, often referred to as 'haws', as opposed to 'hips', which are the fruits of roses.

*Ilex* There are too many berried hollies to list. Practically all female hollies have berries, usually red, but sometimes yellow, and there are also black-berried hollies. It is best to buy hollies for their foliage and to consider the berries as secondary, as quantities vary from year to year but their evergreen foliage is always decorative. Beware of thinking that 'Golden Queen' is female, as it is male; 'Golden King', on the other hand, is not male . . . but female.

*Magnolia* Several magnolias bear fruit. Typically, they look like long, thick, extremely warty sausages, which split open to reveal a

|  | colour | height |
|---|---|---|
| 'Rosy Dawn' | Pink | 15cm (6in) |
| speciosum | Purple, white centre | 15cm (6in) |
| album | White | 15cm (6in) |

The following **colchicums** flower a month earlier:
**autumnale**, lilac, 15cm (6in); **bornmülleri**, violet, 18cm (7½in); **byzantinum**, rosy-lilac, 15cm (6in); **'The Giant'**, large, lilac-mauve, 25cm (10in); **'Violet Queen'**, purple, 15cm (6in); **'Water Lily'**, large, double, rosy-lilac, 10cm (4in).

| **Crocus hadriaticus** | Large, creamy white | 10cm (4in) |
|---|---|---|
| karduchorum | Pale lavender-pink | 12cm (5in) |
| medius | Lilac-purple | 8cm (3in) |
| nudiflorus | Deep violet | 15cm (6in) |
| pulchellus | Pale lilac | 12cm (5in) |
| salzmanii | Lilac | 10cm (4in) |
| sativus (Saffron) | Very large, rosy-lilac | 10cm (4in) |
| speciosus and vars | Blue to lavender | 12cm (5in) |
| zonatus | Pale lilac | 10cm (4in) |

Almost all crocuses have white or yellow throats.

| **Cyclamen cilicium** | Pale rose | 6cm (2½in) |
|---|---|---|
| hederifolium | Rose-pink or white | 10cm (4in) |
| **Galanthus reginae-olgae** | White snowdrop with green markings | 12cm (5in) |
| **Sternbergia lutea** | Yellow, crocus-like | 12cm (5in) |

bright orange seed in each wart. The seeds emerge and dangle for a short while on strings of mucus. That may all sound like a horror movie, but it is in fact very attractive.

*Malus* The crab apples are the best of all fruiting trees for this time of year. Many of them keep their fruits well past the end of next month; indeed, some persist right through the winter. *M.* 'Crittenden', sadly becoming scarce, is about the longest-lasting, with many, bright scarlet crab apples. Of the more readily available ones, 'Golden Hornet' is probably the best bet for quite large, bright yellow fruit retained through most of the winter, while 'John Downie' is the best crab apple of all, with large, orange-red fruit well beyond the New Year, from which, unlike most ornamental, long-lasting crabs, good jelly with a fine flavour can be made.

*Sorbus* This genus consists of the whitebeams and the mountain ashes, of which the latter provide the best fruit, usually seen as large clusters of berries in brilliant red, yellow or white. Most red berries are lost rapidly, soon after their formation in late summer, but those that remain, along with the white and yellow berries, will see the month through, if not persist well into winter.

## ROCK GARDEN

*Crocus* spp
*Cyclamen cilicium*
*Cyclamen hederifolium*
*Erica carnea* – early vars
*Galanthus reginae-olgae*
*Gentiana* – Asiatic spp and hybs
*Zauschneria microphylla*

The best are: *S. commixta* 'Embley', large clusters of orange-red; *S.c.* 'Jermyns', amber, becoming orange-red; *S. aucuparia* varieties, the longest-lasting of which is 'Fructu-luteo', whose berries are yellow; *S. vilmorinii*, red in late summer, becoming pink, then white with a pink flush; *S.* × *kewensis*, very large clusters of orange-red; *S.* 'Joseph Rock', amber-yellow, very long-lasting; *S. hupehensis*, white, dangling, lasting well into winter. Perhaps the longest-lasting red-berried sorbus is *S. esserteauana*, whose berries are rather small but still conspicuous.

### Shrubs
Berried shrubs for autumn will be found in the genera *Aucuba, Berberis, Callicarpa, Chaenomeles, Clerodendrum, Cotoneaster, Euonymus, Gaultheria, Pernettya, Photinia, Pyracantha, Rosa, Sambucus, Skimmia, Symphoricarpos, Vaccinium* and *Viburnum.* There are too many species and varieties to list.

Roses provide perhaps the largest and most effective of all shrub fruit. Varieties of *Rosa rugosa*, and several of the species, notably *R. moyesii*, are worth seeking out for the long extension to their season given by their large, brilliant 'hips'.

# NOVEMBER

November's sky is chill and drear
November's leaf is red and sear
SIR WALTER SCOTT

*It is difficult to speak with dispassion of this time of year. To affect a false cheeriness and declare it to have effects on one's psyche other than those that are real would be to deny that it has any effect at all.*

*In the garden the memory of what was so recently rich with colour, scent and bustle is too fresh. I live in a maritime land, where it is almost unheard of for there to be significant snow this month, and there is no sudden transition, no brilliant carpeting of white, through which berries pierce like wine split upon a cloth of damask. There is just a running down, as if age had crept silently upon the garden and struck it with decrepitude.*

*And yet, as this weary month moves on, minutiae begin to register. Tiny-flowered asters, poor relations of the gaudy Michaelmas daisies, peep as if to ask if they can come out now.*

*Skimmias are wreathed in bud-clusters, the promise of spring. And there are berries.*

*Hydrangeas, their colour changes complete, change texture from their silkiness of late summer to a softness like that of finest kid. Above and among them, perhaps, the tall feathers of pampas grass stand guard.*

*Is there then no magic in late autumn? Of course there is. As when the sun returns one still afternoon and beams its way through the wisps of the morning's mist, setting flame to a liquidambar's ember-glowing leaves, slanting whitely across a birch's trunk, and picking out the crocuses, like amethysts on a tawny carpet.*

*Such moments are short, but full of poignancy. Perhaps that is the true spirit of this lonely month. Its treasures, when found, may be put away among the fondest memories.*

# plants
## OF THE
## *month*

### ASTER
#### *Aster ludoviciana* var. *latifolia*

This late-flowering aster is rare in cultivation and not easy to obtain, but as interest in making the garden more attractive in late autumn and winter increases, it stands a good chance of becoming more accessible. Its clouds of little flowers are infinitely to be welcomed this month.

| | |
|---|---|
| type | Herbaceous perennial |
| flowers | Sprays of small, lilac daisies |
| foliage | Slight, slender leaves |
| height | 90cm (36in) |
| spread | 1m (40in) |
| hardiness | Hardy |
| planting | Plant in spring |
| position | Sun or part shade |
| soil | Any good garden soil, preferably moisture retentive |
| propagation | By division in spring |
| alternatives | There are several small-flowered asters, notably the varieties of *A. ericoides*, but they flower earlier |

### SKIMMIA
#### *Skimmia japonica*

Nurserymen will tell you that it is not easy to sell plants with the sexes on separate individuals. With skimmias, although there is one exception, you need a male and a female if you are to see the brilliant, scarlet berries, and people balk at having to buy two plants. They should not, though, as the male plants have a long-lasting beauty all of their own, with tight clusters of buds studding the bushes from autumn right through until flowering time in spring.

| | |
|---|---|
| type | Evergreen shrub |
| flowers | Terminal panicles, usually white, mid- to late spring. Fragrant |
| fruit | Round, shiny, scarlet, very long-lasting berries, borne on female plants. *S.j.* subsp. *reevesiana* is hermaphrodite and all plants bear berries |
| foliage | Leathery, elliptic leaves |
| height | 90–100cm (36–40in) after 10 years |
| spread | 90–100cm (36–40in) after 10 years |
| hardiness | Hardy |
| position | Very useful shrubs for shady positions, but will also grow in sun |
| soil | Any reasonable garden soil, including chalk. *S.j. reevesiana*, however, is not tolerant of chalk soils |
| pruning | None |
| propagation | By semi-ripe cuttings in autumn in a cold frame, or in summer under mist |
| varieties | 'Veitchii' (syn. 'Foremannii') is a vigorous female with large clusters of bright red fruits. 'Rubella' is a male with conspicuous clusters of dark red buds, which open to white flowers in spring |

*SKIMMIA JAPONICA*

*PHOTINIA DAVIDIANA*

## PHOTINIA
### *Photinia davidiana*

Among the brightest of the berries that bring colour to the flower garden at its lowest ebb are those of *Photinia davidiana*. This plant was until recently a member of the genus *Stranvaesia*, which has now disappeared. Photinias are evergreen in the main, and some are grown for their fine, red young leaves. It is their berries, however, for which those that were stranvaesias are best known.

| | |
|---|---|
| type | Evergreen shrub |
| flowers | White, in branched clusters in spring |
| fruits | Large clusters of bright red berries |
| foliage | Leathery, dark green, fairly slender |
| height | 1.2m (4ft) after 10 years |
| spread | 1m (4ft) after 10 years |
| hardiness | Hardy |
| position | Sun or part shade |
| soil | Any good garden soil. Please note that deciduous photinias are usually lime-hating |
| pruning | None |
| propagation | By semi-ripe cuttings under mist in late summer |
| alternatives | 'Fructu-luteo' has bright yellow berries, 'Palette' is a singularly repellent form with leaves blotched and streaked with white. Unfortunately, it commands a considerable market |

## PAMPAS GRASS
### *Cortaderia selloana* 'Sunningdale Silver'

Pampas grass is so well known as hardly to warrant description. However, it is not generally appreciated that there are several varieties of it, some of which are more suitable for small gardens than the more commonly seen tall ones. 'Sunningdale Silver' is of medium size but 'Pumila' is the variety that should be sought if pampas grass is to be in scale with the average garden.

| | |
|---|---|
| type | Evergreen grass |
| flowers | Tall plumes of silvery white |
| foliage | Long, arching, grassy, sharp edged |
| height | 2m (7ft) |
| spread | 1.5m (5ft) |
| hardiness | Hardy |
| planting | Plant in late spring |
| position | Full sun |
| soil | Any reasonable garden soil |
| propagation | By division in late spring. It is not easy, and should be done without allowing the roots to become dry |
| alternatives | 'Pink Feather' has a pinkish tinge to the flowers. 'Rendatleri' is praised for its lilac-pink plumes, but it is a very large plant up to 3m (10ft) tall |

*CORTADERIA SELLOANA 'SUNNINGDALE SILVER'*

# plants
## IN
# *flower*

**KEY**

\* = evergreen    spp = species

vars = varieties

**PLEASE NOTE**

All the above trees and shrubs flower intermittently over many weeks, often enjoying bursts of bloom as late as the end of winter. Mild spells of weather usually precede or coincide with flowering.

**COTONEASTERS**

Some of the best cotoneaster species for autumn colour, such as *C. lucidus*, are now uncommon in cultivation, probably because of the emphasis that has been laid on berries within the genus.

| TREES | colour | flower type |
|---|---|---|
| *Prunus subhirtella* 'Autumnalis' | Pink | Small, like cherry blossom |

| SHRUBS | colour | flower type |
|---|---|---|
| *Jasminum nudiflorum* | Yellow | On bare branches |
| *Viburnum × bodnantense* vars | Light rose | In clusters, sweet scent |
| *farreri* | Pink | In clusters, highly scented |

*Erica carnea* vars, including '**Myretoun Ruby**', '**Pink Spangles**', '**Foxhollow**', '**Praecox Rubra**', '**Ruby Glow**', '**Vivellii**', '**Springwood White**'.

**CLIMBERS**

| | | |
|---|---|---|
| *\*Clematis cirrhosa balearica* | Pale yellow, red spots | |

**PERENNIALS**

Apart from **Schizostylis coccinea**, forms of which may flower on into this month, flowering of perennials, whether herbaceous or evergreen, has ceased.

| BULBS | colour | height |
|---|---|---|
| *Crocus clusii* | Lilac | 8cm (3in) |
| *longiflorus* | Large, lilac | 10cm (4in) Scented |
| *tournefortii* | Lilac | 10cm (4in) |

| TREES for autumn leaf colour | colour |
|---|---|
| *Acer cappadocicum* 'Rubrum' | Red, then gold |
| *griseum* | Crimson and scarlet |
| *grosseri* var. *hersii* | Yellow, then red |
| *pensylvanicum* | Butter yellow |
| *rubrum* 'October Glory' | Flame red |
| *rufinerve* | Yellow |
| *Amelanchier lamarckii* | Orange and red |
| *Betula* spp | Most turn yellow |
| *Crataegus × lavallei* | Red |
| *Ginkgo biloba* | Yellow, but fall before this month |
| *Koelreuteria paniculata* | Yellow |
| *Liquidambar styraciflua* | Flame crimson |
| *Liriodendron tulipifera* | Gold |
| *Malus* spp and vars – some | Red and gold |
| *Parrotia persica* | Red, orange and yellow. Early |
| *Prunus* (Cherries) – most | Shades of yellow, orange or red |
| *Sorbus* spp – many | Shades of copper, red and orange |

## SHRUBS for autumn leaf colour

| | |
|---|---|
| ***Acer japonicum* 'Aconitifolium'** | *Rich crimson* |
| **'Aureum'** | *Golden leaves with little or no autumn colour* |
| ***palmatum* vars** | *There are currently approximately 150 of these Japanese maples. Virtually all have superb autumn colour, usually in bright yellow or intense, flame red* |
| ***Azalea* – deciduous** | *This branch of Rhododendron is one of the richest sources of autumn colour among shrubs. Colours vary from rich yellow to dazzling red* |
| ***Berberis* deciduous – many** | *Mostly red, some are orange* |
| ***Callicarpa bodinieri* vars** | *Violet-purple* |
| ***Ceratostigma willmottianum*** | *Purplish red* |
| ***Cercidiphyllum japonicum*** | *Pink, red and yellow* |
| ***Cornus florida* vars** | *Orange or scarlet* |
| ***kousa chinensis*** | *Brownish crimson* |
| ***mas*** | *Brownish red* |
| ***Cotinus coggygria* vars** | *Red* |
| ***Cotoneaster adpressus*** | *Scarlet* |
| ***bullatus*** | *Scarlet* |
| ***divaricatus*** | *Brilliant scarlet* |
| ***horizontalis*** | *Rich red* |
| ***Enkianthus campanulatus*** | *Yellow and red* |
| ***Euonymus alatus*** | *Bright scarlet* |
| ***europaeus* 'Red Cascade'** | *Rich scarlet* |
| ***Fothergilla major*** | *Mixed colours: orange, red, yellow on the same leaf* |
| ***Hamamelis* spp and vars** | *Most hamamelis colour richly in autumn. The majority turn yellow. **H. intermedia 'Jelena'** is particularly spectacular, in orange, scarlet and crimson* |
| ***Nandina domestica*** | *Red* |
| ***Rhus typhina*** | *Orange and red* |
| ***Viburnum carlesii*** | *Yellow* |
| ***lantana*** | *Crimson* |
| ***opulus*** | *Orange and red* |

## CLIMBERS for autumn leaf colour

| | |
|---|---|
| ***Parthenocissus* spp** | *The most brilliant red hues of all* |
| ***Vitis coignetiae*** | *Orange and dark crimson* |
| **'Brandt'** | *Pink, orange and dark crimson* |

## AUTUMN COLOURS

Autumn leaf colour is dependent on several factors, only very few of which are in the control of the gardener. The chief of these is wind. During a calm autumn, the leaves will stay for a long time on the trees provided they are not blown off by strong winds. Eventually, of course, the slightest breath will dislodge them, but in the earlier stages it takes more than a mere breeze.

If you shelter the best subjects, particularly the Japanese maples, which need shelter from wind in any case as part of their cultural requirements, the autumn colour in your garden will last much longer. That colour is important to you is implicit in the fact that you are reading this book; there is nothing we can do about the paucity of flowering in late autumn and winter beyond trying to grow the plants that do flower during the short days, but we can provide our gardens with colour by growing trees and shrubs that colour well during the earlier part of the season of sparse flowering.

However, it is a great mistake to take this too far. Autumn colour is at best fleeting; at worst, it hardly happens at all. It depends on climatic conditions and may be very poor in a year in which there is a cool summer and a mild autumn. Wherever those conditions obtain in most years, autumn colour is something for which you should not plant. In those circumstances, you should choose plants for their other virtues and take whatever autumn colour comes as a bonus. You are, if your climate is mild, more likely to enjoy long-lasting berries, as the birds will not become hungry as quickly as they do in climates where winter descends rapidly.

Gardens on acid soils enjoy better opportunities for autumn colour, as so many deciduous acid-loving plants do take on brilliant hues. It is not worth growing a deciduous azalea, for example, in a tub just for its autumn colour, but if it is part of a group of acid-loving plants grown in a large tub or a raised bed made with acid soil where the general garden soil is alkaline, then so much the better for the long-term attractiveness of the group.

# DECEMBER

I dreamed that, as I wandered by the way,
Bare winter suddenly was changed to spring.
SHELLEY

*Poor Shelley! His superb imagination was able to banish winter, and he could envisage 'pied windflowers and violets…faint oxlips, tender bluebells…' but his dramatic nature would not let him rest. He had to turn, stumbling from the scene, no doubt with back of hand to tormented forehead, to show it to someone. 'Oh! to whom?', was his mournful cry.*

*Midwinter is certainly a time for positive thinking. That, after all, is the real reason for the timing of Christmas, which the early church wisely placed in the way of the ancient festivals of mid-winter. As gardeners, we could do much worse than emulate the poet and dream of flowers yet to come. Only it goes without saying that, as good gardeners, our dreaming will be translated into planning, and our planning eventually into execution.*

*There are flowers out this month. The very last crocus, a precocious snowdrop, and a little family of cyclamen snuggle beneath trees or beside shrubs, while a handful of opportunist shrubs bloom whenever there is a spell of settled, mild weather.*

*They do this in the 'hope' that the weather will also tempt pollinating insects from hibernation for a short spell, and press hard for their attention in most cases by being highly fragrant. The middle of winter is no pageant of flowers, but it is fascinating to see how nature is capable of fitting plants into every possible ecological and climatic slot. It is easy to become inordinately fond of the flowers of winter and to ascribe to them virtues which they do not possess. We may think of them as brave, mainly because we like to feel brave when we venture out of doors on cold days, but they are not, of course. They are merely doing what all flowering plants do – taking every opportunity to perpetuate their species.*

# tasks
## FOR THE
## *month*
## 1

*PROTECT TENDER CLIMBERS*
*If you have any frost-tender climbers, such as Passiflora caerulea, Lapageria rosea or Clianthus puniceus, drape them with netting in cold spells and weave into the mesh straw, branchlets of large conifers, or any material such as wood wool.*

*'ROSES' IN WINTER*
*You can force Helleborus niger (Christmas roses) slightly to give you longer stems for cutting. Just cover them with a closed cloche. Do not do this with its hybrids, as their leafy stems will flop.*

## CHECKLIST

- Check the effects of frost, wind and rain regularly
- Whenever the weather is open – ie frost-free and not too wet – continue to plant trees and shrubs from containers
- Examine stored bulbs, corms and tubers regularly for signs of disease
- If your soil is acid and you enjoy growing garden pinks, top dress them with lime. It is one of those jobs that gets forgotten once early spring comes around
- Plant bare-rooted trees and shrubs
- Prune trees and shrubs that have become crowded, overgrown, or have crossed or rubbing branches. Winter pruning encourages growth, so think it out as you go
- Give autumn-sown hardy annuals a thorough weeding to see them through to the start of general plant growth

## MAINTENANCE

### WIND, FROST AND RAIN

Any trees or shrubs that have been loosened by wind should be trodden back. Check alpines and herbaceous plants that were planted in autumn; if they have been lifted by frost, firm them back into the soil.

Look out for 'casual water' after rain. If the soil is compacted or capped, water will lie in puddles for a while. Wait until it has dried and then lightly fork the top few inches.

### PESTS

Have a raid on the slug and snail population. Mild, wet winter days bring them to the surface, where they can be picked up. Snails congregate in rubbly places and at the bases of walls and hedges. Drop the creatures into a bucket of salty water, where they will eventually disintegrate. It is not cruel.

### BULBS IN STORE

Once more, examine dahlia tubers and all the bulbs, corms and tubers you have in store. Cut away diseased portions of tubers and dust with sulphur. Discard any bulbs or corms with fungus infections.

## PLANTING

### BARE-ROOTED DECIDUOUS TREES AND SHRUBS

Larger specimens of many trees and shrubs specifically ordered by customers are lifted by nurseries during winter and despatched or made ready for collection. They represent an investment of your money and the grower's time and skill, so should be planted as well as possible. Magnolias should not be lifted or planted in midwinter, but almost all other deciduous trees and shrubs are safe to move and plant now.

### Planting

- Prepare an area of ground one metre (one yard) square by digging in generous amounts of well-rotted organic matter. This acts as a soil conditioner, as well as food for the plant.

- Take out from this a planting hole sufficiently wide to take the roots at their furthest spread. Look for the 'nursery mark', which is a line on the bottom of the stem where the soil level was in the nursery. Lay a piece of timber across the hole and keep the nursery mark level with its lower surface throughout the planting, as it must end up exactly at soil level once more.

- Backfill the hole, jiggling the stem so that soil filters down among the roots. If necessary, use your hands to make sure the roots are all

## WARNING

*The gardener's boots can do a lot of damage in the garden at this time of year. Reduce the risk by following a few simple rules:*
- *Use duckboards whenever possible for all operations that mean walking on the soil.*
- *Avoid walking on the lawn when it is wet; lay duck boards if you have to reach the washing line.*
- *Never walk on frosted grass. It leaves neat, brown footprints.*

in contact with the soil. Firm with the foot at intervals, but not close to the stem and not so as to damage the roots.

■ There is no need to insert a stake at any of the above stages, as you will be using a modern, short-stake method.

**Staking**

Conventional, long stakes have been shown to cause trees to grow with tubular-shaped trunks, which are inherently weak. They have to be driven into the ground between the roots in order to be close enough to the trunks, and must have about one-third of their length in the soil, otherwise they will pull out. Removing a long stake involves considerable root disturbance and damage, and often the bottom will have rotted and will snap off, remaining as a source of fungal infection in intimate contact with the roots.

A short stake keeps the lowest part of the stem of a tree quite still, so that the roots are not disturbed. It allows the upper part to sway, and this has been proved to promote an Eiffel-Tower-shaped trunk, which is far stronger. Short stakes do not have to be put in before planting is complete, neither do they have to be driven so far in, as the leverage on them is much less. Removing them causes little or no damage to the roots, and there will be no rotten pieces left among the roots that cannot easily be removed.

There are two main methods. In the first, a cross-piece is attached to two uprights, and the stem is attached by a proper tree tie to its centre. In the second, a single stake is driven into the soil at an angle to the stem. The former is the safer for trees; the latter is the one preferred for shrubs, when it can be attached to one of the stems and performs a less demanding anchoring role. It is less suitable for trees, as the greater leverage of the tall stems will tend to pull on the stakes along their length.

Stakes should always be placed so that the stem is on the downwind side of the stake. This prevents rubbing.

## MOVING TREES AND SHRUBS

During winter, deciduous trees and shrubs can be moved within the garden. Lifting them is easy as long as you do not tackle specimens that are too large, and you do not have to be as careful about keeping the soil on the root ball as with evergreens. However, root damage should be kept to an absolute minimum, and it is a good idea in any case to cut back the branches of the plant by about one-third to compensate for it. This will ensure that there is not too great a water demand on the roots when the tree or shrub comes into leaf.

Replanting trees and shrubs should be done in just the same way as planting new ones.

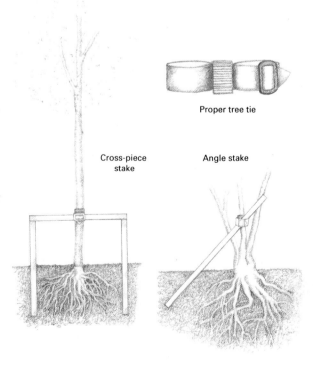

Proper tree tie

Cross-piece stake

Angle stake

# plants
## OF THE
## *month*

### HELLEBORE
### *Helleborus niger* hybrid

*Helleborus niger* itself is the Christmas rose, whose large wide open, almost flat flowers, like white wheels, adorn cool, shady corners of the garden in winter. Often in the past, however, gardeners have found themselves with seedlings that were either poor forms of the species or haphazard hybrids with others. In more recent years, the Christmas rose has been deliberately crossed with other species, such as *H. corsicus* and *H. lividus*, and selections made of those with special qualities. Several are excellent, elegant, very early-flowering hellebores and valuable additions to the winter garden scene.

| | |
|---|---|
| **type** | Partly evergreen perennials |
| **flowers** | Vary in colour and shape. They are usually borne in terminal clusters, and the individual flowers may droop to a greater or lesser degree before becoming more erect. Flower colour is usually based on white, greenish white, or white with a very faint pink flush, and the insides may be unmarked or faintly spotted or splashed. Flowering time varies, but is usually in mid to late winter |
| **foliage** | Also variable, but usually grey-green and tripartite |
| **height** | 30cm (1ft) |
| **spread** | 25cm (10in) |
| **hardiness** | Most are hardy |
| **planting** | Best in spring |
| **position** | Part shade |
| **soil** | A good, leafy, moisture-retentive soil |
| **propagation** | By division after flowering of large, well-established clumps only |
| **alternatives** | None, apart from *H. niger* |
| **special comment** | These plants generally circulate among keen gardeners, but can often be obtained from nurseries specialising in hellebores |

*HELLEBORUS NIGER HYBRID*

### MAHONIA
### *Mahonia* × *media* 'Winter Sun'

The varieties of *Mahonia* × *media* are hybrids between *M. japonica* and *M. lomariifolia*. The former parent brings hardiness, wonderfully long racemes of flowers, scent, and magnificent, bold, pinnate leaves with holly-like leaflets. The latter contributes an increase in the numbers of leaflets, producing a more lacy effect, and clusters of many, boldly upright racemes of richer yellow. Although *M. lomariifolia* is on the tender side, the hybrids that have been selected for distribution are hardy. Some of the hybrids may be only slightly fragrant, but in 'Winter Sun' they are notably so.

| | |
|---|---|
| **type** | Evergreen shrub |
| **flowers** | Many racemes of rich yellow, fragrant flowers |
| **foliage** | Long, pinnate, rigid leaves with spiny leaflets |
| **height** | 1.8m (6ft) after 10 years |
| **spread** | 1.8m (6ft) after 10 years |
| **hardiness** | Hardy, but protect from freezing winds |
| **position** | Best in part shade |
| **soil** | Any garden soil, including chalk |
| **pruning** | None |
| **propagation** | See page 135 |

alternatives  'Buckland' has fewer leaflets and longer, more spreading racemes; 'Charity' can grow very tall and may need cutting hard back to prevent its shooting up into two or three leafless poles. When well grown it is majestic, with leaves over 0.5m (20in) long and large, terminal clusters of very long racemes, closely packed with deep yellow, lightly scented flowers

## VIBURNUM

*Viburnum tinus* 'French White'

*Viburnum tinus* is the well-known laurustinus, unaccountably one of the most popular of all shrubs. One expresses surprise because it is rare for a winter-flowering shrub to catch the attention of the wider gardening public. It is, however, almost indestructible and one of the few evergreens that succeed when exposed to winds from the sea.

| | |
|---|---|
| type | Evergreen shrub |
| flowers | Flat clusters of small, white flowers, produced almost continuously from autumn to spring |
| foliage | Tightly massed, glossy, dark green leaves |
| fruits | Black, small |
| height | 1.5m (5ft) after 10 years |
| spread | 1.5m (5ft) after 10 years |
| hardiness | Hardy |
| position | Sun or shade |
| soil | Any reasonable soil |
| pruning | None. Can be trimmed, after flowering to form a hedge |
| propagation | By semi-ripe cuttings in late summer to early autumn; root earlier ones under mist, later cuttings in a garden frame |
| alternatives | 'Eve Price', buds carmine, flowers pink; 'Gwenllian', compact, deep pink in the bud, opening to white flowers with pink-backed petals |

## CYCLAMEN

*Cyclamen coum*

The botanists are not quite agreed on the status of this cyclamen. Some regard it as a species with several naturally occurring varieties, others as more or less an aggregate of species. From a gardener's point of view, it is a group of cyclamen capable of providing flowers from midwinter to early spring with a

*CYCLAMEN COUM*

variety of colours based on carmine and including white forms, and with round leaves that may be plain green, marked with silver, or even completely silver.

| | |
|---|---|
| type | Tuberous perennial |
| flowers | More truncated than other cyclamen and with the lobes arranged more sideways-on, sometimes giving the appearance of minute ships' propellers |
| foliage | Glossy to matt, silver to plain green, in most forms maroon on the undersides |
| height | 10cm (4in) |
| spread | 10cm (4in) |
| hardiness | Hardy |
| planting | Best purchased 'in the green' in spring from specialist nurseries and planted immediately |
| position | Part shade |
| soil | Any good garden soil, preferably leafy or otherwise organic |
| propagation | From seed sown immediately the pods split |
| varieties | There are several, but the names given are often contradictory. Choose from the catalogue the ones that will give you a good range of flowering times, colours and foliage |

# tasks

## FOR THE

## *month*

## 2

**TREES AND SHRUBS
FOR GRAFTING**

Cherry
Hawthorn
Maple
*Robinia*
*Sorbus*

## PROPAGATION

### GRAFTING

*Camellia reticulata* varieties are as different from other camellias as limousines are from good family cars. They have very large, frilled or wavy-petalled flowers in sumptuous shades of strawberry, but are quite tender. In comparatively recent years they have been hybridised with other species to produce hardier camellias with the same flower characteristics. They appear to be on the threshold of genuine popularity and can be grown where there is much frost but also reliable shelter from cold winds.

Unfortunately, they are not very easy to grow from cuttings. *C. reticulata* cannot be propagated this way at all, and its varieties vary from difficult to impossible, and even the easiest require the use of a mist propagation unit. When you are faced with the purchase of a rather expensive plant, of whose toleration of conditions in your garden you may not be too sure, it is highly likely finally to put you off if you hear that you may not be able to propagate it as insurance against its loss.

However, you may change your mind when you learn that these camellias *can* be grafted. Grafting is little done by amateurs but is not difficult, although it requires some manual dexterity. This is the ideal time to graft camellias and, although they will take up room in a heated frame or propagator, it will be during those few weeks between now and when you will need it for sowing seed.

### Method
The method used for camellias is called 'spliced side-veneer grafting'. Like all other methods, it involves joining a rootstock (the stock) of one plant with a shoot (the scion) of another, by bringing the growing tissues under the barks of each into contact. It is a method particularly used when the stock stem is of larger diameter than that of the scion.

■ The stock should be a strong, pot-grown plant of any variety of *Camellia japonica*. It should be three to four years old at least. It is much better to prepare your own stock in advance from a cutting, as it takes some doing to decapitate (as you must) a plant for which you have paid good money. Bring it into a greenhouse or frame with an operating temperature of 8°C (46°F) or above so that growth may just be starting.

■ Your scion will be a 10cm (4in) shoot of this year's growth of your reticulata hybrid or form of the species. To prepare the stock to receive it, cut about 5mm (¼in) into its stem at a position as low as you can manage, and at a downward angle of about 45°. Now make a slanting cut from about 3cm (1¼in) above the first so that it meets it. Remove the sliver of wood.

■ Next, take the scion and, cutting on the slant towards its base, take off a shaving the same length as the sliver you removed from the stock. Cut the base of the scion at 45° to fit the lip of the stock.

■ Bring the two together so that there is a good, snug fit and the cut surfaces meet each other as much as possible, and bind them together firmly with raffia. There is no need to use grafting wax, as you next put the entire graft into a heated propagating frame. Around 15°C (59°F) will be the best temperature. The atmosphere should be humid to prevent water loss from the scion before union takes place.

■ This should happen in about six to eight weeks. You can tell by a general freshening of the appearance of the foliage of the scion and the start of new shoots. Remove the raffia. Cut the top of the stock at a point just above the union, taking care to cut cleanly and with no pulling. You can now harden off your new plant.

It goes without saying that the tools (knife and secateurs) you use must be keenly sharp. If you have used the secateurs for pruning camellias at any time, use another pair, as a nasty virus that causes yellow mottling of the leaves, to which *C. reticulata* is vulnerable, may have lurked in the sap of other camellias that are reasonably resistant to it. One grafted plant of mine, carelessly operated on with my regular pruning secateurs, was after ten years nothing more than a stunted mass of badly yellowed leaves.

### BRANCHING OUT

Once you have mastered this off-season grafting method, you can try all the other fascinating types of grafting, including 'saddle-grafting' the larger rhododendrons, which looks easy but usually fails in inexperienced hands. The attraction is that you can grow the stocks (*Rhododendron ponticum*) quickly from seed.

Other trees and shrubs with which amateur gardeners can enjoy this most satisfying way of propagating are maples, hawthorns, cherries, robinias and *Sorbus* varieties.

# plants
## IN
# *flower*

| TREES | colour | flower type |
|---|---|---|
| **Prunus subhirtella 'Autumnalis'** | White | Semi-double |
| **'Autumnalis Rosea'** | White, blushed pink | Semi-double |

| SHRUBS | | |
|---|---|---|
| **\*Erica × darleyensis** vars | Pink, rose, magenta or white | Heathers |
| **Hamamelis × intermedia** some vars | Yellow, bronze, copper or red | Spidery, held closely on bare branches |
| **mollis** vars | Shades of yellow | As above |
| **Lonicera fragrantissima** | Cream, fragrant | Tubular |
| **× purpusii** | Cream, fragrant | Tubular |
| **'Winter Beauty'** | As above | As above, free-flowering |
| **standishii** | White, tinged pink, fragrant | Tubular |
| **\*Mahonia × media** vars | Yellow, fragrant | |
| **\*Viburnum tinus** | White or pink | In flat heads |

Also: **Erica carnea** vars, **jasminum nudiflorum**, **Viburnum × bodnantense** vars, **Viburnum farreri**.

| CLIMBERS | | |
|---|---|---|
| **Clematis cirrhosa balearica** | Pale yellow, with red spots | |

| BULBS | colour | height |
|---|---|---|
| **Crocus laevigatus fontanayi** | Violet-blue | 8cm (3in) |
| **Cyclamen coum** aggregate | Carmine to white | 10cm (4in) |
| **Galanthus corcyrensis** | White, green markings | 8cm (3in) |

**KEY**

\* = evergreen     spp = species
vars = varieties

**PLEASE NOTE**
Flowering may be delayed in many cases if the weather is particularly cold, and most of the plants listed may be in flower at any time between now and early spring.

*VIBURNUM TINUS 'FRENCH WHITE'*

# USEFUL ADDRESSES

## UNITED KINGDOM NURSERIES AND GARDEN CENTRES

Hillier Nurseries (Winchester) Ltd.,
Ampfield House, Ampfield,
Romsey, Hampshire SO51 9PA

Largest selection of trees and shrubs

---

Starborough Nursery,
Starborough Road,
Marsh Green,
Edenbridge, Kent TN8 5RB

Hardy and unusual trees and shrubs

---

Knap Hill & Slocock Nurseries,
Barrs Land, Knaphill,
Woking, Surrey GU21 2JW

Rhododendrons and azaleas

---

Four Seasons,
Forncett St. Mary, Norwich,
Norfolk NR16 1JT

Herbaceous perennials (mail order only)

---

Blooms of Bressingham Ltd,
Diss, Norfolk IP22 2AB

Herbaceous perennials, alpines, conifers, shrubs,
ornamental grasses

---

The Valley Clematis Nursery,
Hainton, Lincoln LN3 6LN

Clematis

---

Broadleigh Gardens,
Bishops Hull, Taunton,
Somerset TA4 1AE

Small bulbs, hostas, Pacific Coast irises

---

De Jagers,
Marden, Kent TN12 9BP

Bulbs, general

---

Inshriach Alpine Plant Nursery,
Inshriach, Aviemore,
Inverness-shire,
Scotland

Alpines and woodland plants

---

## CLUBS AND ASSOCIATIONS

The Alpine Garden Society,
AGS Centre,
Avon Bank,
Pershore,
Worcestershire WR10 3JP

---

The Royal Horticultural Society,
80 Vincent Square,
London SW1P 2PE

---

The Hardy Plant Society,
Little Orchard,
Great Comberton,
Near Pershore,
Worcestershire WR10 3DP

---

# USEFUL ADDRESSES

## USA
## NURSERIES AND GARDEN CENTRES

The Greenery,
1451 County Road 616,
Maple City,
Michigan 49664

Hardiest rhododendrons and kalmias

---

Roslyn Nursery,
Box 69, Roslyn,
New York 11576

Hardy plants; rhododendrons, azaleas, camellias, conifers, trees, shrubs, perennials

---

Lilypons Water Gardens,
PO Box 10, Buckeystown,
Maryland 21717

Water lilies

---

Siskyou Rare Plant Nursery,
2825 Cummings Road,
Medford,
Oregon 97501

Alpines, ferns and perennials

---

## CLUBS AND ASSOCIATIONS

For information on 9,286 garden clubs in 50 States and the District of Columbia

The National Council of State Garden Clubs Inc.,
4401 Magnolia Avenue, St Louis,
Missouri 63110

---

For information on hardy plants

The Hardy Plant Society,
124 N. 181st Street, Seattle,
Washington 98133

---

American Horticultural Society,
Box 0105, Mount Vernon,
Virginia 22121

---

## CANADA

C.A. Cruickshank Ltd.,
1015 Mount Pleasant Road,
Toronto, Ontario M4P 2MI

Bulbs

---

# FURTHER READING

*The Hillier Manual of Trees and Shrubs* (David & Charles 1991 Edition).
*Perennial Garden Plants* Graham Stuart Thomas, in association with the Royal Horticultural Society (Dent, Revised, 1990).
*The Heritage of the Rose* David Austin (Antique Collectors Club, Revised, 1990).
*Shrubs Through The Seasons* Roy Lancaster (Harper Collins, 1991).
*A Garden For All Seasons* (Reader's Digest, 1991).
*The All-Seasons Garden* John Kelly (Frances Lincoln (UK), Viking (US), 1987).
*Plants With Impact* John Kelly (David & Charles, 1992).

# INDEX